Getting Started in
OPTIONS

The *Getting Started In* Series

Getting Started in Online Day Trading by Kassandra Bentley
Getting Started in Investment Clubs by Marsha Bertrand
Getting Started in Asset Allocation by Bill Bresnan and Eric P. Gelb
Getting Started in Online Investing by David L. Brown and
    Kassandra Bentley
Getting Started in Online Brokers by Kristine DeForge
Getting Started in Internet Auctions by Alan Elliott
Getting Started in Stocks by Alvin D. Hall
Getting Started in Mutual Funds by Alvin D. Hall
Getting Started in Estate Planning by Kerry Hannon
Getting Started in Online Personal Finance by Brad Hill
Getting Started in 401(k) Investing by Paul Katzeff
Getting Started in Internet Investing by Paul Katzeff
Getting Started in Security Analysis by Peter J. Klein
Getting Started in Global Investing by Robert P. Kreitler
Getting Started in Futures by Todd Lofton
Getting Started in Project Management by Paula Martin and
    Karen Tate
Getting Started in Financial Information by Daniel Moreau and
    Tracey Longo
Getting Started in Emerging Markets by Christopher Poillon
Getting Started in Technical Analysis by Jack D. Schwager
Getting Started in Hedge Funds by Daniel A. Strachman
Getting Started in Options by Michael C. Thomsett
Getting Started in Six Sigma by Michael C. Thomsett
Getting Started in Real Estate Investing by Michael C. Thomsett and
    Jean Freestone Thomsett
Getting Started in Tax-Savvy Investing by Andrew Westham and
    Don Korn
Getting Started in Annuities by Gordon M. Williamson
Getting Started in Bonds by Sharon Saltzgiver Wright
Getting Started in Retirement Planning by Ronald M. Yolles and
    Murray Yolles
Getting Started in Currency Trading by Michael D. Archer and
    Jim L. Bickford
Getting Started in Rental Income by Michael C. Thomsett
Getting Started in Exchange Traded Funds by Todd Lofton
Getting Started in Fundamental Analysis by Michael C. Thomsett
Getting Started in REITS by Richard Imperiale
Getting Started in Swing Trading by Michael C. Thomsett
Getting Started in Property Flipping by Michael C. Thomsett

Getting Started in

OPTIONS

SEVENTH EDITION

Michael C. Thomsett

BICENTENNIAL
1807
WILEY
2007
BICENTENNIAL

JOHN WILEY & SONS, INC.

Published by John Wiley & Sons, Inc., Hoboken, New Jersey.
Published simultaneously in Canada.

Wiley Bicentennial Logo: Richard J. Pacifico

For general information on our other products and services or for technical support, please contact our Customer Care Department within the United States at 800-762-2974, outside the United States at 317-572-3993 or fax 317-572-4002.

Wiley also publishes its books in a variety of electronic formats. Some content that appears in print may not be available in electronic books.

For more information about Wiley products, visit our web site at www.wiley.com.

Library of Congress Cataloging-in-Publication Data:

Thomsett, Michael C.
   Getting started in options / Michael C. Thomsett. – 7th ed.
      p.   cm. – (The getting started in series)
   Includes index.
   ISBN 978-0-470-13806-9 (pbk.)
1. Stock options.   2. Options (Finance)   I. Title.
   HG6042.T46 2007
   332.63'2283–dc22   2007026309

Printed in the United States of America.

10 9 8 7 6 5 4 3 2 1

Contents

Acknowledgments

Thanks to those readers of the previous six editions who took the time to offer their compliments, constructive criticism, or clarifying questions. Their letters have helped to improve the ever-emerging set of explanations, definitions, and examples used in this book.

Thanks also to my editor at John Wiley & Sons, Debra Englander, for her encouragement through many editions of this and other books.

Many thanks to Candlestickchart.com for their permission to use their charts to illustrate points in this book. Thanks also go to the RediNews network, which provided the market data used in the charts.

Finally, thanks go to my wife, Linda Rose Thomsett, for her insights, support, and enthusiasm for this endeavor.

Element Key

Examples: Numerous examples illustrate points made in the discussion surrounding them and are designed to express ideas in practical terms.

 Definitions: This symbol is found in boxed notations providing specific definitions of options terms. These occur at the point of discussion within the book, making definitions applicable to the section being read. (All definitions are also summarized for you in the glossary.)

 Smart Investor Tips: These are useful observations, rules of thumb, resources, and other useful added points every options investor can use.

Introduction

Learning, apparently, is a never-ending process.

No matter how many years you spend mastering the field of options trading, there is invariably more to learn. In this, the 7th edition of *Getting Started in Options,* a lot of new material has been added due to (a) new markets and new concepts in the field; (b) expanded strategic uses of options; and (c) new and important aspects that have grown from previous editions.

Perhaps the most important attribute of options is their flexibility as strategic risk tools. Contrary to the reputation as high-risk instruments, options cover the entire range of risk. They can be quite speculative and even expensive; the short options position can pose a very real risk and may even cause large losses. On the opposite end of the spectrum, conservative and low-risk strategies offer you protection for existing positions in your portfolio, diversification by market position, and additional cash income. The new trader looking at options for any of these uses should also bear in mind that no two people will find the same strategic profile appropriate. All options strategies should be good matches for your individual income, experience, and risk tolerance.

In this edition, all chapters have been changed to some degree; and three new and important chapters and topics have been added in. Chapter 10 explains how paper trading works and can provide you with useful experience before you put real money at risk. Chapter 11 examines the many uses of options beyond the obvious buying and selling, including a means for expanding swing trading, day trading, and sector trading. And Chapter 13 is devoted entirely to calculations of return from options trading. This last chapter deserved its own concentrated discussion. Although return calculations are explained within other chapters, options trading involves additional calculations you need to be aware of, as well as different methods for calculating the outcome.

The purpose of this book is to provide you with a solid foundation in the options market. To achieve this goal, chapters are set up to provide many useful tools, including:

- *Definitions in context*. Terminology in the options world is complex and specialized, often confusing and even overwhelming a newcomer. So as each term is introduced, it is defined in a shaded box on the applicable page.

- *Smart investor tips.* These set-asides give you observations, resources, or summaries to bring home a main point. In fact, one of the best ways to use this book is to skim through and read these tips until you find an area of discussion especially interesting or relevant to your personal questions of the moment.

- *Examples.* A lot of books include examples, and these are often difficult to apply in any context. In this book, examples are specifically designed to expand upon the discussion of the moment. They are kept straightforward to make a point, without going off into excessive detail and discussion.

- *Checklists.* A lot of discussion in this book is arranged by way of checklists, and this makes it easier to absorb information in an organized and logical manner.

- *Illustrations.* Most of what you learn is visual in nature. Options trading can be exceptionally complex, mathematical, and difficult to follow, so the use of a lot of illustrative material helps clarify important points.

- *Tables.* Besides illustrations, whenever a lot of numerical information is needed (and that is often the case when options are involved) that information is set aside in a table. This keeps the narrative segments apart from the numerical, making all of the discussion clearer and more digestible.

As a method for proceeding through this book, don't expect yourself to grasp everything at the beginning. Allow yourself to move through the discussions using the six useful tools summarized above. Set a goal for yourself to master this exciting but complex field of investing, in four steps:

1. Master the terminology of the options field. Of course, you cannot simply memorize definitions without a context, which is why all of the terms you need are introduced as the discussion requires.

2. Be constantly aware of *risk* as you read this book. Options strategies are best defined in terms of risk levels, so the context of risk level is of utmost importance.

3. Watch the market and check options as well as stocks. Become familiar with how option values change as stocks move upward and downward, and become familiar with the degree of movement of options at various value levels.

4. Identify your own risk tolerance levels and decide how options are most appropriate in your own portfolio. Try various strategies through paper

trading (see Chapter 10) before you put any cash at risk, to find out how the market for options actually works. Only when you have a clear idea of what risks are appropriate for you will you be ready to enter the options market; then you can proceed with confidence.

The Wiley *Getting Started* series is designed to provide people like you with a solid base for understanding a particular market or strategy. The use of many learning tools and carefully designed layout make this series a popular one with many varied titles from which to choose. Options and other markets may be considered highly technical or difficult, but one important premise to this series is the belief that anyone can master a new idea. If the information is provided and explained in a user-friendly format, you can acquire and master the field of study, and improve your chances for success in the market.

Chapter 1

Calls and Puts: Defining the Field of Play

Nine-tenths of wisdom is being wise in time.
—Theodore Roosevelt, speech, June 14, 1917

The study of options can expand your perceptions about the range of possibilities. Most people are familiar with two forms of investment: equity and debt. There is a third method, however, and that third method is far more interesting than the other two. Its attributes are unlike any that most people understand—and these differences can be viewed as a troubling set of problems, or as a promising set of opportunities.

Let's begin with a brief review, laying the groundwork about the two basic ways to invest. An *equity investment* is the purchase of ownership in a company. The best-known example of this is the purchase of stock in publicly listed companies, whose shares are sold through the stock exchanges. Each *share* of stock represents a portion of the total capital, or ownership, in the company.

When you buy 100 shares of stock, you are in complete control over that investment. You decide how long to hold the shares and when to sell. Stocks provide you with tangible value, because they represent part ownership in the company. Owning stock entitles you to dividends if they are declared, and gives

equity investment
an investment in the form of part ownership, such as the purchase of shares of stock in a corporation.

5

share
a unit of ownership in the capital of a corporation.

you the right to vote in elections offered to stockholders. (Some special nonvoting stock lacks this right.) If the stock rises in value, you will gain a profit. If you wish, you can keep the stock for many years, even for your whole life. Stocks, because they have tangible value, can be traded over public exchanges, or they can be used as collateral to borrow money.

Example

Equity for Cash: You purchase 100 shares at $27 per share, and place $2,700 plus trading fees into your account. You receive notice that the purchase has been completed. This is an equity investment, and you are a stockholder in the corporation.

Example

Part-way There: You buy an automobile for $10,000. You put down $3,000 and finance the difference of $7,000. Your *equity* is limited to your down payment of $3,000. You are the licensed owner but the financed balance of $7,000 is *not* part of your equity.

debt investment
an investment in the form of a loan made to earn interest, such as the purchase of a bond.

The second broadly understood form is a *debt investment*, also called a debt instrument. This is a loan made by the investor to the company, government, or government agency, which promises to repay the loan plus interest, as a contractual obligation. The best-known form of debt instrument is the bond. Corporations, cities and states, the federal government, agencies, and subdivisions finance their operations and projects through bond issues, and investors in bonds are lenders, not stockholders.

When you own a bond, you also own a tangible value, not in stock but in a contractual right with the lender. The bond issuer promises to pay you interest and to repay the amount loaned by a specific date. Like stocks, bonds can be used as collateral to borrow money. They also rise and fall in value based on the interest rate a bond pays compared to current rates in today's market. In the event an issuer goes broke, bondholders are usually repaid before stockholders as part of their contract, so bonds have that advantage over stocks.

Example

Lending Your Money: You purchase a bond currently valued at $9,700 from the U.S. government. Although you invest your funds in the same manner as a stockholder, you have become a bondholder; this does not provide any equity interest to you. You are a lender and you own a debt instrument.

Example

Helping a Friend: A good friend wants to buy a car for $10,000, but has only $3,000 in cash. This friend asks you to lend him the balance of $7,000 and offers to pay interest to you. The $7,000 you contribute is a debt investment, and the interest you earn is income on that investment. When you act as lender, you have made a debt investment.

The third form of investing is less well known. Equity and debt contain a tangible value that we can grasp and visualize. Part ownership in a company or the contractual right for repayment are basic features of equity and debt investments. Not only are these tangible, but they have a specific lifespan as well. Stock ownership lasts as long as you continue to own the stock and cannot be canceled unless the company goes broke; a bond has a contractual repayment schedule and ending date. The third form of investing does not contain these features; it disappears—expires—within a short period of time. You might hesitate at the idea of investing money in a product that evaporates and then ceases to have any value. In fact, there is no tangible value at all.

So we're talking about investing money in something with no tangible value, that will absolutely be worthless within a few months. To make this even more perplexing, imagine that the value of this intangible is certain to decline just because time passes by. To confuse the point even further, imagine that these attributes can be an advantage or a disadvantage, depending on how you decide to use these products.

These are some of the features of options. Taken alone (and out of context), these attributes certainly do not make this market seem very appealing. These attributes—lack of tangible value, worthlessness in the short term, and decline in value itself—make options seem far too risky for most people. But there are good reasons for you to read on. Not all methods of investing in options are as risky as they might seem; some are quite conservative, because the features just mentioned can work to your advantage. In whatever way you might use options, the many strategies that can be applied make options one of the more interesting avenues for investors. The more you study options, the more you realize that they are flexible; they can be used in numerous situations and to create numerous opportunities; and, most intriguing of all, they can be either exceptionally risky or downright conservative.

Smart Investor Tip

Option strategies range from high-risk to extremely conservative. The risk features on one end of the spectrum work to your advantage on the other. Options provide you with a rich variety of choices.

---

option
the right to buy or to sell 100 shares of stock at a specified, fixed price and by a specified date in the future.

An *option* is a contract that provides you with the right to execute a stock transaction—that is, to buy or sell 100 shares of stock. (Each option always refers to a 100-share unit.) This right includes a specific stock and a specific fixed price per share that remains fixed until a specific date in the future. When you have an open option position, you do not have any equity in the stock, and neither do you have any debt position. You have only a contractual right to buy or to sell 100 shares of the stock at the fixed price.

Since you can always buy or sell 100 shares at the current market price, you might ask: "Why do I need to purchase an option to gain that right?" The answer is that the option fixes the price of stock, and this is the key to an option's value. Stock prices may rise or fall, at times significantly. Price movement of the stock is unpredictable, which makes stock market investing interesting and also defines the risk to the market itself. As an option owner, the stock price you *can* apply to buy or sell 100 shares is frozen for as long as the option remains in effect. So no matter how much price movement takes place, your price is fixed should you decide to purchase or sell 100 shares of that stock. Ultimately, an option's value is going to be determined by a comparison between the fixed price and the stock's current market price.

A few important restrictions come with options:

- The right to buy or to sell stock at the fixed price is never indefinite; in fact, time is the most critical factor because the option exists for a specific time only. When the deadline has passed, the option becomes worthless and ceases to exist. Because of this, the option's value is going to fall as the deadline approaches, and in a predictable manner.

- Each option also applies only to one specific stock and cannot be transferred.
- Finally, each option applies to exactly 100 shares of stock, no more and no less.

Stock transactions commonly occur in blocks divisible by 100, called a *round lot*, which has become a standard trading unit on the public exchanges. In the market, you have the right to buy or sell an unlimited number of shares, assuming that they are available for sale and that you are willing to pay the seller's price. However, if you buy fewer than 100 shares in a single transaction, you will be charged a higher trading fee. An odd-numbered grouping of shares is called an *odd lot*.

So each option applies to 100 shares, conforming to the commonly traded lot, whether you are operating as a buyer or as a seller. There are two types of options. First is the *call*, which grants its owner the right to buy 100 shares of stock in a company. When you buy a call, it is as though the seller is saying to you, "I will allow you to buy 100 shares of this company's stock, at a specified price, at any time between now and a specified date in the future. For that privilege, I expect you to pay me the current call's price."

Each option's value changes according to changes in the price of the stock. If the stock's value rises, the value of the call option will follow suit and rise as well. And if the stock's market price falls, the call option will react in the same manner. When an investor buys a call and the stock's market value rises after the purchase, the investor profits because the call becomes more valuable. The value of an option actually is quite predictable—it is affected by the passage of time as well as by the ever-changing value of the stock.

round lot
a lot of 100 shares of stock or of higher numbers divisible by 100, the usual trading unit on the public exchanges.

odd lot
a lot of shares that contains fewer than the more typical *round lot* trading unit of 100 shares.

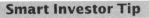

Smart Investor Tip

Changes in the stock's value affect the value of the option directly, because while the stock's market price changes, the option's specified price per share remains the same. The changes in value are predictable; option valuation is no mystery.

call
an option acquired by a buyer or granted by a seller to buy 100 shares of stock at a fixed price within a specified time period.

The second type of option is the *put*. This is the opposite of a call in the sense that it grants a selling right instead of a purchasing right. The owner of a put contract has the right to sell 100 shares of stock. When you buy a put, it is as though the seller were saying to you, "I will allow you to sell me 100 shares of a specific company's stock, at a specified price per share, at any time between now and a specific date in the future. For that privilege, I expect you to pay me the current put's price."

The attributes of calls and puts can be clarified by remembering that either option can be bought or sold. This means there are four possible permutations to option transactions:

1. Buy a call (buy the right to buy 100 shares).
2. Sell a call (sell to someone else the right to buy 100 shares from you).
3. Buy a put (buy the right to sell 100 shares).
4. Sell a put (sell to someone else the right to sell 100 shares to you).

put
an option acquired by a buyer or granted by a seller to sell 100 shares of stock at a fixed price within a specified time period.

Another way to keep the distinction clear is to remember these qualifications: A call buyer believes and hopes that the stock's value will rise, but a put buyer is looking for the price per share to fall. If the belief is right in either case, then a profit may occur.

The opposite is true for sellers of options. A call seller hopes that the stock price will remain the same or fall, and a put seller hopes the price of the stock will rise. (The seller profits if the option's value falls—more on this later.)

Smart Investor Tip

Option buyers can profit whether the market rises or falls; the trick is knowing ahead of time which direction the market will take.

If an option buyer—dealing either in calls or in puts—is correct in predicting the price movement in the stock's *market value*, then the action of buying the option will be profitable. Market value is the price value agreed upon by both buyer and seller, and is the common determining factor in the auction marketplace. However, when it comes to options, you have an additional obstacle besides estimating the direction of price movement: The change has to take place before the deadline that is attached to every option. You might be correct about a stock's long-term prospects, and as a stockholder you have the luxury of being able to wait out long-term change. However, this luxury is not available to option buyers. This is the critical point. Options are finite and, unlike stocks, they cease to exist and lose all of their value within a relatively short period of time—within a few months for every *listed option*. (Long-term options last up to three years; more on these later.) Because of this daunting limitation to options trading, time is one important factor in determining whether an option buyer is able to earn a profit.

market value
the value of an investment at any given time or date; the amount a buyer is willing to pay to acquire an investment and what a seller is also willing to receive to transfer the same investment.

Smart Investor Tip
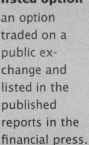

It is not enough to accurately predict the direction of a stock's price movement. For option buyers, that movement has to occur quickly enough for that profit to materialize while the option still exists.

Why does the option's market value change when the stock's price moves up or down? First of all, the option is an intangible right, a contract lacking the kind of value associated, for example, with shares of stock. The option is an agreement relating to 100 shares of a specific stock *and* to a specific price per share. Consequently, if the buyer's timing is poor—meaning the stock's movement doesn't occur or is not substantial enough by the deadline—then the buyer will not realize a profit.

When you buy a call, it is as though you are saying, "I am willing to pay the price being asked to acquire a contractual right. That right provides that I *may* buy 100 shares of stock at the specified fixed price per share, and this right exists to buy those shares at any time between my option purchase date and the specified deadline." If the stock's market price rises above the fixed price indicated in the option agreement, the call becomes

listed option
an option traded on a public exchange and listed in the published reports in the financial press.

more valuable. Imagine that you buy a call option granting you the right to buy 100 shares at the price of $80 per share. Before the deadline, though, the stock's market price rises to $95 per share. As the owner of a call option, you have the right to buy 100 shares at $80, or 15 points below the current market value. This is the purchaser's advantage in the scenario described, when market value exceeds the fixed contractual price indicated in the call's contract. In that instance, you as buyer would have the right to buy 100 shares 15 points below current market value. You own the right, but you are not obligated to follow through. For example, if your call granted you the right to buy 100 shares at $80 per share but the stock's market price fell to $70, you would not have to buy shares at the fixed price of $80; you could elect to take no action.

contract
a single option, the agreement providing the buyer with the terms that option grants. Those terms include identification of the stock, the cost of the option, the date the option will expire, and the fixed price per share of the stock to be bought or sold under the rights of the option.

The same scenario applies to buying puts, but with the stock moving in the opposite direction. When you buy a put, it is as though you are saying, "I am willing to pay the asked price to buy a contractual right. That right provides that I *may* sell 100 shares of the specified stock at the indicated price per share, at any time between my option purchase date and the specified deadline." If the stock's price falls below that level, you will be able to sell 100 shares *above* current market value. For example, let's say that you buy a put option providing you with the right to sell 100 shares at $80 per share. Before the deadline, the stock's market value falls to $70 per share. As the owner of a put, you have the right to sell 100 shares at the fixed price of $80, which is $10 per share above the current market value. You own the right but you are not obligated. For example, if your put granted you the right to sell 100 shares at $70 but the stock's market price rose to $85 per share, you would not be required to sell at the fixed price. You could sell at the higher market price, which would be more profitable. The potential advantage to option buyers is found in the contractual rights that they acquire. These rights are central to the nature of options, and each option bought or sold is referred to as a *contract*.

The Call Option

A call is the right to buy 100 shares of stock at a fixed price per share, at any time between the purchase of the call and the specified future deadline. This time is

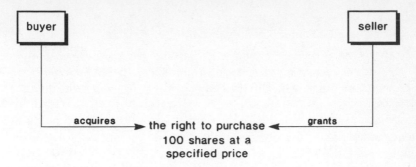

FIGURE 1.1 The call option.

limited. As a call *buyer*, you acquire the right, and as a call *seller*, you grant the right of the option to someone else. (See Figure 1.1.)

Let's walk through an illustration and apply both buying and selling as they relate to the call option.

- *Buyer of a call*: When you buy a call, you hope that the stock will rise in value, because that will result in a corresponding increase in value for the call. This will create higher market value in the call, which can be sold and closed at a profit; or the stock can be bought at a fixed price lower than the current market value.

- *Seller of a call*: When you sell a call, you hope that the stock will fall in value, because that will result in a corresponding decrease in value for the call. This will create lower market value for the call, which can then be purchased and closed at a profit; or the stock can be sold to the buyer at a price above current market value. The order is the reverse from the better-known buyer's position. The call seller will first sell and then, later on, will close the transaction with a buy order. (More information on selling calls is presented in Chapter 5.)

> **buyer**
> an investor who purchases a call or a put option; the buyer realizes a profit if the value of stock moves above the specified price (call) or below the specified price (put).

The backwards sequence used by call sellers is often difficult to grasp for anyone accustomed to the more traditional buy-hold-sell pattern. The seller's approach is to sell-hold-buy. Remembering that time is running for every option contract, the seller, by reversing the sequence, has a distinct advantage over the buyer. Time is on the seller's side.

Smart Investor Tip

Option sellers reverse the sequence by selling first and buying later.
This strategy has many advantages, especially considering the
restriction of time unique to the option contract. Time benefits the
seller.

seller
an investor who grants a right in an
option to someone else; the seller
realizes a profit if the value of the
stock moves below the specified
price (call) or above the specified
price (put).

Prices of listed options—
those traded publicly on exchanges
like the New York, Chicago, and
Philadelphia stock exchanges—are
established strictly through *supply
and demand*. Those are the forces
that dictate whether market prices
rise or fall for stocks. As more buyers want stocks, prices are driven
upward by their demand; and as
more sellers want to sell shares of
stock, prices decline due to increased supply. The supply and demand for stocks,
in turn, affect the market value of options. The option itself has no direct
fundamental value or underlying financial reasons for rising or falling; its market
value is a by-product of the fundamental and technical changes in the stock.

Smart Investor Tip

The market forces affecting the value of stocks in turn affect market
values of options. The option itself has no actual fundamental value; its
market value is formulated based on the stock's fundamentals.

supply and demand
the market forces that determine
the current value for stocks. The
number of buyers represents demand for shares, and the number of
sellers represents supply. The price
of stocks rises as demand increases,
and falls as supply increases.

The orderly process of buying and selling stocks, which establishes stock price values, takes
place on the exchanges through
trading available to the general
public. This overall public trading
activity, in which prices are being
established through ever-changing
supply and demand, is called the
auction market, because value is
not controlled by any forces other

than the market itself. These forces include economic news and perceptions, earnings of listed companies, news and events affecting products and services, competitive forces, and Wall Street events, both positive and negative. Individual stock prices also rise or fall based on index motion.

Stocks issued by corporations are limited in number, but the exchanges will allow investors to buy or sell as many options as they want. The *number* of active options is unlimited. However, the *values* in option contracts respond directly to changes in the stock's value. The two primary factors affecting an option's value are time and the market value of the stock.

Smart Investor Tip

Option value is affected by movement in the price of the stock and by the passage of time. Supply and demand affect option valuation only indirectly.

The owner of a call enjoys an important benefit in the auction market. There is always a *ready market* for the option at the current market price. That means that the owner of an option never has a problem selling that option.

This feature is of critical importance. For example, if there were constantly more buyers than sellers of options, then market value would be distorted beyond reason. To some degree, distortions do occur on the basis of rumor or speculation, usually in the short term. But by and large, option values are directly formulated on the basis of stock prices and time until the option will cease to exist. If buyers had to scramble to find a limited number of willing sellers, the market would not work efficiently. Demand between buyers and sellers in options is rarely equal, because options do not possess supply and demand features of their own. So the Options Clearing Corporation (OCC) acts as the seller to every buyer, and as the buyer to every seller.

Smart Investor Tip

Learn more about the Options Clearing Corporation (OCC) at their web site, http://www.optionsclearing.com. This page includes current market information, resources for options trading, and a link to the options prospectus, "Characteristics and Risks of Standardized Options." The prospectus can also be viewed at the Chicago Board Options Exchange (CBOE) web site,http://www.cboe.com/Resources/intro.aspx.

How Call Buying Works

auction market
the public exchanges in
which stocks, bonds, op-
tions, and other products
are traded publicly, and
in which values are established by everchanging
supply and demand on the
part of buyers and sellers.

ready market
a liquid market, one in
which buyers can easily
sell their holdings, or in
which sellers can easily
find buyers, at current
market prices.

expiration date
the date on which an op-
tion becomes worthless,
which is specified in the
option contract.

underlying stock
the stock on which the
option grants the right
to buy or sell, which is
specified in every option
contract.

When you buy a call, you are not required
to buy the 100 shares of stock. You have the
right, but not the obligation. In fact, the vast
majority of call buyers do *not* actually buy
100 shares of stock. Most buyers are speculating on the price movement of the stock,
hoping to sell their options at a profit rather
than buy 100 shares of stock. As a buyer,
you have until the *expiration date* to decide
what action to take, if any. You have several
choices, and the best one to make depends
entirely on what happens to the market price
of the *underlying stock*, and on how much
time remains in the option period.

Using calls to illustrate, there are three
scenarios relating to the price of the underlying stock, and several choices for action
within each.

1. *The market value of the underlying
stock rises*. In the event of an increase in the
price of the underlying stock, you may take
one of two actions. First, you may *exercise* the
call and buy the 100 shares of stock below
current market value. Second, if you do not
want to own 100 shares of that stock, you
may sell the option for a profit.

Every option has a fixed value at which
exercise takes place. Whenever an option is
exercised, the purchase price of 100 shares of
stock takes place at that fixed price, which is
called the *striking price* of the option. Striking
price is expressed as a numerical equivalent
of the dollar price per share, without dollar
signs. The striking price is normally divisible
by 5, as options are established with striking
prices at five-dollar price intervals for stocks
selling between $30 and $200 per share.
Stocks selling under $30 have options trad-
ing at 2.5-point intervals; and stocks trading
above $200 per share have options trading

at $10 intervals. When a stock splits, new striking price levels may also be introduced. For example, if a stock is split 2-for-1 and it has a current option at 35, the post-split levels would be adjusted to $17^1/_2$. (In cases of splits, the number of shares *and* options are adjusted so that the ratio of one option per 100 shares of stock remains constant. In a 2-for-1 split, 100 shares become 200 shares at half the value; and each outstanding option becomes two options worth half the pre-split value.)

Example

Profitable Decisions: You decided two months ago to buy a call. You paid the option price of $200, which entitled you to buy 100 shares of a particular stock at $55 per share. The striking price is 55. The option will expire later this month. The stock currently is selling for $60 per share, and the option's current value is 6 ($600). You have a choice to make: You may exercise the call and buy 100 shares at the contractual price of $55 per share, which is $5 per share below current market value; or you may sell the call and realize a profit of $400 on the investment, consisting of current market value of the option of $600, less the original price of $200. (This example does not include an adjustment for trading costs, so in applying this and other examples, remember that it will cost you a fee each time you enter an option transaction, and each time you leave one. This should be factored into any calculation of profit or loss on an option trade.)

---

    2. *The market value of the underlying stock does not change*. It often happens that within the life span of an option, the stock's market value does not change, or changes are too insignificant to create the profit scenario you hope for when you buy calls. You have two alternatives in this situation. First, you may sell the call at a loss before its expiration date (after which the call becomes worthless). Second, you may hold on to the option, hoping that the stock's market value will rise before expiration, which would create a rise in the call's value as well, at the last minute. The first choice, selling at a loss, is advisable when it appears there is no hope of a last-minute surge in the stock's market value. Taking some money out and reducing your loss may be wiser than waiting for the option to lose even more value.

exercise
the act of buying stock under the terms of the call option or selling stock under the terms of the put option, at the price per share specified in the option contract.

striking price
the fixed price to be paid for 100 shares of stock, specified in the option contract; the transaction price per share of stock upon exercise of that option, regardless of the current market value of the stock.

Remember, after expiration date, the option is worthless. An option is a *wasting asset*, because it is designed to lose all of its value after expiration. By its limited life attribute, it is expected to decline in value as time passes. If the market value of the stock remains at or below the striking price all the way to expiration, then the *premium value*—the current market value of the option—will be much less near expiration than at the time you purchased it, even if the stock's market value remains the same. The difference reflects the value of time itself. The longer the time until expiration, the more opportunity there is for the stock (and the option) to change in value.

Smart Investor Tip

In setting standards for yourself to determine when or if to take profits in an option, be sure to factor in the cost of the transaction. Brokerage fees and charges vary widely, so shop around for the best option deal based on the volume of trading you undertake.

Example

Best Laid Plans: You purchased a call a few months ago "at 5." (This means you paid a premium of $500). You hoped that the underlying stock would increase in market value, causing the option also to rise in value. The call will expire later this month, but contrary to your expectations, the stock's price has not changed. The option's value has declined to $100. You have the choice of selling it now and taking a $400 loss; or you may hold the option, hoping for a last-minute increase in the stock's value. Either way, you will need to sell the option before expiration, after which it will become worthless.

Smart Investor Tip

The options market is characterized by a series of choices, some more difficult than others. It requires discipline to apply a formula so that you make the best decision given the circumstances, rather than acting on impulse. That is the key to succeeding with options.

3. *The market value of the underlying stock falls.* As the underlying stock's market value falls, the value of all related calls will fall as well. The value of the option is always related to the value of the underlying stock. If the stock's market price falls significantly, your call will show very little in the way of market value. You may sell and accept the loss or, if the option is worth nearly nothing, you may simply allow it to expire and take a full loss on the transaction.

wasting asset
any asset that declines in value over time. An option is an example of a wasting asset because it exists only until expiration, after which it becomes worthless.

Example

Dashed Hopes: You bought a call four months ago and paid 3 (a premium of $300). You were hoping that the stock's market value would rise, also causing a rise in the value of the call. Instead, the stock's market value fell, and the option followed suit. It is now worth only 1 ($100). You have a choice: You may sell the call for 1 and accept a loss of $200; or you may hold on to the call until near expiration. The stock could rise in value at the last minute, which has been known to happen. However, by continuing to hold the call, you risk further deterioration in the call premium value. If you wait until expiration occurs, the call will be worthless.

This example demonstrates that buying calls is risky. The last-minute rescue of an option by a sudden increase in the value of the underlying stock can and does happen, but usually it does not. The limited life of the option works against the call buyer, so that the entire amount invested could be lost. The most significant advantage in speculating in calls is that instead of losing a larger sum in buying 100 shares of stock, the loss is limited to the relatively small premium value. At the same time, you could profit significantly as a call buyer because less money is at risk. The stockholder, in comparison, has the

premium value
the current price of an option, which a buyer pays and a seller receives at the time of the transaction. The amount of premium is expressed as the dollar value of the option, but without dollar signs; for example, stating that an option is "at 3" means its current market value is $300.

advantage of being able to hold stock indefinitely, without having to worry about expiration date. For stockholders, patience is always possible, and it might take many months or even years for growth in value to occur. The stockholder is under no pressure to act because stock does not expire as options do.

Example

Limiting Risk: You bought a call last month for 1 (premium of $100). The current price of the stock is $80 per share. For your $100 investment, you have a degree of control over 100 shares, without having to invest $8,000. Your risk is limited to the $100 investment; if the stock's market value falls, you cannot lose more than the $100, no matter what. In comparison, if you paid $8,000 to acquire 100 shares of stock, you could afford to wait indefinitely for a profit to appear, but you would have to tie up $8,000. You could also lose much more; if the stock's market value falls to $50 per share, your investment will have lost $3,000 in market value.

Smart Investor Tip

For anyone speculating over the short term, option buying is an excellent method of controlling large blocks of stock with minor commitments of capital.

In some respects, the preceding example defines the difference between investing and speculating. The very idea of investing usually indicates a long-term mentality and perspective. Because stock does not expire, investors enjoy the luxury of being able to wait out short-term market conditions, hoping that over several years that company's fortunes will lead to profits—not to mention continuing dividends and ever-higher market value for the stock. There is no denying that stockholders enjoy clear advantages over option buyers. They can wait indefinitely for the market to go their way. They earn dividend income. And stock can be used as collateral for buying or financing other assets. Speculators, in comparison, risk losing all of their investment, while also being exposed to the opportunity for spectacular gains. Rather than considering one method as being better than the other, think of options as yet another way to use investment capital. Option buyers know that their risk/reward scenario is characterized by the ever-looming expiration date. To understand how the speculative nature of call buying affects you, consider the following two examples.

Smart Investor Tip

The limited life of options defines the risk/reward scenario, and option players recognize this as part of their strategy. The risk is accepted because the opportunity is there, too.

Example

Rising Hopes . . . and Prices: You buy an 80 call for 2 ($200), which provides you with the right to buy 100 shares of stock for $80 per share. If the stock's value rises above $80, your call will rise in value dollar-for-dollar along with the stock. So if the stock goes up $4 per share to $84, the option will also rise four points, or $400 in value. You would earn a profit of $200 if you were to sell the call at that point (four points of value less the purchase price of 2). That would be the same amount of profit you would realize by purchasing 100 shares of stock at $8,000 and selling those shares for $8,200. (Again, this example does not take into account any brokerage and trading costs. Chances are that fees for the stock trade would be higher than for an option trade because more money is being exchanged.)

Example

Falling Expectations: You buy an 80 call for 2 ($200), which gives you the right to buy 100 shares of stock at $80 per share. By the call's expiration date, the stock has fallen to $68 per share. You lose the entire $200 investment as the call becomes worthless. However, if you had purchased 100 shares of stock and paid $8,000, your loss at this point would be $1,200 ($80 per share at purchase, less current market value of $68 per share). Your choice, then, would be to sell the stock and take the loss or continue to keep your capital tied up, hoping its value will eventually rebound. Compared to buying stock directly, the option risks are limited. Stockholders can wait out a temporary drop in price, even indefinitely. However, the stockholder has no way of knowing when the stock's price will rebound, or even if it ever will do so. As an option buyer, you are at risk for only a few months at the most. One of the risks in buying stock is the *lost opportunity risk*—capital is committed in a loss situation while other opportunities come and go.

In situations where an investment in stock loses value, stockholders can wait for a rebound. During that time, they are entitled to continue receiving dividends, so their investment is not entirely in limbo. If you are seeking long-term gains, then a temporary drop in market value is not catastrophic as long as you continue to believe that the company remains a viable long-term "hold" candidate; market fluctuations might even be expected. Some investors would see such a drop as a buying opportunity and pick up even more shares. The effect of this move is to lower the overall basis in the stock, so that a rebound creates even greater returns later on.

lost opportunity risk (stock)
the risk stockholders experience in tying up capital over the long term, causing lost opportunities that could be taken if capital were available.

Smart Investor Tip

A long-term investor can hold stock indefinitely and does not have to worry about expiration. Option buyers have to worry continually about expiration date.

The advantage in buying calls is that you are not required to tie up a large sum of capital nor to keep it at risk for a long time. Yet you are able to control 100 shares of stock for each option purchased as though you had bought those shares outright. Losses are limited to the amount of premium you pay.

The Long-Term Call Option

The greatest inhibiting factor in evaluating calls is time. As a call buyer, you need to continually be aware that expiration forces a decision point; profits have to materialize before expiration, or the call buyer loses money.

LEAPS
Long-term Equity Anticipation Security, long-term option contracts that work just like standardized options, but with expiration up to three years.

The listed option has a life span of only a few months, normally eight or so; the price movement of the stock has to be substantial enough to overcome this time factor. For many buyers, the short life span of calls makes them impractical as a speculative position. To overcome this problem, call buyers may also consider using long-term options. These work just like listed options in every respect, with one exception: Their life span lasts up to three years.

A Long-term Equity AnticiPation Security (*LEAPS*) is a long-term option that can be used to solve the problem of time. Unlike the relatively short-lived listed option, LEAPS can be used to expand many strategies that would otherwise be impractical, given the time factor.

The long-term option, because of its extended life, can be employed for some strategies that are not practical with shorter-expiration contracts. LEAPS can be used as an alternative to buying stock and placing large sums of capital at risk. This could change the way that you invest in volatile market conditions. They can also be used to protect paper profits over a period of time, in combination with other strategies, and for speculative or conservative strategies. The choice of using listed options or LEAPS options expands the range of strategies and makes the entire field of options far more flexible; options traders can look beyond the eight-month range that is typical for listed options and achieve far more with a greater amount of time in play.

In considering calls and reviewing the broad range of risk levels, you can consider both short-term and long-term options in developing investment standards. Throughout the remainder of this book, many examples will employ listed options as well as LEAPS options to illustrate how strategies can be used in a number of different ways.

Investment Standards for Call Buyers

Whether using shorter-term listed options or LEAPS calls, you need to not only be aware of risk levels, but also to establish a clear investment standard for yourself. This means much more than merely taking the advice of a stockbroker or financial planner; it means considering a range of ideas and choosing standards that fit well for you, individually.

People who work in the stock market—including brokers who help investors to decide what to buy and sell—regularly offer advice on stocks. If a stockbroker, analyst, or financial planner is qualified, he or she may also offer advice on trading in options. Three important points should be kept in mind when working with a broker, especially where option buying is involved.

1. *You need to develop your own expertise.* The broker might not know as much about the market as you do. Just because someone has a license does not mean that he or she is an expert on all types of investments. In fact, due to the nature of the options market, you may want to become proficient at making your own options-related decisions. In this case, you may wish to continue employing outside help for stock-related decisions, but maintain direct control over options trading.

2. *You cannot expect on-the-job training as an options investor.* Don't expect a broker to train you. Remember, brokers earn their living on commissions and

placement of orders. That means their primary motive is to get clients to buy and to sell. Here again, you may depend on a broker's expertise when it comes to stocks; but you should not assume that the same broker is knowledgeable about options strategies or risks.

3. *There are no guarantees.* Risk is found everywhere and in all markets. While it is true that call buying involves specific risk, this does not mean that buying stock is safe in comparison. You need to distinguish between risk levels for stocks and options. For stocks, your broker should be aware of how volatility in stocks matches with your risk levels; but options change the overall picture, and you need to separate stock and options risks, ignoring the tendency to think that there are any risk-free investments using stocks, options, or the two together. The fact is, once you become comfortable with options trading, you are going to be less likely to depend on a broker for any advice. Options traders tend to think for themselves, and come to realize that they can operate without the services that come with paying full-price commissions.

Smart Investor Tip
Anyone who wants to be involved with options will eventually realize that a broker's advice is unnecessary and could even get in the way of an efficient trading program.

know your customer
a rule requiring brokers to be aware of the risk, knowledge level, and capital profile of each client, designed to ensure that recommendations are suitable for each individual.

Some traders continue using brokers due to personal loyalty or a track record of exceptional advice. Whether you are seeking a broker or using one already, that broker should not give the same recommendations to everyone; advice should be matched to specific risk levels and experience. Brokers are required by law to ensure that you are qualified to invest in options. That means that you should have at least a minimal understanding of market risks, procedures, and terminology, and that you understand the risks associated with options. Brokers are required to apply a rule called *know your customer*. The brokerage firm has to ask you to complete a form that documents your knowledge or experience with options; firms also give out a *prospectus*, which is a document explaining all of the risks of option investing.

The investment standard for buying calls includes the requirement that you know how the market works, and that you invest only funds that you can afford to have at risk. Beyond that, you have every right to decide for yourself how much risk you want to take. Ultimately, you are responsible for your own profits and losses in the market. The role of the broker is to document the fact that the right questions were asked before your money was taken and placed into the option. One of the most common mistakes made, especially by inexperienced investors, is to believe that brokers are responsible for providing guidance. They are not. However, they are required to make sure you know what you're doing before you proceed.

prospectus a document designed to disclose all of the risk characteristics associated with a particular investment.

How Call Selling Works

Buying calls is similar to buying stock, at least regarding the sequence of events. You invest money and, after some time has passed, you make the decision to sell. The transaction takes place in a predictable order. Call selling doesn't work that way. A seller begins by selling a call, and later on buys the same call to close out the transaction.

Many people have trouble grasping the idea of selling *before* buying. A common reaction is, "Are you sure? Is that legal?" or "How can you sell something that you don't own?" It is legal, and you can sell something before you buy it. This is done all the time in the stock market through a strategy known as *short selling*. An investor sells stock that he or she does not own, and later places a "buy" order, which closes the position.

The same technique is used in the options market, and is far less complicated than selling stock short. Because options have no tangible value, becoming an option seller is fairly easy. A call seller grants the right to someone else—a buyer—to buy 100 shares of stock, at a fixed price per share and by a specified expiration date. For granting this right, the call seller is paid a premium. As a call seller, you are paid for the sale but you must also be willing to deliver 100 shares of stock if the call buyer exercises the option. This strategy, the exact opposite of buying calls,

short selling a strategy in the stock market in which shares of stock are first sold, creating a short position for the investor, and later bought in a closing purchase transaction.

has a different array of risks than those experienced by the call buyer. The greatest risk is that the option you sell could be exercised, and you would be required to sell 100 shares of stock far below the current market value.

When you operate as an option buyer, the decision to exercise or not is entirely up to you. But as a seller, that decision is always made by someone else. As an option seller, you can make or lose money in three different ways:

1. *The market value of the underlying stock rises.* In this instance, the value of the call rises as well. For a buyer, this is good news. But for the seller, the opposite is true. If the buyer exercises the call, the 100 shares of stock have to be delivered by the option seller. In practice, this means you are required to pay the difference between the option's striking price and the stock's current market value. As a seller, this means you lose money. Remember, the option will be exercised only if the stock's current market value is higher than the striking price of the option.

Example

Called Away: You sell a call with a striking price of $40 per share. You happen to own 100 shares of the underlying stock, so you consider your risks to be minimal in selling a call. (If the buyer exercises the call, you already own the shares and would be willing to sell them at the striking price.) In addition, the call is worth $200, and that amount is paid to you for selling the call. One month later, the stock's market value has risen to $46 per share and the buyer exercises the call. You are obligated to deliver the 100 shares of stock at $40 per share. This is $6 per share below current market value. Although you received a premium of $200 for selling the call, you lose the increased market value in the stock, which is $600. Your net loss in this case is $400.

The loss in this example would be viewed based on your original cost of the stock. A call seller selects striking prices based on the original cost of the stock. So if you originally paid $42 per share for the stock and it is called away at $40, you break even before trading costs. (A $2-per-share loss is offset by the premium you were paid for selling the call.) On the other hand, if your original cost of the stock was $35 per share, your overall net profit would be $700—a $500 capital gain on the stock plus $200 in option premium.

Example

More Risk, More Loss: Given the same conditions as above, let's now assume that you did not own 100 shares of stock. What happens if the option is exercised? In this case, you are still required to deliver 100 shares at $40 per share. Current market value is $46, so you are required to buy the shares at that price and then sell them at $40, a net loss of $400. ($600 difference in values, less $200 you received for selling the call.) In practice, you would be required to pay the difference rather than physically buying and then selling 100 shares.

Smart Investor Tip

Call sellers have much less risk when they already own their 100 shares. They can select calls in such a way that in the event of exercise, the stock investment will still be profitable.

The difference between these two examples is that in the first case, you owned the shares and could deliver them if the option were exercised. There is even the possibility that you originally purchased those shares below the $40 per share value. So in effect, you exchanged potential gain in the stock for the value of the call premium you received. In the second example, it is all loss because you have to buy the shares at current market value and sell them for less.

When the call is exercised, it doesn't always translate to a loss. If you received enough premium for selling the call, you could still make a profit.

Example

The LEAPS Call Alternative: You sold a LEAPS call with 30 months until expiration. Because that is a long time away, you were paid a much higher premium than you would have received for selling a shorter-term listed option. You were paid 12 ($1,200) when you sold the call. A few months later, the stock is four points higher than the striking price, and your broker notifies you that your option has been called. You are required to pay the difference between current market value and striking price, which is $400. The net effect is a profit of $800 (before considering trading costs). When using a LEAPS call in a short sale, a higher premium grants you more cushion.

2. *The market value of the stock does not change.* In the case where the stock's value remains at or near the price level when the call was sold, the value of the call will decline over time. Remember, the call is a wasting asset. While that is a problem for the call buyer, it is a great advantage for the call seller. Time works

against the buyer, but it works for the call seller. You have the right to close out your short call at any time before expiration date. So you may sell a call and hope that it declines in value; and then buy it to close the position at a lower premium, with the difference representing your profit.

Example

Profiting from Inertia: You sell a call for a premium of 4 ($400). Two months later, the stock's market value is about the same as it was when you sold the call. The option's premium value has fallen to 1 ($100). You cancel your position by buying the call at 1, realizing a profit of $300.

3. *The market value of the stock falls.* In this case, the option will also fall in value. This provides you with an advantage as a call seller. Remember, you are paid a premium at the time you sell the call. You want to close out your position at a later date, or wait for the call to expire worthless. You may do either in this case. Because time works against the buyer, it would take a considerable change in the stock's market value to change your profitable position in the sold option.

Example

Profits from Falling Prices: You sell a LEAPS call and receive a premium of 12 ($1,200). The stock's market value later falls far below the striking price of the option and, in your opinion, a recovery is not likely. As long as the market value of the stock is at or below the striking price at expiration, the option will not be exercised. By allowing the option to expire in this situation, the entire $1,200 you received is profit.

short position
the status assumed by investors when they enter a sale order in advance of entering a buy order. The short position is closed by later entering a buy order, or through expiration.

Remember three key points as a call seller. First, the transaction takes place in reverse order, with sale occurring before the purchase. Second, when you sell a call, you are paid a premium; in comparison, a call buyer pays the premium at the point of purchase. Third, what is good news for the buyer is bad news for the seller, and vice versa.

When you sell a call option, you are a short seller and that places you into what is called a *short position*. The sale is the opening transaction, and it can be closed in one of two ways. First, a buy order can be entered, and that closes out the position. Second, you may wait until expiration, after which the option ceases to exist and the position closes automatically. In comparison, the better-known "buy first, sell later" approach is called a *long position*. The long position is also closed in one of two ways. Either the buyer enters a sell order, closing the position, or the option expires worthless, so that the buyer loses the entire premium value.

long position
the status assumed by investors when they enter a buy order in advance of entering a sell order. The long position is closed by later entering a sell order, or through expiration.

The Put Option

A put is the opposite of a call. It is a contract granting the right to *sell* 100 shares of stock at a fixed price per share and by a specified expiration date in the future. As a put buyer, you acquire the right to sell 100 shares of stock; and as a put seller, you grant that right to the buyer. (See Figure 1.2.)

Buying and Selling Puts

As a buyer of a put, you hope the underlying stock's value will fall. A put is the opposite of a call and so it acts in the opposite manner as the stock's market value changes. If the stock's market value falls, the put's value rises; and if the stock's market value rises, then the put's value falls. There are three possible outcomes when you buy puts.

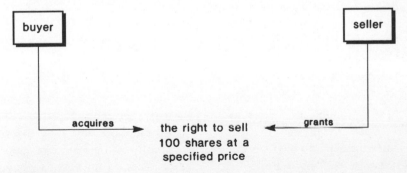

FIGURE 1.2 The put option.

1. *The market value of the stock rises.* In this case, the put's value falls in response. Thus, you may sell the put for a price below the price you paid and take a loss; or you may hold on to the put, hoping that the stock's market value will fall before the expiration date.

Example

Turning It Upside Down: You bought a put two months ago, paying a premium of 2 ($200). You expected the stock's market price to fall, in which case the value of the put would have risen. Instead, the stock's market value rose, so the put's value fell. It is now worth only 0.25, or $25. You have a choice: Sell the put and take a $175 loss, or hold on to the put, hoping the stock will fall before the expiration date. If you hold the put beyond expiration, it will be worthless and your loss will be the full $200.

This example demonstrates the need to assess risks. For example, with the put currently worth only $25—nearly nothing—there is very little value remaining, so you might consider it too late to cut your losses in this case. Considering that there is only $25 at stake, it might be worth the long shot of holding the put until expiration. If the stock's price does fall between now and then, you stand the chance of recovering your investment and, perhaps, even earning a profit.

Smart Investor Tip

Option traders constantly calculate risk and reward, and often make decisions based not upon how they hoped prices would change, but upon how an unexpected change has affected their position.

---

2. *The market value of the stock does not change.* If the stock does not move significantly enough to alter the value of the put, then the put's value will still fall. The put, like the call, is a wasting asset; so the more time that passes and the closer the expiration date becomes, the less value will remain in the put. In this situation, you may sell the put and accept a loss, or hold on to it, hoping that the stock's market price will fall before the put's expiration.

> **Example**
>
> **Choosing between Bad and Worse:** You bought a LEAPS put several
> months ago and paid a premium of 7 ($700). You had expected the
> stock's market value to fall, in which case the put's value would have
> risen. Expiration comes up later this month. Unfortunately, the stock's
> market value is about the same as it was when you bought the LEAPS
> put, but that put is now worth only $100. Your choices: Sell the put for
> $100 and accept the $600 loss; or hold on to the put on the chance that
> the stock's value will fall before expiration.

The choice comes down to a matter of timing and an awareness of how much price change is required to produce a breakeven point or a profit. In the preceding example, the stock would have to fall at least seven points below the put's striking price just to create a breakeven outcome (before trading costs). In this case, even utilizing a longer-term LEAPS put, the option profit simply did not materialize before expiration. If you have more time, your choice would be easier because you could defer your decision to either take a loss or just wait out the price movement of the stock. You can afford to adopt a wait-and-see attitude with a long time to go before expiration, which makes the LEAPS a more flexible choice than shorter-term listed options. The value of any option tends to fall slowly at first, and then more rapidly as expiration approaches.

3. *The market value of the stock falls.* In this case, the put's value will rise. You have three alternatives. First, you may hold the put in the hope that the stock's market value will decline even more, increasing your profit. Second, you may sell the put and take your profit now. Third, you may exercise the put and sell 100 shares of the underlying stock at the striking price. That price will be above current market value, so you will profit from exercise by selling at the higher striking price.

> **Example**
>
> **Having It Both Ways:** You own 100 shares of stock that you bought last
> year for $38 per share, and the price later rose above $40. You were
> worried about the threat of a falling market; however, you also wanted to
> hold on to your stock as a long-term investment. To protect yourself
> against the possibility of a price decline in your stock, you bought a put,
> paying a premium of 0.50, or $50. This guarantees you the right to sell
> 100 shares for $40 per share. Recently, the price of your stock fell to $33
> per share. The value of the put increased to $750, offsetting your loss in
> the stock.

You can make a choice given the preceding example. You may sell the put and realize a profit of $700, which offsets the loss in the stock. This choice is appealing because you can take a profit in the put, but you continue to own the stock. So if the stock's price rebounds, you will benefit twice.

A second alternative is to exercise the put and sell the 100 shares at $40 per share (the striking price of the option), which is $7 per share above current market value (but only $2 per share above the price you paid originally for the stock). This choice could be appealing if you believe that circumstances have changed and that it was a mistake to buy the stock as a long-term investment. By getting out now with a profit instead of a loss, you recover your full investment even though the stock's market value has fallen. This alternative makes sense if and when you would prefer to get out of the stock position; with the put investment, you can make that choice profitably, even though the stock's market value has fallen.

A third choice is to hold off taking any immediate action. The put acts as a form of insurance to protect your investment in the stock against further price declines. That's because at this point, for every drop in the stock's price, the option's value will offset that drop, point for point. If the stock's value increases, the option's value will decline dollar for dollar. So the two positions offset one another. As long as you take action before the put's expiration, your risk is virtually eliminated.

Smart Investor Tip

At times, inaction is the smartest choice. Depending on the circumstances, you could be better off patiently waiting out price movements until the day before expiration.

While you may buy puts believing the stock's market value will fall, or to protect your stock position, you may also sell puts. As a put seller, you grant someone else the right to sell 100 shares of stock to you at a fixed price. If the put is exercised, you will be required to buy 100 shares of the stock at the striking price, which would be above the market value of the stock. For taking this risk, you are paid a premium when you sell the put. Like the call seller, put sellers do not control the outcome of their position as much as buyers do, since it is the buyer who has the right to exercise at any time.

Example

Waiting It Out: Last month, you sold a put with a striking price of $50 per share. The premium was $250, which was paid to you at the time of the sale. Since then, the stock's market value has remained in a narrow range between $48 and $53 per share. Currently, the price is at $51. You do not expect the stock's price to fall below the striking price of 50. As long as the market value of the underlying stock remains at or above that level, the put will not be exercised. (The buyer will not exercise, meaning that you will not be required to buy 100 shares of stock.) If your prediction turns out to be correct, you can make a profit by selling the put once its value has declined.

Your risk in this example is that the stock's market price could decline below $50 per share before expiration, meaning that upon exercise you would be required to buy 100 shares at $50 per share. To avoid that risk, you have the right to cancel the position by buying the put at current market value. The closer you are to expiration (and as long as the stock's market value is above the striking price), the lower the market value of the put—and the greater your profit.

Put selling also makes sense if you believe that the striking price represents a fair price for the stock. In the worst case, you will be required to buy 100 shares at a price above current market value. If you are right, though, and the striking price is a fair price, then the stock's market value will eventually rebound to that price or above. In addition, to calculate the real loss on buying, overpriced stock has to be discounted for the premium you received.

Selling puts is a vastly different strategy from buying puts, because it places you on the opposite side of the transaction. The risk profile is different as well. If the put you sell is exercised, then you end up with overpriced stock, so you need to establish a logical standard for yourself if you sell puts. Never sell a put unless you are willing to acquire 100 shares of the underlying stock, at the striking price.

One advantage for put sellers is that time works for you and against the buyer. As expiration approaches, the put loses value. However, if movement in the underlying stock is opposite the movement you expected, you could end up taking a loss or having to buy 100 shares of stock for each put you sell. Sudden and unexpected changes in the stock's market value can occur at any time. The more volatile a stock's price movement, the greater your risk as a seller. You might also notice as you observe the pricing of options that, due to higher risks, options on volatile stocks tend to hold higher premium values than those on more predictable, lower volatility issues.

Smart Investor Tip

Option price behavior is directly affected by the underlying stock and its attributes. So volatile (higher risk) stocks demand higher option premiums and tend to experience faster, more severe price changes.

Put selling strategies can be more flexible when employing LEAPS. Because there is greater time to go until expiration, the LEAPS put seller has two advantages. First, the potential decline in stock price is limited in comparison to the potential rise in the case of using short calls; and second, the premium is likely to be higher than for shorter-term listed puts.

The potential decline in stock price is limited in two ways. First, the difference between the striking price and zero is a known quantity. Second and more realistically, the price of stock is not likely to fall below tangible book value per share. So risks in short-selling of puts is limited. You will recall that short selling of calls is far riskier because, in theory at least, a stock's price could rise indefinitely.

The second factor—the LEAPS premium—makes put selling practical due to the cushion that premium provides. However, the larger premium also reflects a longer time period that LEAPS put sellers remain at risk; so offsetting the advantage, there is also the disadvantage of having to wait longer for those profits to materialize.

Example

The Premium Cushion: You believe that a particular stock is likely to rise in value. It is currently selling at $41 per share. The 30-month LEAPS puts at a striking price of 40 are available at 9 ($900). You sell a LEAPS put and receive payment of $900.

If the stock's value falls as low as $31 per share, you have downside protection (before trading costs are calculated) due to the nine points you were paid in premium. However, even if that put were to be exercised, you consider $40 per share a reasonable price to pay for the stock. You believe its long-term prospects are strong, so you would not mind picking up shares at that price level. Considering the payment of $900 for the LEAPS put, your net basis in stock upon exercise would be only $31 per share.

Option Valuation

Option values change in direct proportion to the changing market value of the underlying stock. Every option is associated specifically with the stock of a single corporation and cannot be interchanged with others. How you fare in your option positions depends on how the stock's value changes in the immediate future.

The question of selecting stocks is more involved and complex than the method of picking an option. For options, the selection has to do with risk assessment, current value, time until expiration, and your own risk tolerance level; in addition, numerous strategies you may employ will affect the ultimate decision. But option selection is formulated predictably. In comparison, stock selection involves no precise formula that works in every case. Price movement in the stock itself cannot be known in advance, whereas the reaction of option premium value is completely predictable, based on the way the stock's price changes.

The selection of a stock is the critical decision point that determines whether you will succeed with options. This observation applies for buying or selling stock, and also applies when you never intend to own the stock at all but only want to deal with options themselves. It is a mistake to pick options based only on current value and time, hoping to succeed, without also thinking about the particulars of the stock—volatility, relation to striking price of the option, and much more. Of course, to some degree, the features of the option can be used to calculate likely outcomes, but that is only a part of the whole picture. Because option value is tied to stock price and volatility, you also need to develop a dependable method for evaluation of the underlying stock.

fundamental analysis

a study of financial information and attributes of a company's management and competitive position, as a means for selecting stocks.

You may pick stocks strictly on the basis of *fundamental analysis*. This includes a study of financial statements, dividends paid to stockholders, management, the company's position within its industry, capitalization, product or service, and other financial information.

The importance of the fundamentals cannot be emphasized too much, as they define a company's long-term growth prospects, ability to produce consistent profits, and ability to demonstrate market strength over time. However, remember that the fundamentals are historical and have little to do with short-term price changes in the company's stock. It is that very thing—short-term price change—that determines whether a particular option strategy will succeed or fail. While the fundamentals are essential for long-term stock selection, short-term price movement is affected more by perception of value. Indicators involving market price and perception are broadly classified under the umbrella of *technical analysis*.

technical analysis

a study of trends and patterns of price movement in stocks, including price per share, the shape of price movements on charts, high and low ranges, and trends in pricing over time.

Both fundamental and technical indicators have something to offer, and you can use elements of both to study and identify stocks for option trading. The distinctions should be kept in mind, however, including both advantages and disadvantages of each method.

The selection of options cannot be made without also reviewing the attributes of the stock, both fundamental and technical. Whether you treat options only as a form of speculative side bet or as an important aspect associated with being in the market, the judgment you use in selection has to apply to the characteristics and values of both the option and the stock. Criteria for the selection of high-value stocks are at the heart of smart stock market investing. The need for careful, thorough, and continuing analysis cannot be emphasized too much. So attributes such as financial strength, price stability and volatility, dividend and profit history, and others are important, not only to stockholders but to options traders as well. Picking worthwhile options trades depends on your awareness of fundamental and technical indicators for the stock, even while you recognize that short-term indicators may not be reliable.

Smart Investor Tip

In the stock market, the perception of value is of far greater interest in stock valuation than is the actual fundamental value. Perception in the market carries far more weight than even fact itself.

The analysis of stock values for the purpose of determining whether to buy stock is a complex science. When options are added to the equation, it becomes even more complicated. As shown in Table 1.1, you would consider stock price movement to be either a plus or a minus depending on whether you are planning to operate as a seller or buyer, and whether you plan to utilize calls or puts.

TABLE 1.1 Price Movement in the Underlying Security

	Increase in Price	Decrease in Price
Call buyer	Positive	Negative
Call seller	Negative	Positive
Put buyer	Negative	Positive
Put seller	Positive	Negative

Example

All Around the Money: Two months ago, you bought a call and paid a premium of $300. The striking price was $40 per share. At that time, the underlying stock's price was at $40 per share. In this condition—when the call's striking price is identical to the current market value of the stock—the call is said to be *at the money*. If the market value per share of stock increases so that the per-share value is above the call's striking price, then the call is said to be *in the money*. When the price of the stock decreases so that the per-share value is below the call's striking price, then the call is said to be *out of the money*.

These definitions are reversed for puts; "in" and "out of" the money occur in the opposite directions. Figure 1.3 shows the price ranges that represent in the money, at the money, and out of the money for a call.

at the money
the status of an option when the underlying stock's value is identical to the option's striking price.

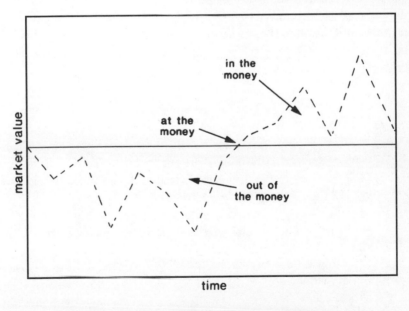

FIGURE 1.3 Market value of the underlying stock in relation to striking price of a call.

in the money
the status of a call option when the underlying stock's market value is higher than the option's striking price, or of a put option when the underlying stock's market value is lower than the option's striking price.

The dollar-for-dollar price movement of an option's value occurs whenever an option is in the money. The tendency will be for the option's value to mirror price movement in the stock, going up or down to the same degree as the stock's market price. These price movements will not always be identical because, as expiration nears, the time factor also affects the option's value.

Example

Staying out of the Money: You bought a put last month with a striking price of 30 and you paid 2. (The striking price is $30 per share and you paid $200 for the put.) At that time, the stock's market value was $34 per share, so the option was four points out of the money. More recently, the stock price has fallen to $31 per share; however, the put's premium remains at 2. Because the put remains out of the money, its premium value cannot be expected to change just because of stock movement—at least not until or unless the stock's market value falls so that the put is in the money.

out of the money
the status of a call option when the underlying stock's market value is lower than the option's striking price, or of a put option when the underlying stock's market value is higher than the option's striking price.

In the preceding example, a significant change would occur if the stock's market price continued to fall below the striking price. Once in the money, the put's value would rise one dollar for each dollar of decline in the stock's market value (not considering the time factor).

The value of options that are in the money relates to the underlying stock's current market value. But in the stock market, value also depends on two additional factors. First is the stock's *volatility*, the tendency to trade within a narrow range (low volatility) or a broad range (high volatility). The degree of volatility will, of course, also affect valuation of the option, as will the time element. But value is also affected by *volume*—the level of trading activity in the stock *and* in the option, or in the market as a whole. The level of volume in a stock might have a similar effect on option value, or option volume could be affected by entirely different factors. Options traders look for clues to explain circumstances when option volume increases but no corresponding increase is seen in the stock. That could indicate that other factors, not yet widely recognized in the market, are distorting the option's value or the stock's value, or that other factors (such as unfounded rumors) are causing distortions in both the stock and the option.

Pick the Right Stock

The usual assumption in using any form of analysis is that you identify stocks you would want to buy or hold, and when the news turns bad, you then want to sell shares. With options, however, a stock that shows inherent weaknesses can also signal the time to use options in a different way. For example, if you are convinced that a stock is overpriced and susceptible to price decline, one reaction would be to buy puts. If you're right and the price falls, your puts will increase in value. Thus, the difference between stock investors and options traders is the reaction to news. Stock investors tend to view bad news—price weakness, negative economic news, overpricing of shares, corporate scandals, and so on—as just bad news. An options trader, though, can use any form of news to make a profitable move in options, even when the news is negative for the company and its stockholders.

volatility
an indicator of the degree of change in a stock's market value, measured over a 12-month period and stated as a percentage. To measure volatility, subtract the lowest 12-month price from the highest 12-month price, and divide the answer by the 12-month lowest price.

volume
the level of trading activity in a stock, an option, or the market as a whole.

Smart Investor Tip

Selecting options wisely depends on also identifying or picking stocks using logical criteria. Using options without also analyzing stocks is a big mistake.

Chapter 6 provides a more in-depth study of stock selection criteria. For now, be aware that checking the facts by reviewing corporate information is a tarting point. A lot of information can be obtained free to let you begin reviewing a corporation's financial strength. You can get current information about any listed company from a number of sources on the Internet. These include several free services allowing downloads of corporate annual reports in addition to direct contact with the companies themselves.

Smart Investor Tip

Get free annual reports for any listed company from one of three online sources: http://reportgallery.com, www.annualreportservice.com, and www.prars.com.

Another source for information concerning stocks is one of several subscription services. Using either online or mail-oriented services, check out Value Line and Standard & Poor's, both of which offer nicely detailed analytical services for investors.

Smart Investor Tip

Check web sites for online subscription services at www.valueline.com and www.standardandpoors.com.

Intrinsic Value and Time Value

intrinsic value
that portion of an option's current value equal to the number of points that it is in the money. One points equals one dollar of value per share; so 35 points equals $35 per share.

Once you become comfortable with methods of stock selection, you will be ready to use that knowledge to study the options market. Remember that options themselves change in value based on movement in the underlying stock. Because option valuation is inescapably tied to stock value and market conditions, options do not possess any fundamental value of their own. By definition, the fundamentals are the financial condition and results of the corporation; an option is related to the stock's market value and exists only for a brief period of time. Every listed option and its pricing structure are more easily comprehended by a study of valuation, which has two parts.

The first of the two segments of value is called *intrinsic value*, which is that part of an option's premium equal to the number of points it is in the money. Intrinsic value, for example, is three points for a call that is three points above striking price, or for a put that is three points below striking price.

Any option premium above the intrinsic value is known as *time value*. This will decline predictably over time, as expiration nears. With many months before expiration, time value can be substantial; if the option is at the money or out of the money, the entire premium is time value. As expiration approaches, time value evaporates at a quickening pace, and at the point of expiration, no time value remains. Time value also tends to fall away when the option is substantially out of the money. In other words, an option that is 2 points out of the money will be likely to have greater time value than one with the same time until expiration, but 15 points out of the money.

> **time value**
> that portion
> of an option's
> current pre-
> mium above
> intrinsic value.

Option valuation can be summed up in this statement: The relative degree of intrinsic value and time value is determined by the distance between striking price and current market value of stock, adjusted by the time remaining until expiration of the option.

Example

Value, But No Real Value: A 45 call is valued currently at 3 ($300 premium value on a $45 striking price). The underlying stock's market value is currently $45 per share. Because the option is at the money, it has no intrinsic value. The entire premium represents time value alone. You know that by expiration, the time value will disappear completely, so it will be necessary for the stock to increase in value at least three points for you to break even were you to buy the call (and without considering transaction fees). The stock will need to rise beyond the three-point level before expiration if you are to earn a profit.

A comparison between option premium and market value of the underlying stock is presented in Table 1.2. Using a call as an example, this table demonstrates the direct relationship between intrinsic value, market value of the underlying stock, and time value of the option. If the option were a put, intrinsic value would be represented by the degree to which the stock's market value was *below* striking price.

Another helpful illustration is shown in Figure 1.4. This summarizes movement in the underlying stock (top graph) and option values (bottom graph). Note than intrinsic value (black portion) is identical to stock price movement in the

TABLE 1.2 The Declining Time Value of an Option

Month	Stock Price	Option Premium (Striking Price of $45)		
		Total Value	Intrinsic Value[1]	Time Value[2]
1	$45	$3	$0	$3
2	47	5	2	3
3	46	4	1	3
4	46	3	1	2
5	47	4	2	2
6	44	2	0	2
7	46	2	1	1
8	45	1	0	1
9	46	1	1	0

[1] Intrinsic value reflects the price difference between the stock's current market value and the option's striking price.

[2] Time value is greatest when the expiration date is furthest away and declines as expiration approaches.

money, and that time value moves independently, gradually dissolving as expiration approaches. From this illustration, you can see how the two forms of value act independently from one another, because different influences—stock price versus time—affect the two segments of the option premium.

The total amount of option premium can be expected to vary greatly between two different stocks at the same price level and identical option features, due to other influences. These include the perception of value, the stock's price history and volatility, stock trading volume, financial status and trends, interest in options among buyers and sellers, and dozens of other possible influences. For example, two stocks at the same current price may have options at 35 and identical expiration dates. But even given identical features, the option premium could be different for each.

It is important to note that the differences will exist solely in time value, even though time until expiration is identical. Intrinsic value is always a factor of the number of in-the-money points in the option, so time value is affected by many elements other than just the time until expiration. It also reflects the market's interest in that option and perceptions about potential for price movement between now and expiration. So two options with identical striking prices and market values may have far different time value premiums because of these perceptions.

In fact, time value is not solely affected by time. It also changes due to the degree of price movement in the stock and, more specifically, based on perceptions about stock price movement. Time value also varies to some degree due to outside influences, like the market *sector* of the stock. For example, information

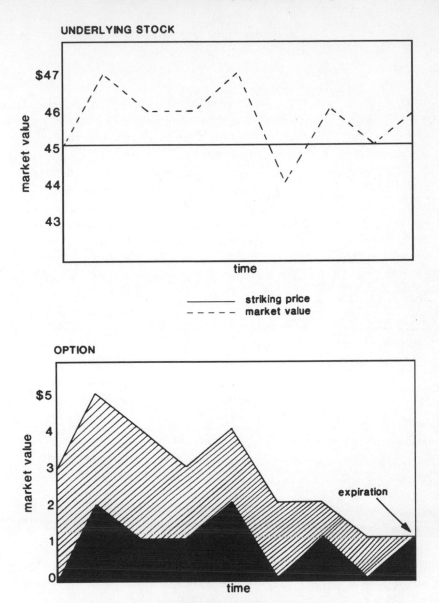

FIGURE 1.4 Time and intrinsic values of underlying stock and options.

sector
a specific seg-
ment of the
market defined
by product or
service offered
by a company.
Factors affecting
value (cyclical,
economic, or
market-based)
make each sec-
tor distinct and
different from
other sectors,
also affecting
option valuation.

extrinsic value
the portion of
an option's pre-
mium generated
from volatility
in the underly-
ing stock and
from market
perception of
potential price
changes until
expiration date;
a nonintrinsic
portion of the
premium value
not specifically
caused by the
element of time.

technology stocks might be more volatile as a group than pharmaceutical or retail stocks; as a result, time value might also be more volatile for options on those stocks.

Because time value is not defined entirely by time, it can be further broken down into two primary parts. Time value—the portion affected strictly by time—is generally quite predictable. As time until expiration approaches, time value declines on an accelerated basis. And the farther out of the money the option is, the more rapidly the decline in time value. But actual volatility in the stock also determines the nonintrinsic option value, and this portion is distinguished from pure time value, and is called *extrinsic value*.

So time value itself becomes quite unpredictable and inconsistent due to extrinsic value. If an option is out of the money, there is no intrinsic value involved; but when an option is in the money, premium contains three parts:

1. *Intrinsic value* is equal to the number of points between current striking price and current stock price.

2. *Time value* refers to all nonintrinsic value in most discussions. However, in a strict sense, "time value" is that portion of premium affected by the passage of time and the time remaining until expiration.

3. *Extrinsic value* is the premium value within time value caused by nontime sources. These include perceived potential for price changes, volatility in the stock, and other external causes.

Throughout the rest of this book, the use of the term "time value" refers to the entire nonintrinsic premium and includes both time and extrinsic value. The term can be confusing because in some options writings, extrinsic value is used as a substitute for time value. For example, Investopedia defines extrinsic value as "the difference between an option's price and the intrinsic value." While this is not entirely accurate, it does agree with a popular definition but makes no distinction between the attributes of time and nontime segments.

Smart Investor Tip

To find definitions for thousands if investment terms, check www.investopedia.com.

Option buyers, as a rule, will be willing to pay more for options when they perceive a greater than normal potential for price movement. Higher levels of volatility increase risks all around, but also increase potential for bigger profits in option speculation. Of course, low-volatility stocks are going to be far less interesting to would-be option buyers, because little price change is expected in the stock. The same arguments apply to sellers; higher-volatility stocks are accompanied by options with higher time value and more potential for profits from selling options (as well as greater risks for exercise).

You can recognize time value easily by comparing the stock's current value to the option's premium. For example, a stock currently priced at $47 per share may have an option valued at 3 and a striking price of 45. To break down the total option premium, subtract striking price from the current market value; the difference is intrinsic value. Then subtract intrinsic value from total premium to find time value. If premium value is at or below striking price (for a call) or above striking price (for a put), there is no intrinsic value. The preceding example is summarized as follows:

Stock Price

Current market value of the stock	$47
Less striking price of the option	−45
Intrinsic value	$ 2

Option Premium

Total premium	$ 3
Less intrinsic value	−2
Time value	$ 1

In the next chapter, several important features of options—striking price, expiration date, and exercise—are more fully explored, especially in light of how these features affect your personal options strategy.

Chapter 2

Opening, Closing, Tracking: How It All Works

Every thinker puts some new portion of an apparently stable world in peril.

—Thomas Dewey, *Characters and Events*, 1929

E very option is characterized by four specific attributes, collectively called the *terms* of the option (also called *standardized terms*). These are striking price, expiration date, type of option (call or put), and the underlying stock.

These are the four essential pieces you need to see the whole picture, to know which option is being discussed, and to distinguish it from all other options. In evaluating risk and potential gain, and even to discuss an option, every buyer and every seller needs to have these four essential pieces of information in hand. Of course, because point of view between buyer and seller is going to be opposite, an advantageous situation to one person may well be disadvantageous to another. That is the nature of investing in options: You can take a position on one side or the other for any particular option, depending upon where you believe the advantage lies.

terms
(also called *standardized terms*) the attributes that describe an option, including the striking price, expiration month, type of option (call or put), and the underlying stock.

To review the four terms:

1. *Striking price.* The striking price is the fixed price at which the option can be exercised. It is the pivotal piece of information that determines the relative value of options based on the proximity of a stock's market value; it is the price per share to be paid or received in the event of exercise. The striking price is divisible by 5 points for stocks traded between $30 and $200. When shares trade below $30 per share, options are sold in increments divisible by 2.5 and other issues end up with fractional values after a stock split. Stocks selling above $200 per share have options selling at intervals divisible by 10 points. The striking price remains unchanged during the life of the option, no matter how much change occurs in the market value of the underlying stock. (When stocks split, both striking price and the number of shares have to be adjusted. For example, after a 2-for-1 split, a $45 option would be replaced with two options of $22.50, and the original 100 shares would be replaced with 200 shares of half the value.)

For the buyer, striking price identifies the price at which 100 shares of stock can be bought (with a call) or sold (with a put). For a seller, striking price is the opposite: It is the price at which 100 shares of stock will be sold (with a call) or bought (with a put) in the event that the buyer decides to exercise.

Example

Call for a Strike: You purchase a call with a strike price of 25, which entitles you to buy 100 shares of stock at $25 per share, no matter how high the market price of stock rises before expiration date. However, the company announces a 2-for-1 stock split. After the split, you own two calls with strike price of $12.50.

2. *Expiration date.* Every option exists for only a limited number of months. That can be either a problem or an opportunity, depending upon whether you are acting as a buyer or as a seller, and upon the specific strategies you employ. The LEAPS provides more time, thus more flexibility on the time limitation. It also commands a higher premium as a result. Every option has three possible outcomes. It will eventually be canceled through a closing transaction, be exercised, or expire, but it never just goes on forever. Because the option is not tangible, the potential number of active options is unlimited except by market demand. A company issues only so many shares of stock, so buyers and sellers need to adjust prices according to supply and demand. This is not true of options, which have no specific limitations such as numbers issued.

Options active at any given time are limited by the risks involved. An option far out of the money will naturally draw little interest, and those with impending expiration will similarly lose market interest as their time value evaporates. Buyers need to believe there is enough time for a profit to materialize, and that the market price is close enough to the striking price that a profit is realistic; or, if in the money, that it is not so expensive that risks are too great. The same considerations that create disadvantages for buyers represent opportunities for sellers. Pending expiration reduces the likelihood of out-of-the-money options being exercised, and distance between market price of the stock and striking price of the call means the seller's profits are more likely to materialize than are the hopes of the buyer.

Example

Expiring Interest: You bought a put two months ago at striking price of 50. This put expires next week, but today the stock's market value is $55 per share. The put is five points out of the money and its current value is fractional. Unless the stock's market value falls within the next week, this put will expire worthless.

3. *Type of option.* Understanding the distinction between calls and puts is essential to success in the options market; the two are opposites. Identical strategies cannot be used for calls and puts, for reasons beyond the obvious fact that they react to stock price movement differently. Calls are by definition the right to buy 100 shares, whereas puts are the right to sell 100 shares. But merely comprehending the essential opposite nature of the two contracts is not enough.

It might seem at first glance that, given the behavior of calls and puts when in the money or out of the money, it would make no difference whether you buy a put or sell a call. As long as expiration and striking price are identical, what is the difference? In practice, however, significant differences do make these two ideas vastly different in terms of risk. When you buy a put, your risk is limited to the amount you pay for premium. When you sell a call, your risk can be far greater because the stock may rise many points, requiring the call seller to deliver 100 shares at a price far below current market value. Each specific strategy has to be reviewed in terms not only of likely price movement given a set of market price changes in the underlying stock, but also how one's position is affected by exposure to varying degrees of risk. Some of the more exotic strategies involving the use of calls and puts at the same time, or buying and selling of the same option with different striking prices, are examples of advanced techniques, which will be explored in detail in later chapters.

Example

Put Me Down for a Call: You have bought two options on two different stocks. The first one, a call, has a striking price of 25. When you bought it, the stock was at $23 per share, but today it has risen to $28. You can sell the call at a profit or exercise it and buy 100 shares at $25 per share. The second option is a put with a strike price of 45. When you bought it, the stock was at $47 per share and you believed the market value would fall. Now, close to expiration, the stock is still at $7 per share and your put has declined in value. The call value increases when stock value rises; and the put value increases when stock value falls.

class
all options traded on a single underlying stock, including different striking prices and expiration dates.

series
a group of options sharing identical terms.

4. *Underlying stock.* Every option is identified with a specific company's stock, and this cannot be changed. Listed options are not offered on all stocks traded, nor are they available on every stock exchange. (Some options trade on only one exchange, while others trade on several.) Options can exist only when a specific underlying stock has been identified, since it is the stock's market value that determines the option's related premium value. All options traded on a specific underlying stock are referred to as a single *class* of options. Thus, a single stock might be associated with a wide variety of calls and puts with different striking prices and expiration months, but they all belong to the same class. In comparison, all of those options with the same combination of terms—identical striking prices, expiration date, type (call or put), and underlying stock—are considered a single *series* of options.

Example

Stuck with the Stock: You bought calls a couple of months ago in a pharmaceutical stock, in the belief that it would rise in value. You realize now that you picked the wrong company. The one on which you hold calls has been lackluster, but a competitor's stock has risen dramatically. You would like to transfer your calls over to the other company, but the rules won't allow you to do this. Every option is identified strictly with one company and cannot be transferred.

A Note on the Expiration Cycle

Expiration dates for options of a single underlying stock are offered on a predictable *cycle*. Every stock with listed options can be identified by the cycle to which it belongs, and these remain unchanged. There are three annual cycles:

cycle
the pattern of expiration dates of options for a particular underlying stock. The three cycles occur in four-month intervals and are described by month abbreviations. They are (1) January, April, July, and October, or JAJO; (2) February, May, August, and November, or FMAN; and (3) March, June, September, and December, or MJSD.

1. January, April, July, and October (JAJO).
2. February, May, August, and November (FMAN).
3. March, June, September, and December (MJSD).

In addition to these fixed expiration cycle dates, active options are available for expiration in the upcoming month. For example, let's suppose that a particular stock has options expiring in the cycle month of April. In February, you may be able to trade in short-term options expiring in March (even though that is not a part of the normal cyclical expiration).

Smart Investor Tip

Some options traders use short-term options as speculative devices. Because they come and go more rapidly than the cyclical options, they often are overlooked as opportunities. For example, they can be used to temporarily protect longer-term short option positions.

An option's expiration takes place on the third Saturday of the expiration month. An order to close an open position has to be placed and executed no later than the *last trading day* before expiration day, and before the indicated *expiration time* for the option. As a general rule, this means that the trade has to be executed before the close of business on the Friday immediately before the Saturday of expiration; however, a specific cut off time could be

last trading day
the Friday preceding the third Saturday of the expiration month of an option.

expiration time
the latest possible time to place an order for cancellation or exercise of an option, which may vary depending on the brokerage firm executing the order and on the option itself.

missed on an exceptionally busy Friday, so you need to ensure that your broker is going to be able to execute your trade in time to comply with the rules.

The last-minute order that you place can be one of three types of transactions. It can be an order to buy in order to close a currently open (previously sold) short position; an order to sell an existing long position to close; or an exercise order to buy or to sell 100 shares of stock for each option involved. If a last-minute exercise is made against your short position, the order is entered without your advance knowledge; you are advised of exercise and instructed to deliver funds (for an exercised call) or to accept and pay for shares (for an exercised put).

Example

A Matter of Timing: You bought a call scheduled to expire in the month of July. Its expiration occurs on the third Saturday in that month. You need to place a sell order or an order to exercise the call (to buy 100 shares of stock at the striking price) before expiration time on the preceding Friday, which is the last trading day prior to expiration. If you fail to place either a sell or exercise order by that time, the option will expire worthless and you will receive no benefit.

With the pending deadline in mind and the unknown potential for a busy Friday in the market—which can occur whether you place orders over the telephone or on the Internet—you need to place that order with adequate time for execution. You can place the order far in advance with instructions to execute it by the end of business on Friday. If the brokerage firm accepts that order, then you will be protected if they fail to execute—as long as you placed the order well in advance of the deadline.

Smart Investor Tip

Even though expiration time is the end of the trading day, it makes practical sense to place a last-day order well before that time—*and* to place the order without restrictions. Only a market order will get executed, so specifying a desired price could prevent the order from going through.

Opening and Closing Option Trades

Every option trade you make must specify the four terms: striking price, expiration month, call or put, and the underlying stock. If any of these terms changes, that means that an entirely different option is involved.

Whenever you have opened an option by buying or selling, the status is called an *open position*. When you buy, it is described as an *opening purchase transaction*. And if you start out by selling an option, that is called an *opening sale transaction*.

open position
the status of a trade when a purchase (a long position) or a sale (a short position) has been made, and before cancellation, exercise, or expiration.

opening purchase transaction
an initial transaction to buy, also known as the action of "going long."

opening sale transaction
an initial transaction to sell, also known as the action of "going short."

closing sale transaction
a transaction to close a long position, executed by selling an option previously bought, closing it out.

closing purchase transaction
a transaction to close a short position, executed by buying an option previously sold, canceling it out.

Example

Open and Close: You bought a call two months ago. When you entered your order, it was an opening purchase transaction. That status remains the same as long as you take no further action. The position will be closed when you enter a *closing sale transaction* to sell the call; you may also exercise the option; if you do not take either of these actions, the option will expire.

Example

The Risk of Exercise: You sold a call last month, placing yourself in a short position. As long as you take no further action, the position remains open. You can choose to wait out the expiration period; or you may execute a *closing purchase transaction*, and cancel the option before expiration. As long as the short position remains open, it is also possible that the call will be exercised and you will have 100 shares called away at the striking price. Exercise will only occur if the stock's market price moves higher than the call's striking price.

Defining Possible Outcomes of Closing Options

Every option will be canceled by an offsetting closing transaction, by exercise, or by expiration. The results of each affect buyers and sellers in different ways.

Results for the Buyer

1. If you cancel your open long position with a closing sale transaction, you will receive payment. If the closing price is higher than the original purchase amount, you realize a profit; if lower, you suffer a loss.

2. If you exercise the option, you will receive 100 shares (if a call) or sell 100 shares (if a put) at the striking price. You will exercise only when that action is advantageous based on current market value of the underlying stock. To justify exercise, market value has to be higher than the striking price (of a call) or lower than the striking price (of a put). At that time, you will be required to pay the striking price plus trading fees, acquiring stock below current market value.

3. If you allow the option to expire, you will lose the entire amount of premium paid at the time of purchase. It will be a complete loss.

Results for the Seller

1. If you cancel your open position with a closing purchase transaction, you pay the premium. If the price you pay to close is lower than the amount you received when you opened the position, you realize a profit; if it is higher, you suffer a loss.

2. If your option is exercised by the buyer you are required to deliver 100 shares of the underlying stock at the specified striking price (of a call), or to purchase 100 shares of stock at the specified striking price (of a put). As a call seller, exercise results in shares being called away. As a put seller, exercise results in shares being put to you. In either case, upon exercise the premium you originally received for going short is yours to keep, and that adjusts your net cost.

3. If the option expires worthless, you earn a profit. Your open position is canceled by expiration, and the premium you received at the time that you sold the option is yours to keep.

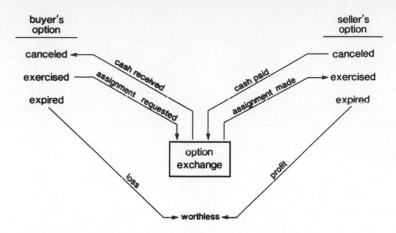

FIGURE 2.1 Outcomes of closing the position.

These outcomes are summarized in Figure 2.1. Notice that buyers and sellers have opposite results for each outcome upon close. The investor who opened the position through buying receives payment upon sale; and the investor who opened the position through selling makes payment upon a later purchase. The buyer elects to exercise, whereas the seller has no choice as to the decision, nor over the timing of exercise. If the option expires worthless, the buyer suffers a total loss, and the seller realizes a total profit.

Smart Investor Tip

Analysis of the possible outcomes is the key to identifying opportunities in the options market. Risk and opportunity evaluation is imperative. Successful options traders need to be shrewd analysts.

Exercising the Option

Option transactions occur through the exchange on which an option has been listed. While several different exchanges handle options trading, and automated trading has become widespread on the Internet (especially in options), there is but one registered clearing agency for all listed option trades in the United States. The Options Clearing Corporation (OCC) has the broad responsibility for *orderly settlement* of all option contracts, which

orderly settlement
the smooth process of buying and selling, in full confidence that the terms and conditions of options contracts will be honored in a timely manner.

takes place through contact between brokerage houses and customers working with the exchange. Orderly settlement means, generally, that buyer and seller both trade in confidence, knowing that they will be able to execute their orders when they want, and finding a ready market. It also means that all terms of the contract are ironclad; exercise price, expiration date, and availability of shares upon exercise are all a part of the orderly settlement. To ensure orderly settlement and in recognition of the probability that option buying and selling does not always match up, the OCC acts in the capacity of buyer to every seller, and as seller to every buyer.

assignment
the act of exercise against a seller, done on a random basis or in accordance with orderly procedures developed by the Options Clearing Corporation and brokerage firms.

When a customer notifies a broker and places an order for execution of an option trade, the OCC ensures that the terms of the contract will be honored. Under this system, buyer and seller do not need to depend upon the goodwill of one another; the transaction goes through the OCC, which depends upon member brokerage firms to enforce *assignment*. Remember that buyers and sellers are not matched together one-on-one. A disparate number of open buy and sell options are likely to exist at any given time, so that exercise will be meted out at random to options in the money—thus the term *assignment*. Since buyers and sellers are not matched to one another as in other types of transactions, how does a seller know whether a specific option will be exercised? There is no way to know. If your short option is in the money, exercise could occur at any time. It might not happen at all, or it might take place on the last trading day.

delivery
the movement of stock ownership from one owner to another. In the case of exercised options, shares are registered to the new owner upon receipt of payment.

When exercise occurs long before expiration date, that exercise is assigned to any of the sellers with open positions in that option. This takes place either on a random basis or on the basis of first-in, first-out (the earliest sellers are the first ones exercised). Upon exercise, 100 shares *must* be delivered. The concept of *delivery* is in relation to the movement of 100 shares of stock from the seller of the option to the exercising buyer. The buyer makes payment and receives registration of the shares, and the seller receives payment and relinquishes ownership of the shares.

What happens if the seller does not deliver shares as demanded by the terms of the option contract? The OCC facilitates the market and enforces assignment. The buyer is given timely possession of 100 shares of stock, even when the seller is unwilling or unable to comply. The broker will deal with the seller by attaching other assets as necessary, or taking legal action, as well as suspending the seller's trading privileges. The buyer would have no awareness of these events if they occur, because the problem is between the violating seller and the system of broker, exchange, and the OCC. So orderly settlement ensures that everyone trading in options in good faith experiences a smooth, dependable system in which terms of the option contract are honored automatically and without fail.

When a buyer decides to exercise, 100 shares are either purchased from ("called from") or sold to ("put to") the option seller. When you have sold a call, exercise means your 100 shares could be called away and transferred to the buyer; and when you sell a put, exercise means that 100 shares of stock can be "put to" you upon exercise, meaning you are required to buy. The entire process of calling and putting shares of stock upon exercise is broadly referred to as *conversion*. Stock is assigned at the time of exercise, a necessity because the number of buyers and sellers in a particular option will rarely, if ever, match. The assignment of an option's exercise, by definition, means that 100 shares of stock are *called away*.

conversion
the process of moving assigned stock from the seller of a call option or to the seller of a put option.

Is exercise always seen as a negative to the seller? At first glance, it would appear that being exercised is undesirable, and it often is seen that way; many sellers take steps to minimize the risk of exercise or to avoid it altogether. However, the question really depends upon the seller's inten-

called away
the result of having stock assigned. Upon exercise, 100 shares of the seller's stock are called away at the striking price.

tions at the time he or she entered the short position. For example, a seller might recognize that being exercised at a specific price is desirable, and will be willing to take exercise with the benefit of also keeping the premium as a profit.

early exercise
the act of exercising an option prior to expiration date.

It is logical that most sellers will close out their short positions or pick options the least likely to be exercised. Sellers have to be aware that exercise is one possible outcome and that it can occur at any time that the option is in the money. The majority of exercise actions are most likely to occur at or near expiration, so the risk of *early exercise* is minimal, although it can and does occur.

Example

The Early Worm: You sold a call with more than six months until expiration. Confident that exercise would not occur until close to expiration, you were not concerned about the possibility. But in the last few days, the stock's market value rose dramatically. You were taken by surprise when you received notice that your call had been exercised early. The lesson to remember from this applies to all option sellers: Exercise can occur any time the option is in the money.

automatic exercise
action taken by the Options Clearing Corporation at the time of expiration, when an in-the-money option has not been otherwise exercised or canceled.

Exercise is not always generated by a buyer's action, either. The Options Clearing Corporation can execute an *automatic exercise* on options in the money on expiration date. The OCC, acting in the role of buyer on the other side of the short position, would benefit from exercise of in-the-money short options. Automatic exercise occurs because in-the-money short positions are not necessarily exercised by buyers; it is more likely that positions will be closed and profits taken. So outstanding in-the-money short positions are automatically exercised by the OCC to absorb the disparity between the two sides.

The decision to avoid exercise is made based on current market value as well as the time remaining until expiration. Many option sellers spend a great deal of time and effort avoiding exercise and trying to also avoid taking losses in open option positions. A skilled options trader can achieve this by exchanging one option for another, and by timing actions to maximize deteriorating time value while still avoiding exercise. As long as options remain out of the money, there is no practical risk of exercise. But once that option goes in the money, sellers have to decide whether to risk exercise or cancel the position with an offsetting transaction.

Example

Reasonable Assumptions: You bought 100 shares of stock several months ago for $57 per share. You invested $5,700 plus transaction fees. Last month, the stock's market value was $62 per share. At that time, you sold a call with a striking price of 60 ($60 per share). You were paid a premium of 7 ($700). You were willing to assume this short position. Your reasoning: If the call were exercised, your profit would be $1,000 before transaction fees. That would consist of 3 points per share of profit in the stock plus the $700 you were paid for selling the option.

Striking price	$60
Less your cost per share	−57
Stock profit	$3
Option premium	+7
Total profit per share	$10

This example shows that it is possible for an investor to sell an in-the-money call, hoping for exercise. The key is in the profit made combining high option premium with a profit on the stock. The premium on the option effectively discounts your basis in the stock, so that exercise creates a nice profit. If the stock's market value falls below striking price and remains there until exercise the profit in the above example is still $700 from option premium; and you would be free to wait out price movement and repeat the process again.

A word of caution: Selling in-the-money calls can affect how profits are taxed. If you have owned shares of stock long enough that a sale would be taxed at favorable long-term capital gain rates, selling an in-the-money call might reset the calculation period to zero. Chapter 12 explains the special tax rules for short option positions.

Example

Repetitive Strategies: You bought 100 shares of stock several months ago for $57 per share. You invested $5,700 plus transaction fees. Last month, the stock's market value was $62 per share. At that time, you sold a call with a striking price of 60, and you were paid a premium of 7 ($700). By expiration, the stock had fallen to $58 per share, and the call expired worthless. At this point, your adjusted basis in the stock is $50 per share ($57 per share paid at purchase less your profit from selling a call and receiving a premium of $700). After the call expires, you sell another call with a striking price of 55 and receive 6. If this option were to be exercised, you would realize an adjusted profit of $1,100 ($500 profit on stock plus $600 profit from selling the call). If the option's time value declines, you can sell the option and realize the difference as profit. If the option expires worthless, you can repeat the process a *third* time, realizing yet more profit, and continue that pattern indefinitely.

current market value

the market value of a stock at any given time.

The decision to act or to wait depends on the time value involved, and on the proximity of the striking price to the market value of the stock. As a general rule, the greater the time until expiration, the higher the time value will be; and the closer the striking price is to market value of the stock, the more important the time value becomes, both to buyer and to seller. For the buyer, time value is a negative, so the higher the time value, the greater the risk. For the seller, the opposite is true. Buyers pay the time value (the amount above intrinsic value) as the difference between the stock's *current market value* and the option's striking price, knowing that this time value will disappear by expiration. The seller picks options to sell with the same thing in mind, but recognizing that more time value means more potential profit.

Example

Quick Changes Artist: You have decided to buy a call with a striking price of 30. The underlying stock's current market value is $32 per share and the option premium is 5 ($500). Your premium includes two points of intrinsic value and three points of time value. If the stock's market value does not increase enough by expiration to offset your cost, then you will not be able to earn a profit. One of two things needs to happen in this situation. Either the stock's current market value needs to rise quickly so that your call premium will be greater than the 5 you paid, or the stock's market value has to rise enough points by expiration to offset time value (3 points) plus grow beyond the intrinsic value level.

This shows how option buyers need to evaluate risk. In the example, time value represents three-fifths of the total premium. If expiration comes up quickly, the stock will need to increase significantly in a short period of time to produce a profit. In thinking about whether it makes sense to buy such a call, consider these alternatives, especially if you believe that the stock will rise in value:

- Buy 100 shares of the stock. If you believe it has potential to increase in value, owning the shares without the built-in deadline of expiration makes ownership more desirable. The added problem of time value could translate to making outright stock purchase not only safer, but more profitable as well.

- Sell a put instead of buying a call. Put sellers have limited exposure compared to call sellers; and if the stock's market price rises, the entire premium will represent profit. Compared to buying a call, the selling of a put often is an overlooked strategy that could make a lot of sense. If you decide to sell a put, your brokerage firm will require you to deposit cash as a reserve in case of exercise, to ensure the money is available to pay for the stock. Going short is a higher-level strategy too, so your brokerage firm may take a harder look at you and your qualifications to engage in short option strategies.

- Buy calls with more point distance between striking price and current market value. This enables you to pay less for the call, but also makes the odds of profit more difficult.

- But calls with longer time until expiration. While this costs more, it leaves the exposure period longer as well, so that your chances of the call's becoming profitable will be greater.

A third opportunity could present itself in taking the opposite approach to buying. Given the previous example, in which significant increase in value would be required to make a profit, it might be viewed as an opportunity to sell a call instead of buying one—as long as you remember the higher risks that are involved. Selling uncovered calls is one of the highest-risk strategies you can use; risk is unlimited, at least in theory. So if you take this route, you will be assuming a much greater risk profile. Call sellers benefit from decline in time value; but uncovered short sales are the highest-risk strategies so, even with attractive profit possibilities, the risks cannot be ignored.

Example

Turning the Tables: Given the same circumstances as those in the previous example, you decide to *sell* a call instead of buying one. Instead of paying the $500 premium, you receive $500 as a seller. Of this, $300 represents time value, which now is an advantage rather than a problem. The possibility of expiration is an advantage as well. The pending expiration places pressure for time value to evaporate, meaning greater profits for you as a seller. As long as the stock's current market value does not increase more than three points between now and expiration, the transaction will be profitable. However, because the call is in the money, you also face the possibility of exercise. The two points of intrinsic value have to be weighed against the five points you receive for the call to make a value judgment about this strategy; in addition, your trading costs have to be factored into the calculation.

---

parity

the condition of an option at expiration, when the total premium consists of intrinsic value and no time value.

By the time of expiration, all of the time value will have disappeared from the premium, and all remaining premium will represent intrinsic value only. To avoid exercise, you would want to buy to close the call and take the $300 profit; however, exercise can occur at any time, so in this position you remain exposed to that possibility. When no time value remains at expiration, the condition is known as *parity*.

Using the Daily Options Listings

Online trading is a natural for the options market. The ability to monitor a changing market on the basis of only a 20-minute delay is a significant advantage over telephone calls to a broker, and for an extra charge you can get real-time quotations (or as close as possible to real time) online. The Internet is also likely to be far more responsive than a broker, who may be on another line, with another client, or away from the desk when you call. For you as an options trader, even a few minutes of inaccessibility can create a lost opportunity. Of course, exceptionally heavy volume market periods translate to slowdowns, even on the Internet.

In the past, options traders depended on alert brokers, hoping they would be able to telephone them if price changes made fast decisions necessary. Some placed stop limit orders, a cumbersome method for managing an options portfolio. And in the worst of all cases, some investors used to wait until the day after to review options listings in the newspaper. None of these antiquated methods are adequate for the modern options trader, who should be able to find a dependable online source for rapid options quotations.

Smart Investor Tip

You can make good use of online sites offering free options and stock quotes. Three sites with exceptional quotation services are quote.com (http://new.quote.com); e*trade (https://us.etrade.com); and Yahoo! Finance (http://finance.yahoo.com). You can also go directly to the Chicago Board Options Exchange (CBOE) to get detailed options quotes (www.cboe.com) or check the major exchanges (www.nyse.com, www.nasdaq.com, and www.amex.com).

Not only are you more able to work on your own through discount service brokers and without expensive and unneeded broker advice; you also need to be online to maximize your market advantage. Option pricing can change from minute to minute in many situations, and you need to be able to keep an eye on the market.

Whether you use an automated system or published options service, you also need to learn how to read options listings. A typical daily options listing from the month of May 2004 is summarized in Table 2.1.

The details of what this table shows are:

First column: The underlying stock and the current market value of the stock. In this example, Wal-Mart's current price was $45.71 per share.

TABLE 2.1 Example of Daily Options Listing

Wal-Mart	(WMT)	Calls			Puts		
		Jan	Feb	Mar	Jan	Feb	Mar
45.71	45	1.35	1.85	2.50	0.50	0.80	1.20
45.71	47.50	0.28	0.65	1.00	1.90	2.15	2.40
45.71	50	0.07	0.20	0.35	4.30	4.40	4.50
45.71	52.50	0.02	0.05	0.10	6.80	6.90	7.00

Second column: This shows the striking price for each available option. The example includes options with striking prices between 45 and 52.50 per share. In this particular case, Wal-Mart included options in between the normal five-point increments.

Third, fourth, and fifth columns: These show current premium levels for calls. Note two trends. As striking prices rises farther above current market value, call values decline; and as time until expiration extends outward, call values rise.

Sixth, seventh, and eighth columns: These show current premium levels for calls. The same two trends are evident here. However, because put valuation moves in a direction opposite that of calls, the farther in the money, the higher the put value. For example, the 52.50 put is almost 7 points in the money. This is reflected in the higher premium value, and additional time further adds to put valuation.

In this example, Wal-Mart trades on the March, June, September, December (MJSD) cycle. However, in all cases, the three months following the current month always have options as well. The report was taken in December, so options are available for January, February, and March (and then for June, September, and December).

For LEAPS, the same information is available but for longer terms. For comparable LEAPS listings, see Table 2.2.

In this example, premium values are considerably higher for the same range of striking prices. Since there is much more time until expiration, time value is also higher for the LEAPS options. This opens up a broader range of strategic possibilities for both buyers and sellers. LEAPS contracts always expire in January each year, so as on the end of 2007, the long-term values show January expirations only. Also, the interim values for LEAPS (47.50 and 52.50) were not available for Wal-Mart two years out; thus, no current value exists for those valuations.

TABLE 2.2　Example of LEAPS Listings

Wal-Mart	(WMT)	Calls		Puts	
		Jan 08	Jan 09	Jan 08	Jan 09
45.68	45	5.10	7.30	2.75	3.70
45.68	47.50	3.70	—	3.96	—
45.68	50	2.70	4.80	5.20	6.30
45.68	52.50	1.95	—	7.00	—

Understanding Option Abbreviations

Option values are expressed in abbreviated form, both in listings and in communication between brokers and customers (or between online brokerage services and customers). The abbreviated expressions in the options market go beyond current premium. Both expiration month and striking price are expressed in shorthand form as well. For example, an October option with a striking price of 35 per share is referred to as an OCT 35 option, and a January option with a 50 striking price is called a JAN 50. Like the premium value, striking price is expressed without dollar signs.

The complete option description must include all four terms plus current premium: underlying stock, expiration month, striking price, and type of option (call or put). The terms, remember, must all be present to distinguish one option from another. In the following example, the single expression gives you the underlying stock, expiration month, striking price, type of option, and current premium. The Wal-Mart call expiring January 2008 with a striking price of 50 was valued at 2.70 (or, $270). This option is fully described and distinguished as:

Wal-Mart JAN 08 $50 Call at 2.70

When you call a broker on the telephone or log onto a web site and place a trade, an additional coding system is used to specify the expiration month and striking price, and to distinguish calls from puts. This helps to avoid misunderstandings and to classify options properly. A large number of options can exist on a single stock, so the coding system used for trading purposes is very helpful and efficient. After trading options actively, you might memorize these codes; however, it also helps to make a chart and keep it handy for quick reference. Figure 2.2 summarizes the symbols used for buying and selling listed options. You will need these for entering correct option designations online or, if you trade by telephone, for communication with a broker.

The expiration month is always expressed first, followed immediately by the striking price. Note that striking prices of 5, 105, and 205 have identical symbols. This works because the market value of the underlying stock quickly determines which range of pricing applies for listed options. The situation for LEAPS options is more complex because price ranges can spread out over a wider range over three years, and symbols also need to distinguish between different years, and not just months. The industry is struggling with the problem of how to reduce LEAPS options to a logical and consistent system of symbols.

expiration month symbols		
MONTH	CALLS	PUTS
January	A	M
February	B	N
March	C	O
April	D	P
May	E	Q
June	F	R
July	G	S
August	H	T
September	I	U
October	J	V
November	K	W
December	L	X

striking price symbols			
STRIKING PRICE			SYMBOL
5	105	205	A
10	110	210	B
15	115	215	C
20	120	220	D
25	125	225	E
30	130	230	F
35	135	235	G
40	140	240	H
45	145	245	I
50	150	250	J
55	155	255	K
60	160	260	L
65	165	265	M
70	170	270	N
75	175	275	O
80	180	280	P
85	185	285	Q
90	190	290	R
95	195	295	S
100	200	300	T
7½	–	–	U
12½	–	–	V
17½	–	–	W
22½	–	–	X

FIGURE 2.2 Option trading symbols.

Example

Abbreviated Form: You want to trade in calls with September expiration and 60 striking price. The symbols to use are I for the month (September is the ninth month and I is the ninth letter); and L for the striking price. In this case, a call would have the designation IL and a September 60 put would be coded as UL.

The complete option quote also includes the abbreviated symbol for the underlying stock. Every listed stock on every stock exchange has a unique abbreviation that distinguishes it from all other listed stocks. Wal-Mart, for example, is abbreviated WMT. So a Wal-Mart option code consists of two sections. First is the symbol for the stock (in this case, three letters). This is followed by a period and then a two-letter code indicating month and striking price. Distinction between call and put is part of the month code. A Wal-Mart September call with a striking price of 60 is designated as WMT.IL A put for the same striking price and month is designated as: WMT.UL.

Smart Investor Tip

If you know the name of the company but not its abbreviated symbol, most online sites offering free quotations also offer cross-reference services. One example is found at http://finance.lycos.com—from this page, go to "Lookup symbol" and type in the company name. This is a free service.

For LEAPS the abbreviations are more difficult. Just as computer programmers in the 1950s and 1960s did not anticipate the problems of the millennium when they assigned only two digits for years, the designers of option trading symbols did not foresee the problems of multiyear LEAPS options. While the abbreviations for traditional listed options are straightforward, abbreviations for LEAPS options would need to take into consideration both the multiple-year problem and the possibility of multiple-level outstanding options.

The exchanges have run out of symbols. With nearly 500 stocks trading LEAPS, the problem is made worse by the fact that some listings exceed the 100-point spread and may have existing LEAPS outstanding for 105 and 205 striking prices, for example. Under today's system, there is no easy way to define the rule for symbols, because it continues to evolve.

Fortunately, you do not need the symbol in order to find a LEAPS listing. You can simply go to one of many web sites offering free listings and look up the contract. The Chicago Board Options Exchange (CBOE) offers one of the best services of this type. As options trading becomes increasingly efficient online, it is also likely that the use of abbreviated options symbols for terms will become obsolete. The need for such abbreviations came from the days when most trades took place by phone. So a trader did not need to tell the broker to buy a "Wal-Mart September 60 call." He could simply instruct the broker to buy a

WMT.IL. If trading takes place online, the whole process will be more automatic than in the past, and the use of symbols—especially given the complexity of LEAPS trading—may fade.

Smart Investor Tip
For free LEAPS listings and a wide range of other LEAPS resources, check the CBOE web site "quotes" link at http://quote.cboe.com.

Calculating the Rate of Return for Sellers

rate of return
the yield from investing, calculated by dividing net cash profit upon sale by the amount spent at purchase.

annualized basis
a method for comparing rates of return for holdings of varying periods, in which all returns are expressed as though investments had been held over a full year. It involves dividing the holding period by the number of months the positions were open, and multiplying the result by 12.

You are guided by your *rate of return* in all of your investments. In a single transaction involving one buy and one sell, rate of return is easily calculated. Simply divide the net profit (after trading fees) by the total purchase amount (including trading fees), and the resulting percentage is the rate of return. When you sell options, though, the rate of return is more complicated. The sale precedes the purchase, so rate of return is not as straightforward as it is in the more traditional investment.

Rate of return can only be looked at in comparative form. In other words, comparing one short position outcome to another, given dissimilar holding periods, makes the comparison invalid. The calculation should be adjusted so that all short position outcomes are reviewed and compared on an *annualized basis*. Because different lengths of time can be involved in a short position—from a few hours up to several months, or even two to three years if LEAPS are involved—it is not realistic to compare calculated rates of return without making the adjustment. A 50 percent return in two months is far more significant than the same rate of return with a 10-month holding period.

To annualize a rate of return, follow these steps:

1. Calculate the rate of return. Divide the net profit by the amount of purchase.
2. Divide the rate of return by the number of months the investment position was open.
3. Multiply the result above by 12 (months).

Example

When 12 Percent Is Not 12 Percent: You realize a net profit of 12 percent on an investment. The annualized rate of return will vary depending upon the holding period.

1. *Three months:*
   Net profit 12%

   > Holding period = 3 months
   > 12 ÷ 3 = 4%
   > 4% × 12 months = 48% annualized

2. *Eight months:*
   Net profit 12%

   > Holding period = 8 months
   > 12 ÷ 8 = 1.5%
   > 1.5% × 12 months = 18% annualized

3. *Fifteen months:*
   Net profit 12%

   > Holding period = 15 months
   > 12 ÷ 15 = 0.8%
   > 0.8% × 12 months = 9.6% annualized

As these examples demonstrate, annualized rate of return differs dramatically depending on the period the position remained open. Annualizing applies for periods above one year, as in example number 3. A short period is properly extended though annualizing, just as a period beyond one year should be contracted to reflect rate of return as *though* the investment were held for exactly 12 months. By making all returns comparable, it becomes possible to study the outcomes realistically, not to calculate your true average yield but to better be able to analyze outcomes side by side. Annualizing can also produce exceptional but unrealistic results. So annualizing is valuable for making accurate comparisons, but it will not necessarily provide you with a realistic future average return using options. You should accept the possibility that you will experience a range of outcomes from options trading; some profits materialize quickly, and others take a long time. Some strategies will also produce losses.

Example

Fast Turnaround: You recently sold a call at 3 and, only two weeks later, closed the position by buying at 1. The profit, $200, is 4,800 percent on an annualized basis (200 percent return dividing by 0.5 month, and multiplied by 12 months, or $[200 \div 0.5] \times 12$). This is impressive, but it is of little use in your comparative analysis. Not only is it atypical of the returns you earn from options trading, but it also reflects an exceptionally brief holding period, which you probably cannot duplicate consistently.

Smart Investor Tip

Annualized basis is helpful in judging the success of a series of transactions employing a particular strategy. It is less useful in looking at individual outcomes, especially those with very short holding periods.

return if exercised
the estimated rate of return option sellers will earn in the event the buyer exercises the option. The calculation includes profit or loss in the underlying stock, dividends earned, and premium received for selling the option.

The calculation of return is made even more complex when it involves more than return on the option premium. When you sell calls against stock you own, you need to adjust the comparative analysis to study the likely outcome based on two possible events. The first is called *return if exercised*. This is the rate of return you will earn if your short call is exercised and 100 shares of stock are called away. It includes both the profit on your option and profit or loss on the stock, as well as any dividends you received during the period you owned the stock.

The second calculation is called *return if unchanged*. This is a calculation of the return to be realized if the stock is not called away and the option is allowed to expire worthless (or it is closed out through a closing purchase transaction).

In both types of return, the calculations take into account all forms of income. The major difference between the two rates has to do with profit or loss on the underlying stock. These factors complicate the previous observation that comparisons should be made on an annualized rate. It is extremely difficult to account for each dividend payment, especially if the stock has been held over many years. In addition, how do you account for the return on stock held but not sold?

Neither of these analytical tools lends itself to annualized return, which is a valuable tool for the study of relatively simple transactions involving only one source of income. The return if exercised and return if unchanged are far more valuable as a method for determining the wisdom of a decision to sell a call *in advance* of actually taking that step. By comparing these potential rates of return, you can determine which options are more likely to yield profits adequate to justify tying up 100 shares of stock with a short call position.

return if unchanged
the estimated rate of return option sellers will earn in the event the buyer does not exercise the option. The calculation includes dividends earned on the underlying stock, and the premium received for selling the option.

The actual steps involved in calculation should always be net of brokerage fees, both for sale and purchase. Remember that no attempt should be made to make comparisons on an annualized basis, however, because complex transactions with differing types of profit, and generated over different lengths of time, make annualized return inappropriate. While the following examples use single option contracts, in practice options traders often use multiple options and involve more than 100 shares of stock.

Example

Many Happy Returns: You own 100 shares of stock that you purchased originally at $58 per share. Current market value is $63 per share. You sell a call with a striking price of 60 and receive a premium of 7. Between the date the option is sold and expiration, you also receive two dividend payments, totaling $68.

Return if exercised:

Striking price	$6,000
Less original cost of stock	−5,800
Profit on stock	$ 200
Dividends received	68
Call premium received	+700
Total profit	$ 968

Return if exercised: ($968 ÷ $5,800) = 16.69%

Return if unchanged:

Call premium received	$ 700
Dividends received	68
Total profit	$ 768

Return if unchanged: ($768 ÷ $5,800) = 13.24%

This side-by-side calculation allows you to see what will happen in either outcome. In the example, it comes down to a difference of about 3.5 percent between the two outcomes. So the question becomes, would it be worth that small difference to accept exercise? In the alternative, would it be better to close out the position before expiration and repeat the transaction subsequently? By avoiding exercise, you can sell a later call and expand profits even further, which should also be considered when comparing these two possible outcomes.

The comparison between "if exercised" and "if unchanged" is further complicated by inclusion of capital gain on the stock. Because one calculation includes this and the other does not, the two outcomes are not truly comparable. Based on the striking price you pick when you sell a call against 100 shares of stock you own, a capital gain could be minimal or quite significant; exercise could even end up with a capital loss. So the gain on the stock cannot be entirely ignored.

Even so, the comparison including stock does distort any attempt to make a true comparison. Ideally, you should consider the corresponding gain or loss on the option only, and separate out capital gains or losses on the stock separately. This is inaccurate, of course, but making valid comparisons of potential outcomes is difficult. The last chapter in this book examines return calculations in more detail, because the difficulty involved makes it especially complex.

Another important factor in this example involves taxes. Because the example includes selling an in-the-money call, the capital gain may be treated as short-term. As part of your option strategy, any short positions have to be made with a tax calculation in mind. Tax strategies are explained in Chapter 12. A net profit comparison should always include brokerage fees and both federal and state tax consequences, which are going to vary by individual as well as by state.

Annualizing the returns if exercised or if unchanged is not recommended because the transactions involve three different time periods: for stock, dividend, and short position in the call. In addition, the purpose here is not to compare results after the transaction has been completed, but to make a comparison in advance to determine whether the transaction would be worthwhile. You can use these calculations not only to compare the two outcomes, but also to compare outcomes between two or more possible option short positions.

Smart Investor Tip

The purpose in comparing returns on option selling is not to decide which outcome is more desirable, but to decide whether to enter into the transaction in the first place.

Succeeding in options trading means entering open positions with complete awareness of all possible outcomes and their consequences or benefits. You need to know when it makes sense to close out a position with a closing transaction; avoid exercise with subsequent trades; or just wait for expiration. You also need to be aware of market conditions and the timing of options trades, as well as the relative degree of risk to which you are exposed by entering into open options positions. Knowledge about potential profit is only part of a more complex picture. The more you study options and participate in the market, the more skill you develop in making an overall assessment and comparison.

Buying Calls: Maximizing the Rosy View

More are taken in by hope than by cunning.
—Luc de Clapiers, *Reflections and Maxims*, ca. 1747

Option buyers have to be optimists. They believe that a stock's price will move enough points within a limited time to produce a profit. If they are right, their return on investment is huge. If they are wrong, they are 100 percent wrong.

When you embark on a program of buying calls, you take the most speculative position that is possible with options. Since time works against you, substantial change in the underlying stock is required in order to produce a profit. Remember, a call grants to the buyer the right to purchase 100 shares of the underlying stock, at an established striking price per shares, and before a firm expiration date in the near-term future. As the buyer, you acquire that right in exchange for paying a premium. You face three alternatives: First, you can sell the call before it expires; second, you can exercise the call and purchase 100 shares of the underlying stock; or third, you can allow the call to expire worthless.

As a call buyer, you are never obligated to buy 100 shares. In comparison, the seller *must* deliver 100 shares upon exercise of a call. As buyer, you have the right to determine which of the three outcomes will occur. The decision depends on:

- Price movement of the underlying stock and the resulting effect on the call's premium value.

- Your reasons for buying the call in the first place, and how related strategies are affected through ownership of the call.

- Your risk posture and willingness to wait for future price movement of both stock and the call, as opposed to taking a profit or cutting a loss today. (This is where setting and following standards comes into play.)

Understanding the Limited Life of the Call

You can become a call buyer simply for the potential profit you could earn within a limited period of time—in other words, buying purely on the chance of earning a profit in the short term. That profit will be realized if and when the call's premium value increases, so that the call can be sold for more than it cost, or by exercising the call and buying 100 shares of stock below current market value. The call also can be used to offset losses in a short position held in the underlying stock. These uses of calls are explored in more detail later in this chapter.

The buyer's risks are not the same as those for sellers; in fact, they often are the exact opposite. Before becoming an options buyer, examine all of the risks, become familiar with potential losses as well as potential gains, and review risk from both sides: as potential buyer or seller. Time value evaporates with ever-increasing speed as expiration nears, which is a disadvantage to you as a buyer but an advantage to the seller. Time is a significant factor that affects your decision about *when* to close out your long position in the option. Because time value disappears by the point of expiration, time itself dictates which options you can afford to buy, and which ones are long shots. More time value usually means more time until expiration, and more price movement that you will need to make a profit. In fact, even when the stock price movement goes the way you want, you still might not make a profit; price movement has to exceed the number of points of time value *and* more to produce a profit.

This is where comparisons between listed options and LEAPS options become interesting. For example, you might look at side-by-side options with identical striking prices and come to different conclusions about their viability.

Example

Into the Stretch: A stock is currently valued at $48 per share. The 50 call expires in eight months and is currently selling for 3. If you buy that call, it will be necessary for the stock to rise at least five points to $53 per share before expiration, just to cover your costs before trading fees (such a rise would produce intrinsic value of 3 points, producing breakeven *before* trading fees).

Example

Taking the LEAPS: The picture is far different when a LEAPS call is reviewed. For the same stock, currently valued at $48, the 50 call that expires in 29 months is valued at 9. In this situation, the call costs three times more—$900 versus $300—but you have 30 months for the stock to move, instead of eight months. You would need the stock to rise 11 points, to $59 per share, to break even in this case.

Which of these scenarios is better? You can buy a short-term call for 3 or a long-term LEAPS call for 9. Depending on the stock and its price volatility, your opinion about future price movement, and your personal risk profile, you could decide to go with either of these calls, or decide to take no action.

Smart Investor Tip

Time works against you as a buyer, so the more time value in the option you buy, the more difficult it will be to make a profit.

Buying short-term options or LEAPS options are not your only choices. A comparison between purchasing stock as a long-term investment and purchasing calls for short-term profit points out the difference between investment and *speculation*. Typically, speculators accept the risk of loss in exchange for the potential for profit, and they take their positions in short-term instruments such as options for the exposure to that potential. Because a relatively small amount of money can be used to tie up 100 shares of stock, call buying is one form of *leverage*, a popular strategy for making investment capital go further. Of course, the greater the degree of leverage, the greater the associated risk.

speculation
the use of money to assume risks for short-term profit, in the knowledge that substantial or total losses are one possible outcome. Buying calls for leverage is one form of speculation. The buyer may earn a very large profit in a matter of days, or could lose the entire amount invested.

When you consider the interaction between intrinsic and time value of calls, you quickly realize that time itself plays a very crucial role in option value. The longer the time until expiration, the more complicated this relationship becomes.

For this reason, the LEAPS option presents many interesting possibilities for speculators.

leverage

the use of investment capital in a way that a relatively small amount of money enables the investor to control a relatively large value. This is achieved through borrowing—for example, using borrowed money to purchase stocks or bonds—or through the purchase of options, which exist for only a short period of time but enable the option buyer to control 100 shares of stock. As a general rule, the use of leverage increases potential for profit as well as for loss.

Intrinsic value rises and falls to match the underlying stock's price. But because a LEAPS call is long-term, the action of time value often obscures the relationship between intrinsic value and underlying stock price. It might appear as though the call's value is not tracking the stock point for point. With a lot of time value remaining in a call's premium (including both time and extrinsic segments), it is possible that the call's value will not respond to changes in the stock as clearly as it does when expiration is imminent.

Example

Making the Long Call: You purchased a LEAPS call last month with a striking price two points above market value of the underlying stock. Since then, the stock's price has risen and the LEAPS call is now in the money. But you have noticed that as the stock's market value rises and falls, the LEAPS call tends to duplicate the change only about 75 percent (so when the stock rises one point, the call rises 75 cents). This is caused by changes in perception of extrinsic value, offsetting the tendency of intrinsic value by itself.

The complexity here is that intrinsic value is not entirely isolated from the call's extrinsic value. Two things occur as expiration nears. First, the pure time value premium tends to deteriorate at an accelerated rate. Seconds, extrinsic value is likely to disappear altogether. If you think of extrinsic value as "potential value" of the call, it makes sense. In other words, extrinsic value exists because of perception that profits may be possible in the call position due to (1) time remaining until expiration; (2) volatility of the underlying stock; and (3) proximity of the striking price and current market value. So in the case of a LEAPS call with many months to go until expiration, a change in the underlying stock will also affect perceptions about the investment or speculative value of the call. Extrinsic value is then likely to affect option value directly.

As expiration approaches, extrinsic value becomes a smaller factor and will disappear from the picture altogether. But as long as many months remain until expiration, intrinsic value cannot operate independently. Some nonintrinsic changes will occur as well. This may be seen as point changes lower than changes in the underlying stock's value, or point changes higher than the point change in the underlying stock. That is the effect of extrinsic value interacting not only with time but also with intrinsic value.

Is call speculation appropriate for you? Questioning risk levels is necessary for every investor and should be an ongoing process of self-examination. Knowing exactly what you are getting into, determining the best strategy, and fully comprehending the risk, add up to the measure of your *suitability* for a particular investment or strategy. Suitability identifies what is appropriate given your income, sophistication, experience, understanding of markets and risks, and capital resources. Avoid the problem of understanding the profit potential of a strategy but not the full extent of risk.

Example

My Friend Told Me: An investor has no experience in the market, having never owned stock; he also does not understand how the market works. He has $1,000 available to invest today, and decides that he wants to earn a profit as quickly as possible. A friend told him that big profits can be made buying calls. He wants to buy three calls at 3 each, requiring $900, plus trading fees. He expects to double his money within one month.

This investor would not meet the minimum suitability standards for buying calls. He does not understand the market, know the risks, or appreciate the specific details of options beyond what a friend told him. He probably does not know anything about time value and the chance of losing money from buying calls. He is aware only of the profit potential, and that information is incomplete. In this situation, the broker is responsible for recognizing that option buying would not be appropriate. One of the broker's duties is to ensure that clients know what they are doing and understand all of the risks. The broker's duty is to refuse to execute the transaction. This does not mean that every broker will follow that rule.

Suitability refers not only to your ability to afford losses, but also to your understanding of the many forms of risk in the options market. If the investor in the preceding example worked with an experienced broker at the onset, it would also make sense to listen to that broker's advice about a proposed option position.

Judging the Call

Most call buyers lose money. Even with thorough understanding of the market and trading experience, this fact cannot be overlooked. This statement has to be qualified, however. Most call buyers who simply buy calls for speculation lose money. There are many additional reasons for buying calls, and there are specific strategies to avoid loss. These are explained in Chapter 9 in detail.

The biggest problem for call buyers is lack of enough time. Typically, an underlying stock's value rises, but not enough to offset the declining time value by the point of expiration. So if the stock rises, but not enough, then the call buyer will not be able to earn a profit. A simple rise in stock price is not adequate in every case, and call buyers have to recognize the need for not just price change, but *adequate* price change to offset declining time value.

Example

When Four Equals Two: You recently bought a call for 4 when it was at $45, at the money (the current market value of the underlying stock was identical to the call's striking price). By expiration, the stock had risen to $47 per share, but the call was worth only 2. Why? The original $400 premium consisted entirely of time value and contained no intrinsic value. The time value was gone by expiration. The $200 value at closing represents the two points of intrinsic value. In this case, you can either sell the call and get half your money back, or wait it out hoping for a last-minute surge in the stock's price. Otherwise, you may simply allow the call to expire and lose the entire $400.

It is a mistake to assume that a call's premium value will rise with the stock in every case, even when in the money. The time value declines as expiration nears, so a rise in the option's premium occurs in intrinsic value, and may only offset lost time value premium. It is likely that even a rising stock price will not reflect dollar-for-dollar gains in the option until the time value has been used up. That's because time value is soft and is likely to evaporate quickly, as opposed to the hard intrinsic value that is more predictable—it changes point for point with in-the-money stock price movement.

Smart Investor Tip

The increase in premium value of an in-the-money option takes place in intrinsic value. Time value has to be absorbed too, and as expiration approaches, time value evaporates with increasing speed.

This means that if you buy a call with several points of time value, you cannot earn a profit unless the stock rises enough to (1) offset the time value premium, and (2) create enough growth above striking price. This double requirement is easy to overlook, but worth remembering.

Example

All for Nothing: You bought a call two months ago and paid 1. At the time, the stock was 7 points out of the money. Now expiration date has arrived. The stock's market value has increased an impressive six points. However, the option is virtually worthless because, with expiration pending, there is no intrinsic value. The call is still out of the money, even though the underlying stock's market value has increased six points.

Call buyers will lose money if they fail to recognize the requirement that the underlying stock needs to increase sufficiently in value. A mere increase is not enough if time value needs to be offset as well. With this in mind, call buyers should set goals for themselves, defining when to leave a position. The goal should relate to gain and to bailout in the case of a loss.

This is always a problem for anyone taking up a long position with options. You buy hoping the call will grow in value, but time works against you. In fact, three-quarters of all options expire worthless, so making a profit consistently buying options is a difficult task. You need to overcome time as well as realizing growth in intrinsic value; and, of course, interim changes in extrinsic value further complicate this requirement. As a buyer, you race against time. It makes a lot of sense to set goals for yourself, but the time may also come when you realize you are going to make a profit because time is evaporation. With this in mind, your goal should include identifying when to take a loss.

Smart Investor Tip

Knowing when to take a profit is only a part of the option trader's goal. It is equally important to know when to take a loss.

Example

Keeping Promises: You are the type of investor who believes in setting goals for yourself. So when you bought a call at 4, you promised yourself you would sell if the premium value fell to 2 or rose to 7. This standard reduces losses in the event that the option declines in value, while also providing a point at which the profit will be taken. You recognize that when it comes to options, time is the enemy and an opportunity might not return. Option buyers often do not get a second chance.

suitability

a standard by which a particular investment or market strategy is judged. The investor's knowledge and experience with options represent important suitability standards. Strategies are appropriate only if the investor understands the market and can afford to take the risks involved.

realized profits

profits taken at the time a position is closed.

paper profits

(also called *unrealized profits*) values existing only on paper but not taken at the time; paper profits (or paper losses) become realized only if a closing transaction is executed.

Goal-setting is important because *realized profits* can occur only when you actually close the position. For buyers, that means executing a closing sale transaction. You need to set a standard and then stick to it. Otherwise, you can only watch the potential for realized profits come and go. Your *paper profits* (also known as *unrealized profits*) may easily end up as losses.

If you buy a call and the stock experiences an unexpected jump in market value, it is possible that the time value will increase as well, but this will be temporary; to realize the profit, it has to be taken when it exists. The wider the out-of-the-money range, the lower your chances for realizing a profit. The leverage value of options takes place when the option is in the money. Then the intrinsic value will change point-for-point with the stock. As shown in Figure 3.1, whenever a stock is five points or more below the call's striking price, it is described as being *deep out* of the money. For puts, the number of points is the same, but the stock's market value would

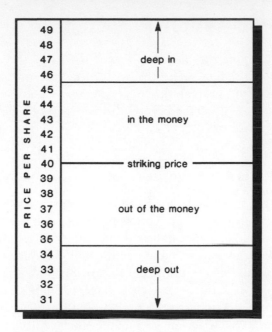

FIGURE 3.1 Deep in/deep out stock prices for calls.

be five points or more above striking price. If the stock's market value is five points or more above striking price (for calls) or below striking price (for puts), it is said to be *deep in* the money.

These definitions are important to call buyers. A deep out of the money option, because it requires significant price movement just to get to a breakeven point, is a long shot; and a deep in the money call is going to demand at least five points of premium just for intrinsic value, in addition to its time value. So the majority of call buyers will buy within the five-point range on either side of the striking price. This provides the maximum opportunity for profit with the least requirement for price increase to offset time value.

deep out
condition when the underlying stock's current market value is five points or more below the striking price of the call or above the striking price of the put.

deep in
condition when the underlying stock's current market value is five points or more above the striking price of the call or below the striking price of the put.

Call Buying Strategies

Buying calls and hoping they increase in value is a basic, speculative strategy. It is the best-known option strategy, as well. More investors select calls than puts, because they tend to think that prices are always going to rise; it is also an obvious strategy. But looking beyond this is where calls become the most interesting. Calls can also be put to work in ways beyond mere speculation.

Strategy 1: Calls for Leverage

Leverage is using a small amount of capital to control a larger investment. While the term usually is applied to borrowing money to invest, it also perfectly describes call buying. For a few hundred dollars placed at risk, you control 100 shares of stock. By "control," we mean that the option buyer has the right (but not the obligation) to buy the 100 shares at any time prior to expiration, with the price frozen by contract. Leverage enables you to establish the potential for profit with a limited amount of at-risk capital. This is why so many call buyers willingly assume the risks, even knowing that the odds of making money on the call itself are against them.

Example

Spotting the Advantage: You are familiar with a pharmaceutical company's management, profit history, and product line. The company has recently announced that it has received approval for the release of a new drug. The release date is three months away. However, the market has not yet responded to the news. You expect that the stock's market price will rise substantially once the market realizes the significance of the new drug. But you are not sure; the lack of response by the market has raised some doubt in your mind. By buying a call with six months until expiration, you expose yourself to a limited risk; but the opportunity for gain is also worth that risk, in your opinion. In this case, you have not risked the price of 100 shares, only the relatively small cost of the option.

Example

Expanded Potential: Given the same circumstances as in the previous example, you also realize that price growth might not occur for one to two years. It may require market response and acceptance, so a short-term option will not provide the leverage you seek. A LEAPS call does provide you the long-term leverage in this situation. Buying a LEAPS call will require more investment, because you have to buy the additional time; but if you believe the stock has growth potential within the window of time, it would make sense to invest.

Profits can take place rapidly in an option's value. If the price of the stock were to take off, you would have a choice: You could sell the call at a profit, or exercise it and pick up 100 shares at a fixed price below market value. That is a wise use of leverage, given the circumstances described. Things can change quickly. This can be demonstrated by comparing the risks between purchase of 100 shares of stock, versus the purchase of a call. (See Figure 3.2.)

In this example, the stock was selling at $62 per share. You could invest $6,200 and buy 100 shares, or you could purchase a call at 5 and invest only $500. The premium consists of 2 points of intrinsic value and 3 points of time value.

If you buy 100 shares, you are required to pay for the purchase within three business days. If you buy the call, you make payment the following day. The payment deadline for any transaction is called the *settlement date*.

	STOCK (1)		CALL (2)	
	PROFIT OR LOSS	RATE OF RETURN	PROFIT OR LOSS	RATE OF RETURN
price increase of 5 points	$500	8.1%	$500	100%
price increase of 1 point	$100	1.6%	$100	20%
no price change	0	0	0	0
price decrease of 1 point	–$100	–1.6%	–$100	–20%
price decrease of 5 points	–$500	–8.1%	–$500	–100%

(1) purchased at $62 per share ($6,200)
(2) striking price 60, premium 5 ($500)

FIGURE 3.2 Rate of return: buying stocks versus calls.

settlement date
the date on which a buyer is required to pay for purchases, or on which a seller is entitled to receive payment. For stocks, settlement date is three business days after the transaction. For options, settlement date is one business day from the date of the transaction.

As a call buyer, your plan may be to sell the call prior to expiration. Most call buyers are speculating on price movement in the underlying stock and do not intend to actually exercise the call; rather, their plan is to sell the call at a profit. In the example, a $500 investment gives you control over 100 shares of stock. That's leverage. You do not need to invest and place at risk $6,200 to gain that control. The stock buyer, in comparison, is entitled to receive dividends and does not have to work against the time deadline. Without considering trading costs associated with buying and selling calls, what might happen in the immediate future?

If a five-point gain occurred by the point of expiration, it would translate to only a two-point net gain for the option buyer:

Original cost	$500
Less evaporated time value	−300
Original intrinsic value	$200
Plus increased intrinsic value	+500
Value at expiration	$700
Profit	$200

A point-for-point change in option premium value would be substantial. An in-the-money increase of 1 point yields 1.6 percent to the stockholder, but a full 20 percent to the option buyer. If there were to be no price change between purchase and expiration, three-fifths of the option premium would evaporate due to the disappearance of time value. The call buyer risks a loss in this situation even without a change in the stock's market value.

As a call buyer, you are under pressure of time for two reasons. First, the option will expire at a specified date in the future. Second, as expiration approaches, the rate of decline in time value increases, making it even more difficult for options traders to get to breakeven or profit status. At that point, increase in market value of the underlying stock must be adequate to offset time value *and* to yield a profit above striking price in excess of the premium price you paid.

It is possible to buy calls with little or no time value. To do so, you will have to select calls that are relatively close to expiration, so that only a short time remains for the stock's value to increase, and fairly close to striking price to reduce the premium cost. The short time period increases risk in one respect; the lack of time value reduces risk in another respect.

Example

Just a Little Time: In the second week of May, the May 50 call is selling for 2 and the underlying stock is worth 51.50 ($1^{1}/_{2}$ points in the money). You buy one call. By the third Friday (the following week), you are hoping for an increase in the market value of the underlying stock. If the stock were to rise one point, the option would be minimally profitable. With only $^{1}/_{2}$ point of time value, only a small amount of price movement is required to offset time value and produce in-the-money profits (before considering trading fees). Because time is short, your chances for realizing a profit are limited. But profits, if they do materialize, will be very close to a dollar-for-dollar movement with the stock, given the small amount of time value remaining. If the stock were to increase 3 points, you could double your money in a day or two. And of course, were the stock to drop 2 points or more, the option would become worthless. Considering trading costs, examples of small-point scenarios like this are most realistic for multiple-contract strategies. For example, if you were to buy 10 calls at $51.50, you would invest $510.50 plus trading costs; but on a per-contract basis, trading costs would be far lower than for a single-contract purchase.

Smart Investor Tip

Short-term call buyers hope for price movement, and they may need only a few points. The risk, of course, is that price movement could go in the wrong direction.

The greater the time until expiration, the greater the time value premium—and the greater the increase you will require in the market value of the underlying stock, just to maintain the call's value. For the buyer, the interaction between time and time value is the key. This is summarized in Figure 3.3.

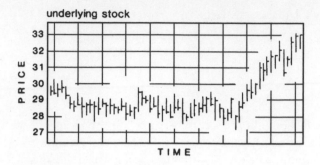

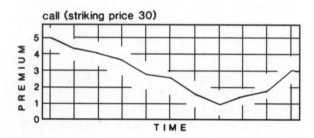

FIGURE 3.3 Diminishing time value of the call relative to the underlying stock.

Example

The Luxury of Time: You buy a call at 5 when the stock's market value is at or near the striking price of 30. Your advantage is that you have six months until expiration. For four months, the underlying stock's market value remains fairly close to the striking price, and the option's premium value—all or most time value—declines over the same period. Then the stock's market value increases to $33 per share. However, because the time value has disappeared, the call is worth only 3, the intrinsic value. You have lost $200.

Buying calls is one form of leverage—controlling 100 shares of stock for a relatively small investment of capital—and it offers the potential for substantial gain (or loss). But because time value is invariably a factor, the requirements are high. Even with the best timing and analysis of the option and the underlying stock, it is very difficult to earn profits consistently by buying calls.

Strategy 2: Limiting Risks

In one respect, the relatively small investment of capital required to buy a call *reduces* your risk. A stockholder stands to lose a lot more if and when the market value of stock declines.

Example

The Lesser of Two Losses: You bought a call two months ago for a premium of 5. It expires later this month and is worth nearly nothing, since the stock's market value has fallen 12 points, well below striking price. You will lose your $500 investment or most of it, whereas a stockholder would have lost $1,200 in the same situation. You controlled the same number of shares for less exposure to risk, and for a smaller capital investment. Your loss is always limited to the amount of call premium paid. This comparison is not entirely valid, however. The stockholder receives dividends, if applicable, and has the luxury of being able to hold stock indefinitely. The stock's market value could eventually rebound. Options traders cannot afford to wait, because they face expiration in the near future.

You enjoy the benefits of lower capital exposure only as long as the option exists. The stockholder has more money at risk, but is not concerned about expiration. It would make no sense to buy calls *only* to limit risks, rather than taking the risks of buying shares of stock. A call buyer believes that the stock will increase in value by expiration date. Risks are limited in the event that the estimate of near-term price movement proves to be wrong, but are inapplicable for long-term risk evaluation.

Strategy 3: Planning Future Purchases

When you own a call, you fix the price of a future purchase of stock in the event you exercise that call prior to expiration. This use of calls goes far beyond pure speculation.

Example

All a Matter of Timing: The market had a large point drop recently, and one company you have been following experienced a drop in market value. It had been trading in the $50 to $60 range, and you would like to buy 100 shares at the current depressed price of $39 per share. You are convinced that market value will eventually rebound. However, you do not have $3,900 available to invest at the moment. You will be able to raise this money within one year, but you believe that by then, the stock's market value will have returned to its higher range level. Not knowing exactly what will happen, one alternative in this situation is to buy a LEAPS call. To fix the price, you can buy calls while the market is low with the intention of exercising each call once you have the capital available. The 40 LEAPS call expiring in 12 months currently is selling for 3, and you purchase one contract at that price. Six months later, the stock's market price has risen to $58 per share. The call is worth 18 just before expiration. The same strategy—looking ahead one year—would not have been possible with shorter-term listed calls.

In this case, you would have two choices. First, you could sell the call at 18 and realize a profit of $1,500. Second, you could exercise the call and buy 100 shares of stock at $40 per share. If you seek long-term growth and believe the stock is a good value, you can use options to freeze the current price, with the idea of buying 100 shares later.

The advantage to this strategy is that your market risk is limited. So if you are wrong and the stock continues to fall, you lose only the option premium. If you are right, you pick up 100 shares below market value upon exercise.

Some option speculators recognize that large drops in overall market value are often temporary, as a single-stock reaction to marketwide short-term trends. So a large price drop could represent a buying opportunity, especially in those stocks that fall more than the average marketwide drop. In this situation, investors are likely to be concerned with the risk of further price drops, so they hold off and miss the opportunity. As an options trader, you can afford to speculate on the probability of a price rebound and buy calls. When the market does bounce back, you can sell those calls at a profit.

Strategy 4: Insuring Profits

Another reason for buying calls is to protect a short position in the underlying stock. Calls can be used as a form of insurance. If you have sold short 100 shares of stock, you were hoping that the market value would fall so that you could close out the position by buying 100 shares at a lower market price. The risk, of course, is that the stock will rise in market value, creating a loss for you as a short seller.

Example

Checking Your Shorts: An investor sells short 100 shares of stock when market value is $58 per share. One month later, the stock's market value has fallen to $52 per share. The investor enters a closing purchase transaction—buys 100 shares—and realizes a profit of $600 before trading costs.

A short seller's risks are unlimited in the sense that a stock's market value, in theory at least, could rise to any level. If the market value does rise above the initial sale price, each point represents a point of loss for the short seller. To protect against the potential loss in that event, a short seller can buy calls for insurance.

Example

Reducing Your Risks: You sell short 100 shares when market value is $58 per share. At the same time, you buy one call with a striking price of 65, paying a premium of $1/2$, or $50. The risk is no longer unlimited. If market value rises above $65 per share, the call protects you; each dollar lost in the stock will be offset by a dollar gained in the call. Risk, then, is limited to seven points (the difference between the short sale price of $58 and the call's striking price of 65).

In this example, a deep out of the money call was inexpensive, yet it provided valuable insurance for short selling. The protection lasts only until expiration of the call, so if you want to protect the position, the expired call will have to be replaced with another call. This reduces your potential loss through buying offsetting calls, but it also erodes a portion of your profits. As a short seller, like anyone buying insurance, you need to assess the cost of insurance versus the potential risk.

Example

The Need for More: A short seller pays a premium of 2 and buys a call that expires in five months. If the value of the stock decreases two points, the short seller might take the profit and close the position; however, with the added cost of the call, a two-point change represents a breakeven point (before calculating the trading costs). The short seller needs more decrease in market value to create a profit.

Calls serve an important function when used by short sellers to limit risks. They also take part of their potential profit for insurance, so short sellers hope that the strategy will be profitable enough to justify the added expense. Using LEAPS calls in this situation will cost more but provide the same insurance for a longer period of time. The selection of a call to insure a short position depends on the length of time you plan to remain in the short stock position.

Example

The Effect of Rumors: An investor sold short 100 shares of stock at $58 per share. At the same time, he bought a call with a striking price of 65 and paid a premium of 2. A few weeks later, the underlying stock's market price rose on rumors of a pending merger, to a price of $75 per share. The short seller is down $1,700 in the stock (shares were sold at $58 and currently are valued at $75). However, the call is worth $1,000 in intrinsic value plus whatever time value remains. To close the position, the investor can exercise the call and reduce the loss to $700—the sales price of the stock ($58), versus the striking price of the exercised call ($65 per share). In this case, an additional call with later expiration and higher striking price could be purchased to continue providing additional insurance. This overall strategy makes sense only if the investor continues to believe that the stock's value will eventually fall and recognizes that the use of calls is a valuable strategy while waiting out the short sale move. If the investor now believes that the stock is not going to fall, then continuing with the short sale in stock would not make sense; the smart move would be to close out the position and take the loss, before a larger loss occurs. Otherwise, if the stock's value continues to rise *after* the call has been closed, the investor risks further losses.

Strategy 5: Premium Buying

A final strategy involves buying calls to average out the cost of stock held in the portfolio. This is an alternative to dollar cost averaging (see Chapter 6). Stockholders who desire to hold shares of a company's stock for the long term may want to buy stock while prices are stable or falling, on the idea that lower prices represent an averaging-down of the overall net price per share. However, the dollar cost averaging strategy, as effective as it is in a declining market situation, is not as desirable when stock prices rise. In that case, hindsight shows that you would have been better off to buy more shares at the original price.

This is a dilemma. If you plan to keep a stock as an investment over the long term, but you do not want to put all of your capital into the stock right now (fearing possible decline in value), one alternative is call premium buying. When you purchase a call using this strategy, you seek longer-term out-of-the-money calls for relatively low premium levels. Then, if the stock's value does rise, you can purchase additional shares below market value.

Example

Climbing the Wall of Worry: You own 400 shares of a particular company and you want to buy another 200 to 400 shares in coming months. You originally planned to buy more shares any time the stock's price dropped, creating a lower average cost with each subsequent purchase. However, at the same time you are concerned about losing the opportunity to buy at today's price in the event the stock's price rises. You purchase two calls, one two points out of the money expiring in three months, the other seven points out expiring in six months.

By employing this strategy, you can have it both ways. If the stock's market value falls, you buy additional shares and reduce your overall basis in stock; if the stock's market value rises, you can exercise your calls and fix the stock purchase price at the call striking prices, even if the stock's market value goes far above those levels.

Buying *more* shares of a company whose prospects are increasingly poor is never sensible. However, in utilizing an options strategy such as premium buying in conjunction with downward dollar cost averaging, we assume that the investor has performed the required level of fundamental analysis to be confident in the company's long-term value. This has to be offset against the cost of premium buying; you need to ensure that the money paid for call premium is not so excessive that the dollar cost averaging advantages are less than the advantages of simply buying stock at a higher price.

Defining Profit Zones

Whatever strategy you employ in your portfolio, always be aware of how much price movement is required to create a profit, the risks involved in the strategy, and the range of potential losses to which you are exposed. Throughout the rest of this book, we will use illustrations to define the *breakeven price* as well as *profit zone* and *loss zone* for each strategy. See

breakeven price
(also called the *breakeven point*) the price of the underlying stock at which the option investor breaks even. For call buyers, this price is the number of points above striking price equal to the call premium cost; for put buyers, this price is the number of points below striking price equal to the put premium cost.

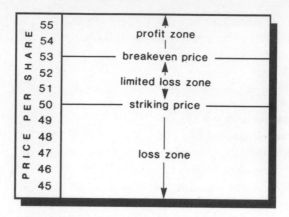

FIGURE 3.4 A call's profit and loss zones.

Figure 3.4 for a sample. Note that prices per share are listed at the left in a column, and the various zones are divided according to price levels. (As with all examples, these zones are simplified for illustration purposes, do not allow for the cost of trading, and usually involve single option trades. Be sure to add brokerage fees to the cost of all transactions in calculating your own breakeven, profit, and loss zones.)

Example

A Math Quiz: You buy a call and pay a premium of 3, with a striking price of 50. What must the stock's price become by point of expiration, in order for you to break even (not considering trading costs)? What price must the stock achieve in order for a profit to be gained, assuming that only intrinsic value will remain at the time? And at what price will you suffer a loss?

profit zone

the price range of the underlying stock in which the option investor realizes a profit. For the call buyer, the profit zone extends upward from the breakeven price. For the put buyer, the profit zone extends downward from the breakeven price.

In this example, a loss occurs if the option expires out of the money, as is always the case. Because you paid a premium of 3, when the underlying stock's market value is 3 points or less above striking price, the loss will be limited. (Striking price was 50, so if the stock reaches 52, there will be 2 points of intrinsic value at point of expiration,

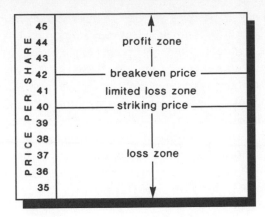

FIGURE 3.5 Example of call purchase
with profit and loss zones.

for example.) With limited intrinsic value between striking price and 53, there is
not enough increase in market value to produce a profit. Once the stock reaches
$53 per share, you are at breakeven, because you are three points in the money
and you paid 3 for the option. When the stock rises above the $53 per share
level, you enter the profit zone.

Defining breakeven price and profit
and loss zones helps you to define the range
of limited loss in cases such as option buying, so that overall risk can be quantified
more easily. An example of a call purchase
with defined profit zone and loss zones is
shown in Figure 3.5. In this example, the
investor bought one May 40 call for 2. In
order to profit from this strategy, the stock's
value must increase to a level greater than
the striking price of the call plus 2 points
(based on the assumption that all time value
will have disappeared). So $42 per share is

loss zone

the price range of the
underlying stock in which
the option investor loses.
A limited loss exists for
option buyers, since the
premium cost is the max-
imum loss that can be
realized.

the breakeven price. Even when buying a call scheduled to expire within a few
months, you need to know in advance the risks and how much price movement
is needed to yield a profit.

Example

Timing Your Move: You have been tracking a stock with the idea of
buying calls. Right now, you could buy a call with a striking price of 40
for a premium of 2. The stock's market value is $38 per share, two points

out of the money. In deciding whether to buy this call, you understand that between the time of purchase and expiration, the stock will need to rise by no less than four points: two points to get to the striking price plus two more points to cover your cost. If this does occur, the option will be worth exactly what you paid for it, representing a breakeven level (before trading costs). Because the entire premium consists of time value, the stock needs to surpass striking price and develop enough intrinsic value to cover your cost. If price movement were to take place quickly, you could earn a profit consisting of both time and intrinsic value. So the illustration of breakeven and profit zones invariably assumes that all time value will be gone by the time you are ready to close a position.

Example

Going with Higher Potential: Another stock you have been following has an option available for a premium of 1 and currently is at the money. Expiration is two months away and the stock is only 1 point below breakeven (because of your premium cost). Considering these circumstances, this option has greater potential to become profitable. You need relatively little price movement to create a good profit. If the stock moves adequately at any time in the next two months, you will earn a profit.

In the first example, a breakeven price was four points above current market value of the stock, and the option premium was $200. In the second example, only one point of price movement is required to reach breakeven. The lower premium also means you are exposed to less potential loss in the event the stock does not rise.

You could make as much profit from a $100 investment as from an equally viable $200 investment, as the previous examples demonstrate. The size of the initial premium cost cannot be used to judge potential profit, whereas it can be used to define potential losses. Premium level can be deceptive, and a more thoughtful risk/reward analysis often is required to accurately compare one option choice to another.

Smart Investor Tip

The option's premium level cannot be used reliably to judge the viability of a buy decision. It can be used to define potential losses, however.

Another factor to consider when evaluating potential profit is the tax effect of buying options. By definition, a buyer's listed option profits and losses are always short-term because listed stock options expire within one year or less; LEAPS profits may be either short-term or long-term depending on how long the positions are open (see Chapter 12). So you need to consider the tax consequences of profits as part of the breakeven analysis. The transaction cost also has to be calculated on both sides of the transaction, of course. You probably need to calculate the *aftertax breakeven point*, which is the profit required to break even when also allowing for the federal, state, and (if applicable) local taxes you will owe.

aftertax breakeven point
the point level at which you will break even on an option trade, considering the taxes due on capital gains you will be required to pay for trading options.

Option profits are taxed in the year a transaction is closed. So option sellers receive payment in one year, but the option may expire or be closed in the following year. In that situation, the option profit is taxed in the latter year, when the option has been closed, exercised, or expires. This raises individual tax planning questions. Chapter 12 explains the tax considerations in detail.

Example

A Taxing Matter: You bought a call two months ago and you want to identify the aftertax breakeven point. Your effective tax rate (combining federal and state) is 50 percent, so your breakeven cannot simply be restricted to the calculation of pretax profit. Even though the true breakeven point is variable (because as you earn more, a higher amount of taxes will be due), you should build in a 50 percent cushion to the breakeven calculation. If you were to make $200 on an option transaction, $100 would have to go to pay a combined federal and state tax liability, so you would have to raise the breakeven by two more points to create an aftertax breakeven of $200 ($400 pretax profit minus $200 tax liability).

The important point to remember about taxes is how that figures into your overall goal setting. A "profit" is going to be much smaller if your tax rate is high, and combined federal and state rates can take a significant share of your pretax profit.

The aftertax breakeven point has to be calculated figuring both federal and state rates. The only way you can keep 100 percent of your profits is when you have a carryover loss, which can be deducted only at the rate of $3,000 per year on your federal return. However, if you have profits in the current year, you can offset those profits against your unused carryover losses and shelter current-year profits. These are among the many considerations to keep in mind when developing a strategy for buying options.

Before buying any option, evaluate the attributes of the underlying stock and the profit or loss potential of the option. The analysis of the underlying stock should include, at a minimum, a study of market price, dividend history and rate, price volatility, P/E ratio, earnings history, and other fundamental and technical features that define a stock's safety and stability. There is no point to selecting an option that has price appeal, when the underlying stock has undesirable qualities, such as price unpredictability, inconsistent financial results, weak position within a sector or industry, or an inconsistent dividend history. At the very least, determine from recent history how responsive the stock's market price is to the general movement of the market. Options cannot be evaluated apart from their underlying stock, because that would ignore the important risk attributes of the stock and its potential volatility. The value and profit potential in your options strategy grows from first selecting stock candidates that are a good fit with your own risk profile. It is the wise selection of a range of "good" stocks (by the definition you use to make stock value judgments) that determines viable option selection.

You may also evaluate the entire stock market before deciding whether your timing is good for buying calls. For example, do you believe that the market has been on an upward climb that may require a short-term correction? If so, it is possible that buying options, even on the best stock choices, could be ill timed. No one truly knows how markets will move, or why they behave as they do, even though you may find yourself on a continual quest to find a method to gain such insights. The process of buying and selling is based, invariably, on timing and opinion. See Chapter 6 for a more in-depth and expanded study and discussion of stock selection.

Beyond the point of stock and option analysis, observe the time factor and how the passage of time affects option premium. Time value changes predictably, but in different degrees by stock and from one period to another. Changes in time value can be elusive and unpredictable in the degree and timing. The only certainty is that at expiration, no time value will remain in the option premium.

In the next chapter, strategies for buying puts will be examined in depth.

4

Buying Puts: The Positive Side of Pessimism

Blessed is he who expects nothing, for he shall never be disappointed.
—Alexander Pope, letter, October 16, 1727

D o you believe the market is headed down? If so, puts could serve as a valuable weapon in your pessimistic market strategy.

Call buyers acquire the right to *buy* 100 shares of an underlying stock. In contrast, a put grants the buyer the opposite right: to *sell* 100 shares of an underlying stock. Upon exercise of a put, the buyer sells 100 shares at the fixed contract price, even if the stock's current market value has fallen below that level.

It is easy to get confused because calls and puts are opposites. In other words, if the underlying stock's value goes down, the put's value goes up. The put works in the other direction. So buying puts, which can be done for several reasons, is an action you will take if you expect declining stock prices; if you want to protect a long stock position in the event of a decline in price; or when entering a more advanced strategy combining puts with calls—more on all of this later.

As a put buyer, you have a choice to make in the near future. You may sell the put before it expires; you may exercise the put and sell 100 shares of the underlying stock at the fixed striking price; or you may let the put expire worthless.

You are not obligated to sell 100 shares by virtue of owning the put. That decision is entirely up to you, and is a right but not an obligation. The seller, however, would be obligated to buy 100 shares if you did decide to exercise the put.

Smart Investor Tip
The buyer of an option always has the right, but not the obligation to exercise. The seller has no choice in the event of exercise.

As a put buyer, your decisions will depend on the same features that affect and motivate call buyers:

- Price movement in the underlying stock and how that affects the put's premium value.

- Your motives for buying the put, and how today's market conditions meet or do not match with those motives.

- Your willingness to wait out a series of events between purchase date and expiration and see what develops, versus your desire for a sure profit in the short term.

Additionally, the same rules apply to puts and to calls regarding the trend in extrinsic value. If you make a distinction between extrinsic and time value, you will recall the important rule: Time value declines over time and is a factor strictly related to the time remaining until expiration. Extrinsic value (usually included as part of time value in a discussion of option valuation) is more complicated.

Extrinsic value, the nonintrinsic portion of option value *not* related solely to the time element, is affected by numerous things, including:

- *Volatility of the underlying stock.* The more volatile the stock, the greater the related volatility in extrinsic value. This is especially applicable when the stock's price is erratic and chaotic.

- *Trading range of the stock.* A fairly narrow trading range tends to hold down extrinsic value, but when a stock's market value moves back and forth within a broader trading range, that will be reflected in greater extrinsic value. (This is not the same as volatility of the underlying stock. A volatile stock is erratic and unpredictable. A broad trading range may remain predictable but with greater distance between its likely high and low price range.)

- *Breakout from established trading range.* When a stock's price moves above or below an established trading range, option extrinsic value will increase as well. Depending on whether movement means that puts (or calls) go in the money, the increased intrinsic value may also be augmented with greater extrinsic (nontime) value within the same trend.

- *Proximity between current market value of stock and striking price of the put.* When the two are within close proximity, extrinsic value—which you might think of as potential for increased value in the future—is going to be greater as well. This is especially true when the put is out of the money but the stock's current market value is three points or less above the striking price.

- *The time element.* While extrinsic value is distinguished from time value, it is going to vary based on (1) time itself and (2) the other considerations listed here.

The Limited Life of the Put

If you believe the underlying stock's market value will decline in the near future, you can take one of three actions in the market: sell short on shares of the stock, sell calls, or buy puts. When you buy a put, your desire is that the underlying stock value will fall below the striking price; the more it falls, the higher your profit. Your belief and hope is opposite that of a call buyer. In that respect, many people view call buyers as optimists and put buyers as pessimists. It is more reasonable when using puts to define yourself as someone who recognizes the cyclical nature of prices in the market, and who believes that a stock is overvalued. Then put buying is sensible for two reasons. First, if you are correct, it may be a profitable decision. Second, buying puts contains much lower risk than short selling stock or call selling.

Your risk is limited to the premium paid for the put. As a put buyer, you face identical risks to those experienced by the call buyer. But when compared to selling short 100 shares of stock, put buyers have far less risk *and* much less capital requirement. The put buyer does not have to deposit collateral or pay interest on borrowed stock, is not exposed to exercise as a seller would be, and does not face the same risks as the short seller; yet the put buyer can make as much profit. The only disadvantage is the everpending expiration date. Time works against the put buyer, and time value premium evaporates with increasing speed as expiration approaches. If the stock's market value declines, but not enough to offset lost time value in the put, you could experience a loss or only break even. The strategy requires price drops adequate to produce a profit.

Compare the various strategies you can employ using shares of stock or options, depending on what you believe will happen in the near-term future to the market value of the underlying stock:

	you believe that the market will:	
	Rise	**Fall**
Stock strategy	Buy shares (long)	Sell shares (short)
Option strategy (long)	Buy calls	Buy puts
Option strategy (short)	Sell puts	Sell calls

Example

Perfect Timing: You have been watching a stock over the past few months. You believe it is overpriced today, and you expect market value to decline in the near term. Originally, you had planned to buy shares, but now you think the timing is wrong. Instead, you borrow 100 shares from your brokerage firm and sell them short. A few weeks later, the stock has fallen 8 points. You close the position by buying 100 shares. Your profit is $800, less trading costs and interest.

Example

Limiting Risk Exposure: You believe that a particular stock's market value will decline, but you do not want to sell short on the shares, recognizing that the risks and costs are too high. You also do not want to sell a call. That leaves you with a third choice, buying a put. You find a put with several months until expiration, whose premium is 3. If you are right and the stock's market value falls, you could make a profit. But if you are wrong and market value remains the same or rises (or falls, but not enough to produce a profit), your maximum risk exposure is only $300.

As a put buyer, you benefit from a stock's declining market value, and at the same time you avoid the cost and risk associated with short positions. Selling stock short or selling calls exposes you to significant market risks, often for small profit potential.

The limited loss is a positive feature of put buying. However the put—like the call—exists for only a limited amount of time. To profit from the strategy, you need to see adequate downward price movement in the stock to offset time value and to exceed your initial premium cost. So as a put buyer, you trade limited risk for limited life. If you use LEAPS puts, premium costs will be higher, but you also buy more time; so for some speculators, the LEAPS put is a viable alternative to the short-term listed put.

Smart Investor Tip

As a put buyer, you eliminate risks associated with going short, and in exchange, you accept the time restrictions associated with option long positions.

The potential benefit to a particular strategy is only half of the equation. The other half is risk. You need to know exactly how much price movement is needed to break even and to make a profit. Given time until expiration, is it realistic to expect that much price movement? There will be greater risks if your strategy requires a six-point movement in two weeks, and relatively small risks if you need only three points of price movement over two months or, in the case of LEAPS, over many more months.

You can view a LEAPS put in terms of risk in one of two ways. Of course, the extrinsic and time value problems and opportunities remain as they do with all options. But the extended period of time has an offsetting element to remember. First, you pay more for the additional time. Second, your risk is reduced because the added time provides more opportunities for favorable price movement. Thus, potential profits are improved for higher initial option premium cost. For anyone purchasing puts, this trade-off is the ultimate judgment call. You seek bargain prices, but you also seek the most time. So the offset between opportunity and risk is defined by the offset between time and cost.

Example

The Time-versus-Cost Decision: You want to buy a put on Motorola (MOT) in the month of December. You review three different possibilities, those expiring in four months (April), in 13 months (the following January), and in 25 months (January a year later). At the time, Motorola's market value was $20.67 per share. The put values were:

| | Put Striking Prices | | |
Striking Prices	4 Months	13 Months	25 Months
17.50	0.30	0.95	1.35
20	0.95	1.75	2.30
22.50	2.35	3.10	3.50
25	4.40	4.80	5.00
30	9.40	9.65	9.75

The selection of one put over another should depend on your preferences: in- or out-of-the-money, proximity between striking price and current market value of the stock, and, of course, the price of each put. The 17.50 and 20 puts are only slightly out of the money and so the distances between premium value reflect this potential. Extrinsic value is greater, thus the distances between put values based on the proximity issue. But when you study the in-the-money puts (those higher than current market value of $20.67 per share), you can spot some advantageous situations. Extrinsic value again affects the situation; for example, the 22.50 puts are relatively close to current market value, but study the prices of the 30 puts. These are quite far in the money, considering striking price of 30 and current market value of 20.67—more than nine points.

If you were inclined to invest in a long put on this stock and favored in-the-money puts, the 30 is more expensive, but the extrinsic value is very low. If you were to select the 25-month put rather than the 13-month put, the added cost would be only $10, the difference between 9.65 and 9.75. In other words, for only $10, you "buy" an additional 12 months in the put, giving you that extra year of potential. Thus, if Motorola were to decline several points over 25 months, this added cost provides you with much greater potential for profit. The 25 put can be subjected to the same argument, with the added cost only $20, the difference between 4.80 and 5.00.

The point to this comparison is that the farther away from striking price, the smaller the increments in extrinsic value. This gives you the opportunity to extend the put's lifetime for very little added cost.

Put buying is suitable for you only if you understand the risks and are familiar with price history and volatility in the underlying stock, not to mention the other fundamental and technical aspects that make a particular stock a good prospect for your options strategy. Without a doubt, buying puts is a risky strategy, and the smart put buyer knows this from the start.

Example

Calling the Market Correctly: You have $600 available and you believe that the market as a whole is overpriced. You expect it to fall in the near future. So you buy two puts at 3 each. The market does fall as expected; but the underlying stock remains unchanged and the puts begin to lose their time value. At expiration, they are worth only 1.

Your perception of the market was correct: Prices fell. But put buyers cannot afford to depend on overall impressions. The strategy lost money because the underlying stock did not behave in the same way as the market in general. The problem with broad market indicators is that such indicators cannot be reliably applied to single stocks. Each stock has its own attributes and reacts differently in changing markets, as well as to its own internal changes—revenues and earnings, capitalization, competitive forces, and the economy, to name a few. Some stocks tend to follow an upward or downward price movement in the larger market, and others do not react to markets as a whole. It is important to study the attributes of the individual stock rather than assuming that overall indicators and index trends are going to apply accurately to a specific stock.

In the preceding example, it appears that the strategy was inappropriate. First, capital was invested in a high-risk strategy. Second, the entire amount was placed into puts on the same stock. By basing a decision on the overall market trend without considering the indicators for the specific company, you lost money. It is likely, too, that you did not understand the degree of price change required to produce a profit. If you do not know how much risk a strategy involves, then it is not an appropriate strategy. More study and analysis is required.

Smart Investor Tip

When it comes to market risk, the unasked question can lead to unexpected losses. Whatever strategy you employ, you need to first explore and understand all of the risks involved.

It is not unusual for investors to concentrate on potential gain without also considering the potential loss, especially in the options market. In the previous example, one reason you lost was a failure to study the individual stock. One aspect not considered was the company's strength in a declining market, its ability to hold its price. This information might have been revealed with more focused analysis and a study of the stock's price history in previous markets. Options traders may lose not because their perception of the market is wrong, but because there was not enough time for their strategy to work—in other words, because they did not fully understand the stock-specific implications and option-specific timing aspects of the decision.

Once you understand the risks and are convinced that you can afford the losses that could occur, you might decide that it is appropriate to buy puts in some circumstances. Remember, though, that the evaluation has to involve not only the option—premium level, time value, and time until expiration—but also the attributes of the underlying stock.

Example

Losses You Can Afford: You are an experienced investor and you have a well-diversified investment portfolio. You own shares in companies in different market sectors and also own shares in two mutual funds, plus some real estate. You have been investing for several years, fully understand the risks in these markets, and consider yourself a long-term and conservative investor. In selecting stocks, you have always used their potential for long-term price appreciation and a history of stability in earnings as your primary selection criteria. Short-term price movement does not concern you with these longer-term aspects in mind. Outside of this portfolio, you have funds available that you use for occasional speculation. You believe the market will fall in the short-term, including the value of shares of stock that you own. You buy puts with this in mind. Your theory: Any short-term losses in your permanent portfolio will be offset by gains in your put speculation. And if you are wrong, you can afford the losses.

You are aware of the difference between long-term investment and short-term speculation in the preceding example. You have established a base in your portfolio, and you thoroughly understand how the market works. You can afford some minor losses with capital set aside purely for speculation. Buying puts is an appropriate strategy given your belief about the market, particularly since you understand that stocks in your portfolio are likely to fall along with broader market trends. Your ability to afford losses, and the proper selection of stocks on which to buy puts, add up to a greater chance of success.

Judging the Put

Time works against all option buyers. Not only will your option expire within a few months, but time value will decline even if the stock's price does not change. Buyers need to offset lost time value with price movement that creates intrinsic value in its place.

You can select low-priced puts—ones that are out of the money—but that means you require many points of price movement to produce a profit. In other words, those puts are low-priced for a good reason. The likelihood of gain is lower than it is for higher-priced puts. When you buy in-the-money puts, you will experience a point-for-point change in intrinsic value; but that can happen in either direction. For put buyers, a downward movement in the stock's market value is offset point-for-point with gains in the put's premium; but each upward movement in the stock's market value is also offset, by a decline in the put's intrinsic value.

Example

A Losing Proposition: You bought a put and paid a premium of 5. At the time, the stock's market value was 4 points below the striking price. It was 4 points in the money. (For calls, "in the money" means the stock's market value is higher than striking price, but the opposite for puts.) However, by expiration, the stock has risen 4.50 points and the option is worth only 0.50 ($50). The time value has disappeared and you sell on the day of expiration, losing $450.

Example

Time Running Out: You bought a put several months ago, paying a premium of 0.50 ($50). At that time, the stock's market value was five points out of the money. By expiration, the stock's market value has declined 5.50 points, so that the put is 0.50 point in the money. When you bought the put, it had no intrinsic value and only 0.50 point of time value. At expiration, the time value is gone and there remains only 0.50 point of intrinsic value. Overall, the premium value has not changed; but no profit is possible because the stock's market value did not decline enough.

The problem is not limited to picking the right direction a stock's market value might change, although many novice options traders fall into the trap of believing that this is true. Rather, the *degree* of movement within a limited period of time must be adequate to produce profits that exceed premium cost and offset time value (and to cover trading costs on both sides of the transaction). This time-related problem exists for LEAPS puts as well. However, with much longer time involved, many put buyers view the normal market cycles as advantageous even when speculating. For example, you may need to spend more premium dollars to acquire a LEAPS put, but with up to three years until expiration, you will also have many more opportunities to realize a profit.

Whether using listed options or LEAPS to buy puts, it remains a speculative move to go long when time value is involved. Some speculators attempt to bargain hunt in the options market. The belief is that it is always better to pick up a cheap option than to put more money into a high-priced one. This is not always the case; cheap options are cheap because they are *not* necessarily good bargains, and this is widely recognized by the market overall. The question of quality has to be remembered at all times when you are choosing options and comparing prices. The idea of value is constantly being adjusted for information about the underlying stock, but these adjustments are obscured by the double effect of (1) time to go until expiration and the effect on time value, and (2) distance between current market value of the stock and the striking price of the option. When the market value of the stock is close to the striking price, it creates a situation in which profits (or losses) can materialize rapidly. At such times, the proximity between market and striking price will also be reflected in option premium. It's true that lower-priced puts require much less price movement to produce profits; but these low-priced puts remain long shots.

> ### Smart Investor Tip
> A bargain price might reflect either a bargain or a lack of value in the option. Sometimes, real bargains are found in higherpriced options.

> ### Example
> **Fast Profits:** You bought a put last week when it was in the money, paying a premium of 6. You believed the stock was overpriced and was likely to fall. Two days after your purchase, the stock's market value fell two points. You sold the put and received $800. This represents a return on your investment of 33.3 percent in two days (not considering trading costs).

In this example, you turned the position around rapidly and walked away with a profit. So the bargain existed in this put because you were right. The return was substantial, but that does not mean that the experience can be repeated consistently. Remember, when you buy puts on speculation, you are gambling that you are right about *short-term* price changes. You might be right about the general trend in a stock but not have enough time for your prediction to become true before expiration. With this in mind, it is crucial to set goals for yourself, knowing in advance when you will sell a put—based on profit goals as well as loss bailout points.

> ### Example
> **Know When to Quit:** You bought a put last month, paying a premium of 4. At that time, you decided to set a few goals for yourself. First, you decided that if the put's value fell by 2 points, you would sell and accept a loss of $200. Second, you promised yourself that if the put's value rose by 3 points, you would sell and take a profit. You decided you would be willing to accept either a 50 percent loss or a 75 percent gain. And failing either of these outcomes, you decided you would hold the put until just before expiration and then sell for the premium value at that time.

Setting goals is the only way to succeed if you plan to speculate by bu___
options. Too many speculators fall into a no-win trap because they program
themselves to lose; they do not set standards, so they do not know when or how
to make smart decisions.

Example

Missed Opportunities: You bought a LEAPS put last month and paid
5. With 26 months to go before expiration, you thought there was
plenty of time for a profit to materialize. Your plan was to sell if the value
went up 2 points. A month after your purchase, the stock's market value
fell and the put's value went up to 8, an increase of 3 points. You did not
sell, however, because you thought the stock's market value might
continue to fall. If that happened and the put's value increased, you did
not want to lose out on future profits. But the following week, the stock's
value rebounded 4 points, and the put followed, losing 4 points. The
opportunity was lost. This pattern repeated several times and the put
ended up worthless at the point of expiration.

This example demonstrates the absolute need for firm goals. Even with a
lot of time, you cannot expect to realize a profit unless you also know when to
close the position. Inexperienced option speculators do not recognize the need
to take profits when they are there, or to cut losses—either decision based upon
a predetermined standard. When the put becomes more valuable, human nature
tells us, "I could make even more money if I wait." When the put's value falls,
the same voice says, "I can't sell now. I have to get back to where I started."

Ask yourself: If you listen to that voice, when do you sell? The answer,
of course, is that you can never sell. Whether your option is more valuable or
less valuable, the voice tells you to wait and see. Lost opportunities are unlikely
to repeat themselves, given the time factor associated with options; and even
when those opportunities do reappear with a LEAPS put, it does not mean that
the right decision will be made. The old stock market advice, "Buy in a rising
market," cannot be applied to options, because options expire. Not only that,
but time value declines, which means that profits you gain in intrinsic value
could be offset if you wait too long. You need to take profits or cut losses at the
right moment.

Example

Hesitate—and Lose: You bought a put last month for 6, and resolved
that you would sell if its value rose or fell by two points. Two weeks ago,

the stock's market value rose two points and the put declined to your bailout level of 4. You hesitated, hoping for a recovery. Today, the stock has risen a total of five points since you bought the put, which is now worth 1.

In this example, you would lose $300 by not following your own standard and bailing out at 4. Even if the stock did fall later on, time would work against you. The longer it takes for a turnaround in the price of the underlying stock, the more time value loss you need to overcome. The stock might fall a point or two over a three-month period, so that you merely trade time value for intrinsic value, with the net effect of zero; it is even likely that the overall premium value will decline if intrinsic value is not enough to offset the lost time value.

The problem of time value deterioration is the same problem ex-perienced by call buyers. It does not matter whether price movement is required to go up (for call buyers) or down (for put buyers); time is the enemy, and price movement has to be adequate to offset time value as well as produce a profit through more intrinsic value. If you seek bargains several points away from the striking price, it is easy to overlook this reality. You need a substantial change in the stock's market value just to arrive at the price level where intrinsic value will begin to accumulate. The relationship between the underlying stock and time value premium is illustrated in Figure 4.1.

Example

Good Trend But Not Enough: You bought a LEAPS put for 5 with a striking price of 30, when the stock was at $32 per share. There were 22 months to go until expiration and the entire put premium was time value; you estimated that there was plenty of time for the price of the stock to fall, producing a profit. Between purchase date and expiration, the underlying stock falls to 27, which is 3 points in the money. At expiration, the put is worth 3, meaning you lose $200 upon sale of the put. Time value has evaporated. Even though you are 3 points in the money, it is not enough to match or beat your investment of $500.

The further out of the money, the cheaper the premium for the option—*and* the lower the potential to ever realize a profit. Even using LEAPS and depending on longer time spans, you have to accept the reality: The current time value premium reflects the time until expiration, so you will pay more time value premium for longer-term puts. That means you have to overcome more points to replace time value with intrinsic value.

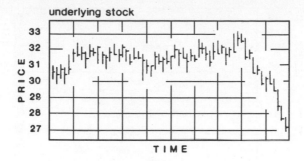

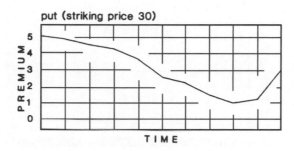

FIGURE 4.1 Diminishing time value of the put relative to the underlying stock.

If you buy an in-the-money put and the underlying stock increases in value, you lose one point for each dollar of increase in the stock's market value—as long as it remains in the money—and for each dollar lost in the stock's market value, your put gains a point in premium value. Once the stock's market value rises above striking price, there remains no intrinsic value; your put is out of the money and the premium value becomes less responsive to price movement in the underlying stock. While all of this is going on, time value is evaporating as well.

Smart Investor Tip

For option buyers, profits are realized primarily when the option is in the money. Out-of-the-money options are poor candidates for appreciation, because time value rarely increases.

Whether you prefer lower-premium, out-of-the-money puts or higher-premium in-the-money puts, always be keenly aware of the point gap between the stock's current market value and striking price of the put. The further out of the money, the less likely it is that your put will produce a profit.

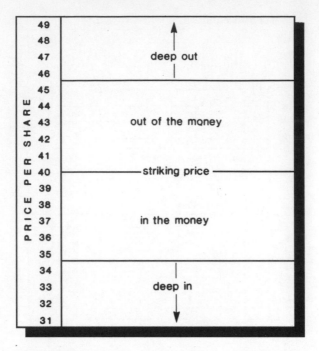

FIGURE 4.2   Deep-in/deep-out stock prices for puts.

To minimize your exposure to risk, limit your speculation to options on stocks whose market value is within five points of the striking price. In other words, if you buy out-of-the-money puts, avoid those that are deep out of the money. What might seem like a relatively small price gap can become quite large when you consider that *all* of the out-of-the-money premium is time value, and that no intrinsic value can be accumulated until your put goes in the money. Added to this problem is the time factor. As shown in Figure 4.2, you may want to avoid speculating in puts that are either deep in the money or deep out of the money. Deep-in-the-money puts are going to be expensive—one point for each dollar below striking price, plus time value—and deep-out-of-the-money puts are too far from striking price to have any realistic chances for producing profits.

Put Buying Strategies

There are three reasons to buy puts. The first is purely speculative: the hope of realizing a profit in a short period of time, with relatively small risk exposure. This leveraged approach is appealing but contains higher risks along with the potential for short-term profits. The second reason to buy puts is as an alternative to short selling of stock. And third, you may buy puts to provide yourself with a form of insurance against price declines in a stock long position.

Strategy 1: Gaining Leverage

There is value in the leverage gained using the put. With a limited amount of capital, the potential for profits is greater for put buyers than through stock short selling, and with considerably less risk.

Example

Safer than Shorting Stock: A stock currently is valued at $60 per share. If you sell short 100 shares and the stock drops five points, you can close the position and take a profit of $500. However, rather than selling short, you could buy 12 puts at 5, for a total investment of $6,000. A five-point drop in this case would produce a profit of $6,000, a 100 percent gain (assuming no change in time value). So by investing the same amount in puts, you could earn a 100 percent profit, compared to an 8.3 percent profit through short selling.

This example demonstrates the value in leverage, but the risk element for each strategy is not comparable. The short seller faces risks not experienced by the put buyer and has to put up collateral and pay interest; in comparison, the put buyer has to fight against time. Risking $6,000 by buying puts is highly speculative and, while short selling is risky as well, the two strategies have vastly different attributes. The greater profit potential through leverage in buying puts is accompanied by equally higher risk of loss. However, even without a large sum of capital to speculate with, you can still use leverage to your advantage. This comparative analysis shows the flaw in analyzing two dissimilar strategies. Because the risk attributes are so different for each, it is not accurate to draw conclusions based only on potential returns.

Example

Comparing Apples to Oranges: You buy a LEAPS put for 5 with a striking price of 60 and 18 months until expiration. The stock currently is selling at $60 per share; your option is at the money. Aware of the potential profit or loss in your strategy, your decision to buy puts was preferable over selling short the stock. The luxury of 18 months in the LEAPS put is preferable over remaining exposed to short selling of stock. As shown in Figure 4.3, a drop of five points in the stock's market value would produce a $500 gain with either strategy (assuming no change in time value premium).

	STOCK (1)		PUT (2)	
	PROFIT OR LOSS	RATE OF RETURN	PROFIT OR LOSS	RATE OF RETURN
price decrease of 5 points	$500	8.1%	$500	100%
price decrease of 1 point	$100	1.6%	$100	20%
no price change	0	0	0	0
price increase of 1 point	–$100	–1.6%	–$100	–20%
price increase of 5 points	–$500	–8.1%	–$500	–100%

(1) sold short at $62 per share ($6,200)

(2) striking price 60, premium 5 ($500)

FIGURE 4.3   Rates of return: selling short versus buying puts.

The short seller, like the put buyer, has a time problem. The short seller has to place collateral on deposit equal to a part of the borrowed stock's value, and pay interest on the borrowed amount. Thus, the more time the short position is left open, the higher the interest cost—and the more decline in the stock's value the short seller requires to make a profit. While the put buyer is concerned with diminishing time value, the short seller pays interest, which erodes future profits, if they ever materialize, or which increases losses.

A decline of five points in the preceding example produces an 8.1 percent profit for the short seller and a 100 percent profit for the put buyer. Compare the risks with this yield difference in mind. Short selling risks are unlimited in the sense that a stock's value could rise indefinitely, creating ever-increasing losses. The put buyer's risk is limited to the $500 investment. A drop of $1 per share in the stock's value creates a 1.6 percent profit for the short seller, and a 20 percent profit for the put buyer.

Potential losses can be compared between strategies as one form of risk evaluation. When a short seller's stock rises in value, the loss could be substantial. It combines market losses with continuing interest expense and tied-up collateral (creating a lost opportunity). The put buyer's losses can never exceed the premium cost of the put.

Strategy 2: Limiting Risks

It is possible to double your money in a very short period of time by speculating in puts. Leverage increases even a modest investment's overall potential (and risk). Risks increase through leverage due to the potential for loss. Like all forms of investing or speculating, greater opportunity also means great risk.

Example

Profits Becoming Unlikely: You recently bought a put for 4. However, expiration date is coming up soon and the stock's market value has risen above striking price. When the put expires, you face the prospect of losing the entire $400 premium. Time has worked against you. Knowing that the stock's market value might eventually fall below striking price, but not necessarily before expiration, you realize it is unlikely that you will be able to earn a profit.

Risks are lower for puts in comparison to short selling. A short seller in a loss position is required to pay the difference between short-sold price and current market value if the stock has risen in value, not to mention the interest cost. The limited risk of buying puts is a considerable advantage.

Example

Big Problems or Small: You sold short 200 shares of stock with market value of $45 per share; you were required to borrow $9,000 worth of stock, put up a portion as collateral, and pay interest to the brokerage company. The stock later rose to $52 per share and you sold. Your loss on the stock was $1,400 plus interest expense. If you had bought puts instead, the maximum loss would have been limited to the premium paid for the two puts. The fear of further stock price increases that would concern you as a short seller would be a minimal problem for you as a put buyer.

The advantage enjoyed by the put buyer typifies the long position over the short position. Losses are invariably limited in this situation. Although both strategies have the identical goal, risks make the long and short positions much different.

Strategy 3: Hedging a Long Position

Put buying is not always merely speculative. You can also buy one put for every 100 shares of the underlying stock owned, to protect yourself against the risk of falling prices. Just as calls can be used to insure against the risk of rising prices in a short sale position, puts can serve the same purpose, protecting against price declines when you are long in shares of stock. When a put is used in this manner, it is called a *married put*, since it is tied directly to the underlying stock.

This strategy is also one form of a *synthetic position*. The use of a long put with long stock creates a synthetic call. (When you use a long call to protect your position with short stock, it is called a synthetic put.) The risk of declining market value is a constant concern for every investor. If you buy stock and its value falls, a common reaction is to sell in the fear that the decline will continue. In spite of advice to the contrary, you may have sold low and bought high. It is human nature. It requires a cooler head to calmly wait out a decline and rebound, which could take months, even years. Special tax rules apply to married puts so, in calculating the cost and benefit to this strategy, you also need to evaluate the tax status for your stock. Check Chapter 12 for more tax information on married puts.

The married put is a form of insurance protection. This strategy makes sense, whether you end up selling the appreciated put or exercising it. In the event of a decline in the stock's value, you have the right to exercise and sell the stock at the striking price. However, if you believe the stock remains a sound investment, it is preferable to offset losses by selling the put at a profit. When you exercise a put, that action is referred to as *put to seller*.

married put
the status of a put used to hedge a long position. Each put owned protects 100 shares of the underlying stock held in the portfolio. If the stock declines in value, the put's value will increase and offset the loss.

synthetic position
a strategy in which stock and option positions are matched up to protect against unfavorable price movement. When you own stock and also buy a put to protect against downward price movement, it creates a synthetic call. When you are short on stock and buy a call, it creates a synthetic put.

put to seller
action of exercising a put and requiring the seller to purchase 100 shares of stock at the fixed striking price.

Example

A Profitable Dilemma: You own 100 shares of stock that you purchased for $57 per share. This stock tends to be volatile, meaning the potential for short-term gain or loss is significant. To protect yourself against possible losses, you buy a put on the underlying stock. It costs 1 and has a striking price of 50. Two months later, the stock's market value falls to $36 per share and the put is near expiration. The put has a premium value of 14.

In this situation, you have two choices:

1. Sell the put and take the $1,300 profit. Your adjusted cost was $58 per share (purchase price of $5,700 plus $100 for the put). Your net cost per share is $44 ($5,700 less $1,300 profit on the put). Your basis now is eight points above current market value. By selling the put, you have the advantage of continuing to own the stock. If its market value rebounds to a level above $44 per share, you will realize a profit. Without the put, your basis would be 21 points above current market value. Selling the put eliminates a large portion of the loss.

2. Exercise the put and sell the stock for $50 per share. In this alternative, you sell at 8 points below your basis. You lose $100 paid for the put, plus seven points in the stock.

Regardless of the choice taken in these circumstances, you end up with a smaller loss by owning the married put than you would have just owning the stock. The put either cuts the loss by offsetting the stock's market value decline, or enables you to get rid of the depreciated stock at higher than market value. You have a loss either way, but not as much of a loss as you would have had without buying the put.

The married put in this application provides you with *downside protection*, which reduces potential profits because you have to pay a premium

downside protection

a strategy involving the purchase of one put for every 100 shares of the underlying stock that you own. This insures you against losses to some degree. For every in-the-money point the stock falls, the put will increase in value by one point. Before exercise, you may sell the put and take a profit, offsetting stock losses, or exercise the put and sell the shares at the striking price.

to buy the insurance. If you intend to own shares of stock for the long term, puts will have to be replaced upon expiration, so that the cost is repetitive. However, as a long-term investor, you are not normally concerned with short-term price change, so the strategy is best employed only when you believe your shares currently are overpriced, given the rate of price change and current market conditions. In this situation, using puts for insurance is speculative but may remain a prudent choice.

In the event the stock's market price rises, your potential losses are frozen at the level of the put's premium and no more. This occurs because as intrinsic value in the put declines, it is offset by a rise in the stock's market value. Whether you end up selling the put or exercising, downside protection establishes an acceptable level of loss in the form of insurance, and fixes that loss at the striking price of the put, at least for the duration of the put's life. This strategy is appropriate even when, as a long-term investor, you expect instability in the market in the short term.

Example

Damage Assessment: You recently bought 100 shares of stock at $60 per share. At the same time, you bought a put with a striking price of 60, paying 3. Your total investment is $6,300. Before making your purchase, you analyzed the potential profit and loss and concluded that your losses would probably not exceed 4.8 percent ($300 paid for the put, divided by $6,300, the total invested). You also concluded that an increase in the stock's market value of 3 points or less would not represent a profit at all, due to the investment in the put. So profits will not begin to accumulate until the stock's market value exceeds $63 per share.

A summary of the insurance strategy is shown in Figure 4.4. Note that regardless of the severity of decline in the stock's market value, the loss can never exceed 4.8 percent of the total amount invested (the cost of the put). That is because for every point of decline in the stock's market value, the put increases one point in intrinsic value. This status continues until the put expires.

The insurance strategy is also a powerful tool when you plan to sell stock within the next three years, and you are concerned about the potential for losses by that deadline. Insurance protects your value and ensures that, even if the stock's value declines dramatically, you will not lose by continuing to own the stock.

PRICE MOVEMENT, UNDERLYING STOCK	PROFIT OR LOSS		NET PROFIT OR LOSS (3)	
	STOCK (1)	PUT (2)	AMOUNT	RATE
down 20 points	-$2,000	$1,700	-$ 300	- 4.8%
down 5 points	-$ 500	$ 200	-$ 300	- 4.8%
down 3 points	-$ 300	0	-$ 300	- 4.8%
no change	0	-$ 300	-$ 300	- 4.8%
up 3 points	$ 300	-$ 300	0	0
up 5 points	$ 500	-$ 300	$ 200	3.2%
up 20 points	$2,000	-$ 300	$1,700	27.0%

(1) stock purchased at $60 per share
(2) put striking price 60, premium 3
(3) return based on total cost of $6,300

FIGURE 4.4 Downside protection: buying shares and buying puts.

Example

A Wise Financial Planning Move: Several years ago you invested in 1,000 shares of stock and it has appreciated consistently over the years. You are planning to sell the stock in two years and use the funds as a down payment on a home. You don't want to sell the stock until it is needed, for several reasons. You will be taxed on profits in the year sold, so you want to defer that until the latest possible moment. In addition, you would prefer to continue earning dividends and, potentially, additional profits in the stock. But you also know the stock's value could fall. Even a temporary decline would be serious because you will need those funds at a specific date in the future. The solution: Buy 10 puts to insure the value at the striking price. Select puts with expiration dates at or beyond your target date. This reduces your stock's value by the cost of the puts; but it also ensures that any in-the-money declines in the stock's price will be offset by gains in the puts' value.

In this case, the decision to use puts is not merely speculative; it is necessary to insure the stock's market value. A decline might be reversed within 6 to

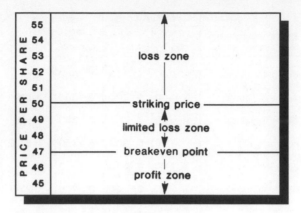

FIGURE 4.5 A put's profit and loss zones.

12 months, but that could create a hardship if you have a specific date in mind to buy a house. The use of puts as insurance can be applied in many ways to protect capital invested in stocks. Even the best stocks can experience a price decline in cyclical markets. When you cannot afford even a temporary decline, puts can be used to lock in a striking price value.

Defining Profit Zones

To decide whether buying puts is a reasonable strategy for you, always be aware of potential profits *and* losses, rather than concentrating on profits alone. Comparing limited losses to potential profits when using puts for downside protection is one type of analysis that helps you pick value when comparing puts. And when looking for a well-priced speculative move, time to expiration coupled with the gap between current market value and striking price—which dictates the amount of time value premium—will help you to find real bargains in puts. Premium level is not a reasonable criterion for your selection.

The profit and loss zones for puts are the reverse of the zones for call buyers, because put owners anticipate a downward movement in the stock, whereas call buyers expect upward price movement. See Figure 4.5 for a summary of loss and profit zones and breakeven point using the following example.

Example

Canceling Out the Losses: You buy a put with a striking price of 50, paying 3. Your breakeven price is $47 per share. If the underlying stock falls to that level, the option will have intrinsic value of 3 points, equal to the price you paid for the put. If the price of stock goes below $47 per share, the put will be profitable point-for-point with downward price movement in the stock. Your put can be sold when the underlying stock's market value is between $47 and $50 per share, for a limited loss. And if the price of the stock rises above $50 per share, the put will be worthless at expiration.

Before buying any put, determine the profit and loss zones and breakeven price (including the cost of trading on both sides of the transaction). For the amount of money you will be putting at risk, how much price movement will be required to produce a profit? How much time remains until expiration? Is the risk a reasonable one?

Another example of a put purchase with defined profit and loss zones is shown in Figure 4.6. In this example, the put was bought at 3 and has a May 40 expiration. The outcome of this transaction would be exactly opposite for the purchase of a call, given the same premium, expiration, and price of the underlying stock. You will gain a profit if the stock falls below the breakeven point of 37 (40 strike less 3 premium).

Remember this rule: As a buyer, don't depend on time value to produce profits between purchase date and expiration, because that is highly unlikely to occur. If you do not experience a price decline in the stock's price adequate to exceed the price you paid for the put, then you will have a loss. Like call purchasing, time works against you when you buy puts. The greater the gap between market price of the stock and striking price, the more time problem you will have to overcome.

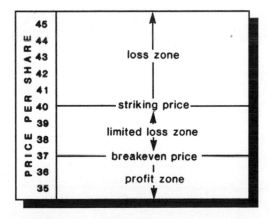

FIGURE 4.6 Example of put purchase with profit and loss zones.

The mistake made by many investors is failing to recognize what is required to produce a profit, and failing to analyze a situation to determine whether buying puts makes sense. Analyze these points in evaluating put buying:

- Your motive (leverage, reduction of risk, or downside protection).
- The premium level and amount of time value premium.
- Time remaining until expiration.
- Gap between the stock's current market value and the put's striking price.
- The number of points of movement in the underlying stock required before you can begin earning a profit.
- The characteristics of the underlying stock (see Chapter 6 for guidelines for selecting stocks appropriate for your option strategy).

Collectively, these guidelines define an investment strategy and work for you as tools for evaluating risks and identifying profit potential. You could earn substantial short-term profits; you also face a corresponding high risk level represented by time, the buyer's enemy.

On the opposite side of the option transaction is the seller. Unlike buyers, sellers have an *advantage* with pending expiration. Time is the seller's friend, and higher time value represents an opportunity rather than a risk. Because time value declines as expiration approaches, the seller benefits in the same degree as the buyer is penalized. You can purchase puts or sell calls and achieve the same strategic position, but the risks may be far different. Calls offer some interesting strategic possibilities for sellers, both high-risk and very conservative. The next chapter examines strategies and risks of selling calls.

Chapter

Selling Calls: Conservative and Profitable

Strategic planning is worthless—unless there is first a strategic vision.
—John Naisbitt, *Megatrends*, 1984

One of the more interesting aspects of options is that they can be extremely speculative and risky, or the most conservative of strategies. It all depends on whether you are a buyer or a seller, and on whether you own the underlying stock.

The idea of going short—selling first, and buying to close later—is a tough idea to grasp. Most of us think about investing in a precise sequence. First, you buy a security; then, at a later date, you sell. If the sale price is higher than the purchase price, you earn a profit; if it is lower, you suffer a loss. However, when you are a call seller, this sequence is reversed.

By starting out the sequence with an opening sale transaction, you are paid the premium at the time the order is placed. You will pay a purchase price later when you close the position or, if the option expires worthless, you never pay at all. In that case, the entire sale premium is yours to keep as profit. If this all sounds like a pretty good deal, you also need to remember that taking a short position is accompanied by inevitable risks. These risks are explained in this chapter and demonstrated through examples. Some types of call selling are extremely high risk and others are very low risk and conservative.

Smart Investor Tip

Sellers receive payment when they initiate the opening transaction. That is compensation for accepting exposure to the risks.

Call sellers enjoy significant advantages over call buyers. In the previous two chapters, many examples demonstrated how time value works against the buyer; in fact, the time value premium makes it very difficult for buyers to earn profits with options; the odds are against them. The problem of declining time value is the primary risk of option buying. Even when the underlying stock's market value moves in the desired direction, it might not happen soon enough or with enough point value to offset the time value premium. This buyer's disadvantage is the seller's advantage.

Because time value evaporates, buyers see time as the enemy. For sellers, though, time is a great ally. The more time value involved, the higher the potential profit; and the more that time value falls, the better. When you enter the order for an opening sale transaction, you are better off if you have the maximum time value possible. While buyers seek options with the lowest possible time value and with the stock's market value within reasonable proximity to striking price, sellers do the opposite. They seek calls with the highest possible time value and the largest possible gap between striking price of the option and market value of the stock.

Smart Investor Tip

Time is the buyer's enemy, but the opposite is true for the seller. The seller makes a profit as time value evaporates.

When you sell a call, you grant the buyer the right to buy 100 shares of the underlying stock at the striking price, at any time prior to expiration. That means that you assume the risk of being required to sell 100 shares of the underlying stock to the buyer, potentially at a striking price far below current market value. The decision to exercise is the buyer's, and that decision can be made at any time. Of course, as long as the call is out of the money, it will not be exercised. That risk becomes real only if and when the call goes in the money (when the stock's market value is higher than the call's striking price).

> ### Example
>
> **Stuck with the Strike:** You sold a call two months ago with a striking price of 50. At the time the stock's market value was $46 per share. At the beginning of this week, the stock had risen to $58 per share and the buyer exercised your call. You are required to deliver 100 shares at $50 per share. If you own 100 shares of stock, you relinquish ownership and receive $50 per share rather than current market value of $58. If you do not own 100 shares, your brokerage firm will complete the transaction and deduct the difference from your account, or $800 ($58 per share current market value *less* striking price of $50 per share). Transaction fees will also apply.

All investment strategies contain specific risk characteristics, and these should be clearly identified and fully understood by anyone undertaking the strategy. The risks tend to have unchanging attributes. For example, the risks of buying stocks are consistent from one moment to another. The experienced stock market investor understands this and accepts the risk. However, call selling has a unique distinction. It can be extremely risky or extremely conservative, depending upon whether you also own 100 shares of the stock at the time you sell the call.

Selling Uncovered Calls

When call selling is reviewed in isolation, it is indeed a high-risk strategy. If you sell a call but you do not own 100 shares of the underlying stock, the option is classified as a *naked option* or *uncovered option*. You are exposing yourself to an unlimited risk. In fact, call selling in this situation is one of the most risky strategies you could take, containing high potential for losses. A buyer's risks are limited to the premium cost; depending on how many points a stock moves up, a call seller's losses can be much higher.

When you take a short position in a call, the decision to exercise belongs to the buyer. You

naked option
an option sold in an opening sale transaction when the seller (writer) does not own 100 shares of the underlying stock.

uncovered option
the same as a naked option—the sale of an option not covered, or protected, by the ownership of 100 shares of the underlying stock.

need to be able and willing to deliver 100 shares in the event that the call is exercised, no matter how high current market value has gone. If you do not already own 100 shares, you will be required upon exercise to buy 100 shares at current market value and deliver them at the striking price of the call. The difference in these prices could be significant.

Example

Unacceptable Risks: You sell a call for 5 with a striking price of 45 and expiration month of April. At the time, the underlying stock has a market value of $44 per share. You do not own 100 shares of the underlying stock. The day after your order is placed, your brokerage firm deposits $500 into your account (less fees). However, before expiration, the underlying stock's market price soars to $71 per share and your call is exercised. You will lose $2,100—the current market value of 100 shares, $7,100; less the striking price value, $4,500; less the $500 premium you received at the time you sold the call:

Current market value, 100 shares	$7,100
Less striking price	−4,500
Less call premium	−500
Net loss	$2,100

When a call is exercised and you do not own 100 shares of the underlying stock, you are required to deliver those 100 shares at the striking price. This means you have to buy the shares at current market value, no matter how high that price. Because upward price movement, in theory at least, is unlimited, your risk in selling the call is unlimited as well.

Smart Investor Tip

Selling uncovered calls is a high-risk strategy, because in theory, a stock's price could rise indefinitely. Every point rise in the stock above striking price is $100 more out of the call seller's pocket.

The risks of selling calls in this manner are extreme. With that in mind, a brokerage firm will allow you to sell calls only if you meet specific requirements. These include having enough equity in your portfolio to provide protection in the event of an unusually high loss. The brokerage firm will want to be able to sell other securities in your account to pay for losses if you cannot come up with the cash. You will need approval in advance from your brokerage firm before you will be allowed to sell calls. Each firm is required to ensure that you understand the risks involved, that you fully understand the options market, and that you have adequate equity and income to undertake those risks.

You will not be allowed to write an unlimited number of naked calls. The potential losses, both to you and to the brokerage firm, place natural limits on this activity. Everyone who wants to sell calls is required to sign a document acknowledging the risks and stating that they understand those risks. In part, this statement includes the following:

Special Statement for Uncovered Option Writers[1]

There are special risks associated with uncovered option writing which expose the investor to potentially significant loss. Therefore, this type of strategy may not be suitable for all customers approved for options transactions.

1. The potential loss of uncovered call writing is unlimited. The writer of an uncovered call is in an extremely risky position, and may incur large losses if the value of the underlying instrument increases above the exercise price.

2. As with writing uncovered calls, the risk of writing uncovered put options is substantial. The writer of an uncovered put option bears a risk of loss if the value of the underlying instrument declines below the exercise price. Such loss could be substantial if there is a significant decline in the value of the underlying instrument.

3. Uncovered option writing is thus suitable only for the knowledgeable investor who understands the risks, has the financial capacity and willingness to incur potentially substantial losses, and has sufficient liquid assets to meet applicable margin requirements. In this regard, if the value of the underlying instrument moves against an uncovered writer's options position, the investor's broker may request significant additional margin payments. If an investor does not make such margin payments, the broker may liquidate stock or options positions in the investor's account, with little or no prior notice in accordance with the investor's margin agreement.

The requirement that your portfolio include stocks, cash, and other securities in order to sell calls is one form of *margin* requirement imposed by your broker. Such requirements apply not only to option transactions, but also to short selling of stock or, more commonly, to the purchase of securities using funds borrowed from the brokerage firm.

---

[1] From the Options Clearing Corporation, "Risk Disclosure Statement and Acknowledgments," at www.optionsclearing.com.

margin

an account with a brokerage firm containing a minimum level of cash and securities to provide collateral for short positions or for purchases for which payment has not yet been made.

writer

the individual who sells (writes) a call or a put.

When you enter into an opening sale transaction, you are referred to as a *writer*. Call writers (sellers) hope that the value of the underlying stock will remain at or below the striking price of the call. If that occurs, then the call will expire worthless and the writer's profits will be made from declining time value (as well as any decline in intrinsic value resulting from the stock's price moving from above the striking price, down to or below the striking price). For the writer, the breakeven price is the striking price plus the number of points received for selling the call.

Example

Gains Offsetting Losses: You sell a call for 5 with a striking price of 40. Your breakeven is $45 per share (before considering trading costs). Upon exercise, you would be required to deliver 100 shares at the striking price of 40; as long as the stock's current market value is at $45 per share or below, you will not have a loss, even upon exercise, since you received $500 in premium when you sold the call.

It is possible to write a call and make a profit upon exercise. Given the preceding example, if the call were exercised when the stock's market price was $42, you would gain $300 before trading costs:

Current market value, 100 shares	$4,200
Less striking price	−4,000
Loss on the stock	$−200
Option premium received	$500
Profit before trading costs	$300

Smart Investor Tip

Exercise does not necessarily mean you lose. The call premium discounts a minimal loss because it is yours to keep, even after exercise.

As a writer, you do not have to wait out expiration; you have another choice. You can close out your short position at any time by purchasing the call. You open the position with a sale and close it with a purchase. There are four events that could cause you to close out a short position in your call:

1. The stock's value falls. As a result, time value and intrinsic value, if any, fall as well. The call's premium value is lower, so it is possible to close the position at a profit.

2. The stock's value remains unchanged, but the option's premium value falls due to loss of time value. The call's premium value falls and the position can be closed through purchase, at a profit.

3. The option's premium value remains unchanged because the underlying stock's market value rises. Declining time value is replaced with intrinsic value. The position can be closed at no profit or loss, to avoid exercise.

4. The underlying stock's market value rises enough so that exercise is likely. The position can be closed at a loss to avoid exercise, potentially at greater levels of loss.

Example

Taking Profits to Escape Risk: You sold a call two months ago for 3. The underlying stock's market value has remained below the striking price without much price movement. Time value has fallen and the option is now worth 1. You have a choice: You can buy the call and close the position, taking a profit of $200; or you can wait for expiration, hoping to keep the entire premium as a profit. This choice exposes you to risk between the decision point and expiration; in the event the stock's market price moves above striking price, intrinsic value could wipe out the profit and lead to exercise. Purchasing to close when the profit is available ensures that profit and enables you to avoid further exposure to risk. If the stock does rise, your breakeven price is three points higher than striking price, since you were paid 3 for selling the call.

naked position
status for investors
when they assume
short positions in calls
without also owning
100 shares of the un-
derlying stock for each
call written.

Whenever you sell a call and you do not also own 100 shares of stock, your risk is described as a *naked position*, which refers to the continuous exposure to risk from the moment of sale through to expiration. Remember, the buyer can exercise at any time, and exercise can happen at any time that your naked call is in the money. Even though exercise is most likely at the time just before expiration, there is no guarantee that it will not happen before that time.

Example

Going Naked, More than Just Embarrassing: You sold a naked call last week that had four months to go until expiration. You were not worried about exercise. However, as of today, the stock has risen above the striking price and your call is in the money. Your brokerage firm has advised that your call was exercised. You are required to deliver 100 shares of the underlying stock at the striking price. Your call no longer exists.

In this example, you experience a loss on the stock because you are required to purchase 100 shares at current market value and deliver them at the striking price. Even so, you may have an overall profit if the gap between current market value and striking price is less than the amount you received when you sold the call.

liquid market
a market in
which buyers
and sellers are
matched to one
another, and
the exchange
absorbs any im-
balances between
the two sides.

You can never predict early exercise, since buyer and seller are not matched one-to-one. The selection is random. The Options Clearing Corporation (OCC) acts as buyer to every seller, and as seller to every buyer. This ensures a *liquid market* even when one side of the transaction is much larger than the other. When a buyer decides to exercise a call, the order is assigned at random to a seller, or on the basis of first-in, first-out. You will not know that this has happened to you until your broker gets in touch to inform you of the exercise. In-the-money options are automatically exercised by the OCC on exercise date.

Smart Investor Tip

Because exercise can happen at any time your call is in the money, you need to be aware of your exposure; early exercise is always a possibility. If you sell an in-the-money call, exercise could happen quickly, even on the same day.

In order to profit from selling calls, you will need the underlying stock to act in one of two ways:

1. Its market value must remain at or below the striking price of the call, waiting out the evaporation of time value. The option will expire worthless, or it can be closed with a purchase amount lower than the initial sales price.

2. The market value must remain at a stable enough price so that the option can be purchased below initial sales price, even if it is in the money. The decline in time value still occurs, even when accompanied by consistent levels of intrinsic value.

The profit and loss zones for uncovered calls are summarized in Figure 5.1. Because you receive cash for selling a call, the breakeven price is higher than the

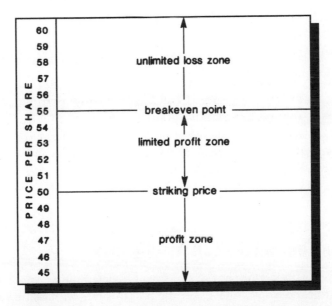

FIGURE 5.1 An uncovered call's profit and loss zones.

striking price. In this illustration, a call was sold for 5; hence, breakeven is five points higher than striking price. (This example does not take into account the transaction fees.) To enter into a naked call position, you will need to work with your brokerage firm to meet its requirements.

Example

Setting Limits: You have advised your broker that you intend to write uncovered calls. Your portfolio currently is valued at $20,000 in securities and cash. Your broker restricts your uncovered call writing activity to a level that, in the broker's estimation, would not potentially exceed $20,000. However, as market conditions change, your portfolio value could fall, in which case your broker has the right to restrict your uncovered call activity to a lower dollar amount, or even to require you to deposit additional funds. When you do not have funds available, the brokerage firm has the right to sell some of your securities to cover the shortfall.

Potential loss in call writing is conceivably unlimited because no one knows how high a stock's price could rise. Put writers, in comparison, face a limited form of potential loss. The maximum is the difference between the striking price and zero; in practical terms, the real risk level is the difference between striking price and tangible book value per share.

Example

Worst Case, But Limited: You want to write puts in your portfolio as part of your investment strategy (See Chapter 8). Your portfolio is valued at $20,000. Your brokerage firm will place restrictions on uncovered put writing activity based on an estimation of potential losses. However, when you write puts, your liability is not as great; stocks can fall only so far, whereas they can rise indefinitely. So the worse case for selling puts is known; it is the striking price of the short puts.

Assessing Uncovered Call Writing Risks

Don't forget the importance of risk assessment in determining what is an appropriate investment or strategy. Consider the risks involved with writing uncovered calls, especially in light of limitations that are placed on your activity by brokerage firms. These limitations are necessary due to the risk of potential losses.

Restrictions that are placed on naked call writing limit your ability to participate in the high-risk end of this market.

The risks of uncovered call writing include the following:

- The stock might rise in value; you will be required to buy the call to close your position and avoid further loss.

- The stock might rise in value, leading to exercise, perhaps early exercise.

- Although the stock might remain at or below striking price for a period of time, it could rise unexpectedly and suddenly, leading to exercise; you are at risk from the moment you sell the call, all the way to expiration.

- You lose opportunities to move your capital around in the market because your brokerage firm wants to limit your risk of loss as well as theirs; so your equity is committed as collateral for your open uncovered call positions.

- If you do suffer unexpected large losses, your brokerage firm may sell other securities in your portfolio to pay for those losses. This may include securities whose sale is poorly timed, so you lose long-term value in your portfolio, not to mention control over the timing of a stock's sale.

- Although you set standards for yourself, you might fail to take action when you should, so that today's profit disappears and you end up losing money upon exercise or having to buy the call at a loss to avoid exercise.

Smart Investor Tip

It is smart to know all of the risks involved with uncovered call selling. Not knowing can lead to some very expensive surprises.

A Question of Suitability   Are uncovered calls suitable for you? Every investor and trader has to ask this question at the very beginning of consideration for any strategy. Uncovered calls are extremely risky because, in theory at least, a stock's market value can rise indefinitely. As a practical matter, a stock's potential price increase is limited, but it is impossible to know by how much; and that is where the risk factor is so extreme.

The level of suitability is determined by several crucial factors. These include:

1. *Risk level and your ability to accept it.* The most important test for any strategy is whether the risk level is appropriate. Can you afford the "worst-case" outcome? In the example of a covered call, the maximum risk is unknown, and it could be substantial. For example, what happens

if you sell an uncovered call with a striking price of 50 and receive a premium of 6 ($600)? Without considering transaction fees, you would break even if the call were exercised when the stock's market value had risen to $56 per share. But what if the stock rises to $66. Or $76?

Some options traders are willing to undertake the risk involved with uncovered calls. Because three-quarters of all options expire worthless, the law of averages mandates that in a majority of instances, short options will not be exercised. But a string of modest profits can be easily wiped out by one unexpected rise in a stock's market price.

2. *Knowledge about the strategy and risk.* No one should ever enter into a strategy without fully understanding the risks involved. Many first-time options traders become excited by the potential for profits, but ignore the equally important potential for loss. So a strategy like writing uncovered calls can be lucrative but also high risk.

Every brokerage firm is required to determine whether a customer has adequate knowledge to trade options. Before you are allowed to do any options trading, you will be asked to complete an options application and state your level of experience. But this requirement is only one aspect of the requirement for knowledge, and it is a requirement intended not only to protect you but also to protect your brokerage firm. Equally important is the more practical requirement that your actual experience match the strategies. You can easily claim to have extensive knowledge when you fill out a form, but you might not be fully aware of the actual risks you face when writing uncovered calls or undertaking other high-risk strategies.

3. *Experience as an investor or trader.* Knowing the risks of an options strategy is all-important, but so is experience. Having a book-smarts understanding of uncovered calls is a good start, but you also need actual experience. For example, the knowledge that three-quarters of all options expire worthless might compel you to make a logical assumption: That uncovered call risks are not all that high. Since time value evaporates over time, selling calls with high time value reduces risks, as the logical argument goes. However, once you actually enter into a short option position, you are likely to discover that the strategy is not nearly as comfortable as you had thought.

Actual, real-money experience is an essential requirement for options trading. There is no substitute for it. The syndrome of theoretical experience versus real-world experience has misled many people. For example, in recent years, online gambling has become widespread. Anyone who has practiced card games online with artificial pots of money knows that the strategic play level is not the same as the play level with actual money. You might believe you are an exceptionally lucky card player.

But when you put real dollars on the table, a man named Doc might quickly clean you out.

The same caution applies to options trading. Some strategies are highly conservative (as you will see in the next section of this chapter). Other strategies, specifically writing uncovered calls, are extremely high risk and not appropriate for everyone. Your experience as a stock investor and options trader is invaluable in knowing quite well what levels of risk you can afford to take, and what levels you are willing to take.

4. *Income and investment capital.* You need to have enough money in your portfolio to afford writing uncovered calls. Even if you believe you can manage the risk to this strategy, you cannot write an unlimited number of short calls. Your brokerage firm has to limit your exposure by law.

Regulation T
a Federal Reserve Board (FRB) rule defining customer cash account minimum levels based on strategies employed.

The Federal Reserve Board (FRB) has a hand in regulating how much risk you can have outstanding in your brokerage account. The FRB enforces *Regulation T*, which defines the level of credit you can have in your brokerage account. Reg T limits your borrowing power to 50 percent of the purchase price of securities. So when you write an uncovered call, your brokerage firm has to limit your risk by requiring that you keep the required cash level in your account.

Uncovered calls have a very specific margin requirement. When you write an uncovered call, you are required to maintain at least 20 percent of the stock's current price plus the amount of the call premium, and minus the dollar value that the stock is below the striking price. You are always required to maintain at least 10 percent of the stock's price even when this computation ends up with an amount below that level. Examples are summarized in the table:

Call Written	Current Stock Price	Call Price	20% of Price	Difference	Margin Required
60	$65	$600	$1,100	$0	$1,700
50	50	300	1,000	0	1,300
40	37	200	800	300	700
30	21	200	600	900	210*

*The margin cannot be less than 10% of the stock price.

In the summary, the calculation is performed based on four different uncovered call scenarios. In the first two cases, the stock price is higher than striking price or equal to it; so no in-the-money difference applies. In the last case, the calculation is performed in the same way as in the other cases (call price plus 20 percent of stock value, minus in-the-money difference), but it produces a negative. The minimum required is 10 percent of the current stock price ($21 per share × 10% = $210).

5. *Personal investment goals.* If you want to preserve your capital and take low risks, uncovered call writing is clearly inappropriate for you. Everyone has a set of personal investment goals, and it is not always a clear-cut issue of a strategy's being 100 percent appropriate or inappropriate. This is why some self-analysis is useful before putting money at risk. If you are a speculator and you want only high-risk and high-return strategies, then uncovered call writing is a great concept. But if you are saving for retirement, a child's college education, or to purchase your first home, uncovered call writing would be reckless. The approach calling for higher risk as a means for making profits more rapidly is often ill advised. If you cannot afford to lose money, you should not enter into strategies in which losses are very real possibilities.

approval level
a brokerage house's limitation on types of options strategies customers are allowed to enter, based on experience, knowledge, and account value.

6. *Brokerage approval level.* Finally, your brokerage firm is going to assign you an *approval level* based on your experience as an options trader. These levels vary slightly among brokerage firms, but generally they follow the same restrictions.

For example, at level 0, customers are approved for the most conservative of strategies, such as writing covered calls. Level 1 allows customers to buy calls and puts and to enter other long-side advanced strategies in addition to all trading allowed under level 0. (Long-side means you cannot open uncovered short positions.) At level 2, customers can enter all strategies in level 1 plus more complex strategies known as spreads (more on this later in the book). Level 3 is the highest level, allowing customers to enter virtually every kind of option strategy and limited only by margin and brokerage restrictions. These include uncovered options and advanced strategies (short straddles and strangles, for example, which are discussed in a later chapter).

Your personal suitability is not limited to knowledge and experience. Brokerage firms assign levels based on capital available in your account, in addition to your skill level. For example, if the total value of your account is only $5,000, it is unlikely that you will get the highest approval level.

Risk and suitability are much different when you sell covered calls, as the next section explains.

Selling Covered Calls

When you sell uncovered calls, potentially large losses can result if you are required to deliver shares upon exercise, or to close out positions at a loss to avoid exercise. Imagine being able to sell calls without that risk—meaning that you would never be required to suffer large losses due to an unexpected rise in the stock's market value.

cover
the ownership of 100 shares of the underlying stock for each call sold, providing sellers the ability to deliver shares already held, in the event of exercise.

There is a way. By selling a call when you also own 100 shares of the underlying stock, you *cover* your position. If the option is called away by the buyer, you can meet the obligation simply by delivering shares that you already own.

covered call
a call sold to create an open short position, when the seller also owns 100 shares of stock for each call sold.

You enjoy several advantages through the *covered call*.

- You are paid a premium for each call that you sell, and the cash is placed in your account at the time you sell. While this is also true of uncovered call writing, the same risks do not apply. You can afford exercise because you own 100 shares of stock. Upon exercise, you would not be required to buy shares at market price; you simply relinquish ownership of the shares you already own.

Example

A Premium Deal: You owned 100 shares of Merck that you had originally bought at $38 per share. You sold a covered call shortly after buying the stock at 40 and were paid 3 ($300). However, when the stock rose to $42 per share shortly before expiration, your covered call was exercised. Your stock was called away at the striking price of $40 per share. During the period you owned the stock, you received four quarterly dividends at $38 each. Your total profit on this transaction was:

Profit on stock ($40 less original cost of $38)	$200
Call premium received	300
Dividends received	152
Total	$652

- The actual net price of your 100 shares of stock is reduced by the value of the option premium. The covered call discounts your basis because you receive cash when you sell the call. This gives you flexibility and downside protection, as well as greater versatility in selling calls with high time value.

Example

Discounted Basis: You owned 100 shares of Merck you had originally bought at $38 per share, as in the previous example. You waited a few months until the stock's market value had risen to $42 per share. At that time you sold a covered call with a striking price of 45 and received a premium of 2 ($200). Your *net basis* is reduced to $36 per share (original cost less premium on the option). While you continue to face the possibility of exercise at $45, that would be nine points higher than your net basis in the stock.

net basis

the cost of stock when reduced by premium received for selling covered calls; the true net cost of stock after discounting original cost.

- Selling covered calls provides you with the freedom to accept moderate interim price declines, because the premium you receive reduces your basis in the stock. Simply owning the stock without the discount means that declines in the stock's market value represent paper losses.

Example

Riding the Price Waves: You own stock originally purchased at $38 per share. Since the purchase date, the price has moved between $38 and $44 per share. When the price was on the high side, you sold covered calls, closing out those positions when the stock's price retreated. You have made a series of modest but consistent profits on the movement in the stock, without having to take profits. The sum of your profits have also reduced your net basis in the stock.

- By selling calls against appreciated stock, you are able to augment profits and, in the case of exercise, build in a capital gain as well.

Example

Tax and Profit Planning: You employ a strategy of buying stock and waiting for price appreciation, and then selling covered calls. If the calls are exercised, you achieve a capital gain on the stock as well as dividend income and option premium. If the calls are not exercised, you augment your current income by closing out those calls at a lower price, or waiting until expiration.

The disadvantage to covered call selling is found in lost opportunity risk that may or may not materialize. If the stock's market value rises dramatically, your call will be exercised at the specified striking price. If you had not sold the call, you would benefit from higher market value in shares of stock. So covered call sellers trade the certainty of premiums received today, for the potential lost profits in the event of exercise.

Smart Investor Tip

The major risk associated with covered call writing is the possibility of lost income from rising stock prices. But that might not happen at all; when you sell a call, you accept the possibility of lost capital gains income in exchange for the certainty of call premium income.

Example

Profit Alternatives, a Nice Dilemma: You own 100 shares of stock, which you bought last year at $50 per share. Current market value is $54 per share. You are willing to sell this stock at a profit. You write a November 55 call and receive a premium of 5. Now your net basis in the stock is $45 per share (original price of $50 per share, discounted five points by the option premium). If the stock's market value remains between the range of $45 and $55 between the date you sell the call and expiration, the short call will expire worthless. It would not be exercised within that price range, since striking price is 55. You can wait out expiration or buy the call, closing it out at a profit. However, if the stock's value does rise above $55 per share and the call were exercised, you would not receive any gain above $55 per share. While exercise would still produce a profit of $1,000 ($500 stock profit plus $500 option premium), you would lose any profits above the striking price level.

One of three events can take place when you sell a covered call: an increase in the stock's price, a decrease in the stock's price, or no significant change. As long as you own 100 shares of the underlying stock, you continue to receive dividends even when you have sold the call. The value of writing calls should be compared to the value of buying and holding stock, as shown in Table 5.1.

TABLE 5.1 Comparing Strategies

	Outcomes	
Event	Owning Stock and Writing Calls	Owning Stock Only
Stock goes up in value.	Call is exercised; profits are limited to striking price and call premium.	Stock can be sold at a profit.
Stock remains at or below the striking price.	Time value declines; the call can be closed out at a profit or allowed to expire worthless.	No profit or loss until sold.
Stock declines in value.	Stock price is discounted by call premium; the call is closed or allowed to expire worthless.	Loss on the stock.
Dividends.	Earned while stock is held.	Earned while stock is held.

Before you undertake any strategy, assess the benefits or consequences in the event of all possible outcomes, including the potential for lost future profits that might or might not occur in the stock. To ensure a profit in the outcome of writing covered calls, it is wise to select those calls with striking prices above your original basis, or above original basis when discounted by the call premium you receive.

Example

The Discounting Effect: You bought stock last year at $48 per share. If you sell a covered call with a striking price of 50 and receive a premium of 3, you have discounted your basis to $45 per share. Given the same original basis, you may be able to sell a call with a striking price of 45 and receive a premium of 8. That discounts your basis to $40 per share; in both instances, exercise would net a profit of $500. (Exercise at $50, discounted basis of $45 per share; or exercise at $45, discounted basis of $40 per share.) In the latter case, chances of exercise are greater because the call is five points deeper in the money. Selling out-of-the-money calls also affects your capital gain, so if your profit in the stock is substantial, this strategy could be expensive; if you lose the long-term gain status in the stock, it could offset the overall pretax gain. (See Chapter 12 for more information concerning taxes and covered calls.)

In comparing potential profits from various strategies, you might conclude that writing in-the-money calls makes sense in some circumstances, even with possible tax consequences in mind. A decline in the stock's price reduces call premium dollar-for-dollar, with the added advantage of declining time value. If this occurs, you can close out the position at a profit, or simply wait for exercise. As a call seller, you are willing to *lock in* the price of the underlying stock in the event of exercise; this makes sense only if exercise will produce a profit to you, given original purchase price of the shares, discounted by the call premium, and given the net tax consequences involved.

lock in
to freeze the price of the underlying stock by selling a covered call. As long as the call position is open, the writer is locked into the striking price, regardless of current market value of the stock. In the event of exercise, the stock is delivered at the locked-in price.

Assessing Covered Call Writing Risks

The seller of uncovered calls faces potentially large losses. As a covered call writer, your risks are reduced significantly. That risk is limited on the upside to lost future profits that do not always take place. On the downside, the risk is the same for simply owning shares; a decline in price represents a paper loss. The call writer discounts the basis in stock, providing a degree of downside protection and lowering those risks. When you write calls against stock using striking prices above your original basis, you have created a built-in profit factor. Whereas uncovered call selling is very high-risk, covered call writing is on the opposite side of the spectrum; it is very low-risk.

Smart Investor Tip
The covered call seller has fewer risks than others because it is a safe, conservative strategy. Even if the stock falls in value, writing calls provides you with downside protection.

You may be concerned with the lost opportunity risk associated with potential future profits in the stock. Once you sell a call, you commit yourself to selling 100 shares at the striking price, even if the stock's market value rises far above that price. Owning 100 shares covers the short position in the call; it also limits potential profit overall if the call is exercised. Profits are not limited as a certainty; if you close the position or roll into a different short position, or if the call expires worthless, then the lost profit risk is eliminated.

By properly structuring a covered call writing strategy, you can learn to manage the risk of losing potential future gains, in exchange for predictability and the certainty of current profits. The covered call writing strategy is going to produce profits consistently when applied correctly. So a very good return on your investment—including double-digit returns—is possible through writing covered calls. You might lose the occasional spectacular profit when a stock's price rises suddenly; but for the most part, your rate of return will exceed what you could expect in your portfolio without writing covered calls. Some pitfalls to avoid in your covered call writing strategy:

- *Setting up the call write so that, if exercised, you end up losing money in the underlying stock.* This is possible if you sell calls with striking prices below your original basis in the stock.

- *Getting locked into positions that you cannot afford to close out.* If you become involved in a high level of covered call writing, you may eventually find yourself in a position where you want to close out the calls, but you do not have the cash available to take advantage of the situation. You need to set up an adequate cash reserve so that you can act when the opportunity is there.

- *Writing calls on the wrong stock.* When you begin comparing premium values, you might spot an unusually rich time value in a particular option. The stock is likely to be volatile, which is the cause of the exceptionally high premium in the call; this means that the risks associated with owning that stock are greater than for less volatile issues.

Calculating Rate of Return

If your purpose in owning stock is to hold it for many years, writing calls may not be an appropriate strategy—although, in some instances, this strategy can be used to enhance returns with only a moderate risk of exercise. But the call writer's objective often is quite different from that of the long-term investor and, while the two objectives can coexist, it is more likely that you will use the covered call writing strategy on a portion of your portfolio, while avoiding even moderate risks of exercise on another portion. You have three potential sources of income as a covered call writer:

1. Call premium
2. Capital gain on stock
3. Dividends

Example

Double Digit Returns: You bought 100 shares of stock and paid $32 per share. Several months later, the stock's market value rose to $38 per share. You wrote a March 35 call and received 8. Your reasoning: Your original basis in the stock was $32, and selling the call discounts that basis to $24. If the call were exercised, you would be required to deliver the shares at $35, regardless of current market value of those shares. Your profit would be $1,100 if that occurred, a return of 34.4 percent. The option premium at the time you sold contained 3 points of intrinsic value and 5 points of time value. If the stock's market value remained at the same level without exercise, that 5 points eventually would evaporate and the call could be closed through purchase at a lower premium. If the stock's market value were to rise far above the striking price, you would still be required to deliver shares at the striking price upon exercise; the potential future gain would be lost. By undertaking this strategy, you exchange the certainty of a 34.4 percent gain for the uncertainty of greater profits later, if they materialize.

This example shows how a potential future profit may be lost, a fact that covered call writers need to accept. Simply owning stock and not writing calls against it could produce profits in the event of a large run-up in price; but it also produces losses in the event of price decline, and selling calls provides downside protection in addition to the certainty of profit.

We have to deal with *averages* in order to compare straight stock ownership to covered call writing. If we simply hold shares of stock, some will soar in value and others will perform dismally. On average, we may expect to realize a return that beats inflation. For example, the compound rate of return for the S&P 500 from 1926 to 1997 was 12.4 percent. During the same period, the Consumer Price Index averaged 3.1 percent, so stock investments (measured by the S&P 500) beat inflation.[2] If we accept the premise that a portfolio is likely to perform on average at that rate, can we do better by utilizing stocks through covered call writing? Remember, the exceptional stock could return triple digits due to unexpected price growth, and, equally likely, exceptions will involve price declines or stagnation. On average, a compound rate of return should be about 12.4 percent. If we select stocks wisely and employ smart covered call strategies, can we enhance this rate of return? Even given the exceptions on both upside and downside, covered call writing *does* improve overall returns on portfolios, often dramatically.

A realistic point of view may be to count profits only if they are taken. In other words, potential future profits do not exist at the time to sell an option, and by the same argument, profits in open option positions are not profits unless you close those positions. Covered call writers can earn consistent returns on their strategies, but they also have to accept the occasional lost profit from a stock's unexpected price change. Because covered call writing provides downside protection and discounts your basis in the stock, the strategy also reduces the potential for losses due to short-term price decline.

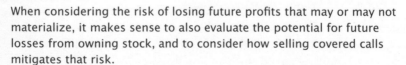

Smart Investor Tip

When considering the risk of losing future profits that may or may not materialize, it makes sense to also evaluate the potential for future losses from owning stock, and to consider how selling covered calls mitigates that risk.

[2]Source: Statistics at www.ameritrade.com.

buy stock $50 per share,
sell 1 call for 5:

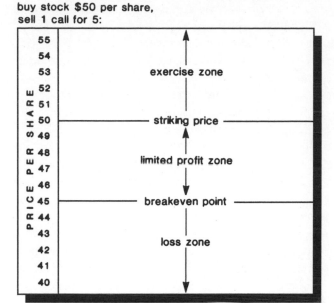

FIGURE 5.2 A covered call's profit and loss zones.

By accepting the limitation associated with writing covered calls, you trade off the potential gain for the *discount* in the price of the stock. This downside protection is especially desirable when you remember that you also continue to receive dividends even though you have sold calls.

You also need to study profit and loss zones applicable in every strategy, and one example is shown in Figure 5.2. A covered call's profit and loss zones are determined by the combination of two factors: option premium value and the underlying stock's current market value. If the stock falls below the breakeven price (price paid for the stock, minus the premium received for selling the call) there will be a loss. Of course, as a stockholder, you decide when and if to sell, so the loss is not necessarily realized. You have the luxury of being able to let the option expire worthless, and then wait for a rebound in the stock's price. The option premium discounts your basis, so by selling the call, you lower the required rebound level.

discount
the reduction in the basis of stock, equal to the amount of option premium received. A benefit in selling covered calls, the discount provides downside protection and protects long positions.

total return

the combined return including income from selling a call, capital gain from profit on selling the stock, and dividends earned and received. Total return may be calculated in two ways: return if the option is exercised, and return if the option expires worthless.

You also need to calculate the rate of return that will be realized given different outcomes. Apply one critical rule for yourself: Never sell a covered call unless you would be satisfied with the outcome in the event of exercise. Figure the *total return* before selling the call, and enter into the transaction only when you are confident that the numbers work for you.

Total return in the case of exercise includes appreciation of stock market value, call premium, and dividend income. If the option expires worthless, one rate of return results; if you close the option by buying it before expiration, a different return results. Because the second outcome does not include selling the stock, the rate of return can vary considerably. The return is calculated based on the original purchase of the stock. The fact that a different base applies for the different calculations makes a yield comparison elusive. So the relative return calculations should not be used to compare outcomes, but to evaluate your overall risk in entering into a particular covered call strategy. The acceptable strategy is one in which you would be happy with the rate of return in any of the outcome scenarios.

Example

A Table of the Elements: You own 100 shares of stock that you bought at $41 per share. Current market value is $44 per share, and you have sold a July 45 call for 5. Between now and expiration, you will receive a total of $40 in dividend income.

Given this information, return if exercised would consist of all three elements:

Stock appreciation	$400
Call premium	500
Dividends	40
Total return	$940
Yield	22.9%

If the call is not exercised but expires worthless, total return does not include appreciation from the underlying stock, since it would not be called away. (Current value compared to purchase price is a paper profit only and is not included in the rate of return.) In this case, return will be as follows:

Call premium	$500
Dividend income	40
Total return	$540
Yield	13.5%

Although the yield in the second instance is lower, you still own the stock after the expiration of the call. So you are free to sell another call, sell the stock, or continue to hold the stock for long-term appreciation. This makes the point that comparisons between the outcomes are not reliable; they should be used to decide whether you would be satisfied with outcome in either instance.

Timing the Decision

Exercise can occur at any time that your call is in the money. It is more likely to occur close to expiration date, but you need to be prepared to give up 100 shares of stock at any time the short option remains open. This is the contractual agreement you enter when you sell the call.

Smart Investor Tip

Whenever you sell a covered call, be prepared for exercise at any time when the call is in the money. The covered call strategy makes sense only if you are willing to have your 100 shares called away.

As shown in Figure 5.3, during the life of a call, the underlying stock might swing several points above or below striking price. If you own 100 shares and are thinking of selling a covered call, keep these points in mind:

- When the striking price of the call is higher than the original price you paid for the stock, exercise is not a negative; it automatically triggers a triple profit—from appreciation of the stock, call premium, and dividend income.

- If you sell a call for a striking price below your original cost of stock, be sure the premium you receive is greater than the loss you will experience in the stock in the event of exercise.

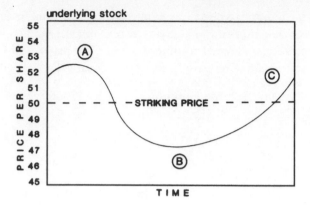

A in the money—best time
   to sell a call

B out of the money—best
   time to buy a call

C in the money at expiration
   —calls will be exercised

FIGURE 5.3 Timing of call transactions
relative to price movement of underlying stock.

- In calculating potential yields, be sure to allow for trading costs on both stock and option, and for both entering and leaving the positions.

- For the benefit of producing a consistent profit from writing calls, remember that you give up the potential for greater gains if and when the stock's current market value rises.

- The tax consequences of covered call writing have to be included in your calculation, especially if you have a substantial paper gain in the stock and have owned that stock long enough that gains would be long-term. In instances when you write in-the-money calls against stock, you could lose the long-term status of stock, so tax planning has to be a part of your strategy unless you restrict your short positions to out-of-the-money contracts.

Example

Alternative to Selling: You buy 100 shares of stock at $51 per share, and it rises to $53. Rather than sell the stock, you choose to sell a call with a striking price of 50, and you are paid a premium of 7.

In this example, the premium contains only 3 points of intrinsic value. The 4 points of time value indicates the probability of a long time to go to expiration. Selling a call in this case provides several advantages to you:

- If the stock's current market value falls below your purchase price, you can buy the option and close the position at a profit, or wait for it to expire worthless.

- By selling the call, you discount your basis in the stock from $51 to $44 per share, providing yourself with 7 points of downside protection. In the event of a price decline in the stock's market value, this is a substantial degree of protection.

- You continue to receive dividends as long as the option is not exercised.

You can also choose to sell a covered call that is deep in the money, as long as you are aware of the tax consequences of that decision.

Example

Going Deep: You bought stock at $51 per share and it is now worth $53. You will receive a premium of at least 8 if you sell a call with a striking price of 45 (because there would be 8 points of intrinsic value). That also increases the chances of exercise substantially. For the 8 points in intrinsic premium, you would lose 6 points in the stock upon exercise (your original basis of $51 less exercise price of $45). These outcomes would change if time value were also available. For example, a 45 call might have current premium of 11, with the additional 3 points representing time value. Upon exercise, the additional 3 points would represent additional profit: $1,100 for selling the call, minus a loss of $600 on the stock, for a net profit of $500 upon exercise. The tax consequences have to be calculated as well. A long-term gain could be subject to short-term treatment for writing deep in-the-money calls.

Smart Investor Tip

Selling deep in-the-money calls can produce high profits for call sellers, especially if they want to sell their stock anyway.

This is not an unreasonable method for producing profits. The outcome occurs only if the call is exercised; in the event the stock's market value falls, the call premium falls one dollar for each dollar lost in the stock's market value. You can buy the call to close the position, with the profit discounting your basis in the stock. Once the position has been closed at a profit, you can repeat the strategy, further reducing your basis in the stock. There is no limit as to how many times you can sell covered calls after a closing purchase, or after expiration.

Example

Exercise or Fast Profits: You bought shares of stock at $51 per share, and it is worth $53 at the time that you sell a 45 call. You receive a premium of 11. The market value of the stock later falls three points, to $50 per share. The call is worth 7, representing a drop of three points of intrinsic value and one point of time value. You can close the position and buy the call for 7, realizing a $400 profit. You still own the stock and are free to sell covered calls again.

Always select options and time covered call sales with these considerations in mind:

- The original price per share of the stock.
- The premium you will be paid for selling the call.
- The mix between intrinsic value and time value.
- The gap between current market value of the stock and striking price of the call.
- The time until expiration.
- Total return if the call is exercised, compared to total return if the option expires worthless.
- Your objective in owning the stock (long-term growth, for example), compared to your objective in selling the call (immediate income and downside protection, for example).

Avoiding Exercise

If you sell a call on stock originally purchased as a long-term investment, you might want to take steps to avoid exercise. This is not contradictory; as a specific strategy, you can write covered calls with the willingness to accept exercise, but with a preference to avoid it. If your primary purpose is to hold stock as a long-term investment, covered call selling enhances current income without necessarily requiring that you give up stock. The overall guideline remains the same: Never sell a covered call unless you are willing to go through exercise and give up 100 shares of stock at the striking price. The strategy is twofold: If you would prefer to keep the stock for long-term investment growth, you need to view calls as current income generators, while also accepting the possibility that the calls might be exercised.

Call sellers—even after picking strategies well—may experience a rise in the stock and later wish to avoid exercise, in order to (a) achieve higher potential capital gains, (b) augment call premium income, and (c) put off selling a stock that is increasing in value.

You avoid exercise in two primary ways: by canceling the option or by rolling out of one option and replacing it with another. The following examples are all based on a situation in which unexpected upward price movement occurs in the underlying stock, placing you in the position where exercise is likely.

Example

Paper Profit Problems: You sold a May 35 call on stock when the stock's market value was $34 per share. The stock's current market value is $41, and you would like to avoid exercise to take advantage of the higher market value of the stock.

Method 1: Cancel the option. You can cancel the option by purchasing it. Although this creates a loss in the option, it is offset by a corresponding increase in the value of the stock. If time value has declined, this strategy makes sense—especially if the increased value of stock exceeds the loss in the option.

Example

Short-Term Loss, Long-Term Gain: You bought 100 shares of stock at $21 per share and later sold a June 25 call for 4. The stock's current market value is $30 per share and the call's premium is at 6. If you buy the call, you will lose $200; however, by getting around exercise, you avoid having to sell the $30 stock at $25 per share. You now own 100 shares at $30, and are free to sell an option with a higher striking price, if you want.

In this example, the outcome can be summarized in two ways. First, remember that by closing the call position at a loss, you still own the 100 shares of stock. That frees you to sell another call with a striking price of 30 or higher, which would create more option premium. (If you could sell a new option for 2 or more, it offsets your loss in the June 25 call.)

You can also analyze the transaction by comparing the exercise price of the option to the outcome of closing the option and selling shares at current market value. The flaw in this method is that it assumes a sale of stock, which is not necessarily going to occur; however, the comparison is valuable to determine whether avoiding exercise makes sense. A summary:

	Exercise	*Sale*
Basis in 100 shares of stock	−2,100	−2,100
Call premium received	400	400
Call premium paid		−600
100 shares deliver at $25	2,500	
100 shares sold at $30		3,000
Net profit	$800	$700

This comparison appears to conclude that you have a better outcome by allowing exercise of the call. That is a fair conclusion only if you would be willing to give up the 100 shares; but it excludes two very important considerations. First, upon exercise you have a capital gain on the stock and a tax consequence. Second, if you keep stock you are free to write covered calls again after expiration or close of the current positions, meaning more income in the future. Exercise ends that possibility.

Smart Investor Tip

A careful comparison between choices is the only way to decide whether to accept exercise or to close out the whole position.

roll forward

the replacement of one written call with another with the same striking price, but a later expiration date.

Method 2: Roll options to avoid exercise. A second technique to avoid exercise involves exchanging one option for another, while making a profit or avoiding a loss in the exchange. Since the premium value for a new option will be greater if more time value is involved until expiration, you can trade on that time value. Such a strategy is likely to defer exercise even when the call is in the money, when you remember that the majority of exercise decisions are made close to expiration date. This technique is called a *roll forward*.

Trading Expirations: The May 40 call you wrote against 100 shares of stock is near expiration and is in the money. To avoid or delay exercise, you close the May 40 option by buying it; and you immediately sell an August 40 call—this has the same striking price but a later expiration.

You still face the risk of exercise at any time; however, it is less likely with a call three months further out. In addition, if you believe that expiration is inevitable, this strategy provides you with additional income. Because the August 40 call has more time until expiration, it also has more time value premium. The roll forward can be used whether you own a single call or several. The more lots of 100 shares you own of the underlying stock, the greater your flexibility in rolling forward and adding to your option premium profits. Canceling a single call and rolling forward produces a marginal gain; however, if you cancel one call and replace it with two or more later-expiring calls, your gain will be greater. For example, you own 300 shares and have previously sold one call; you can roll forward, replacing one call with either two or three which expire later. This strategy is called *incremental return*. Profits increase as you increase the number of calls sold against stock.

incremental return
a technique for avoiding exercise while increasing profits with written calls. When the value of the underlying stock rises, a single call is closed at a loss and replaced with two or more call writes with later expiration dates, producing cash and a net profit in the exchange.

Avoiding Exercise with More Cash: You own 300 shares of stock that you bought for $31 per share. You sold one call with a striking price of 35, and received a premium of 4. Now the stock is worth $39 per share and you would like to avoid or delay exercise. You buy the original call and pay 8, accepting a loss of $400, and replace it by selling three 35 calls with a later expiration for 4 each, receiving a total premium of 12. The net transaction yields you an extra $400 in cash: $1,200 for the three calls, minus $800 paid to close the original position.

In this example, you trade exposure on 100 shares of stock for exposure on 300 shares, but you avoid or delay exercise as well. At the same time, you net out additional cash profits, which reduces your overall basis in the stock. This makes exercise more acceptable later on. Of course, you can continue to use rolling techniques to avoid exercise. Another important point worth evaluating is the potential tax advantage or consequence. Options are taxed in the year that positions are closed; so when you roll forward, you recognize a loss in the original call transaction, which can be deducted on your current year's federal income tax return. At the same time, by rolling forward you receive a net payment while deferring profits, perhaps to the following year. However, because the roll forward may involve in-the-money positions, the stock profit may revert to a short-term gain instead of the more favorable long-term gain. Strategies involving tax problems are examined in Chapter 12.

roll down

the replacement of one written call with another that has a lower striking price.

The roll forward maintains the same striking price and buys you time, which makes sense when the stock's value has gone up. However, the plan does not always suit the circumstances. Another rolling method is called the *roll down*.

Example

Repetitive Profits: You originally bought 100 shares of stock at $31 per share, and later sold a call with a striking price of 35, for a premium of 3. The stock has fallen in value and your call now is worth 1. You cancel (buy) the call and realize a profit of $200, and immediately sell a call with a striking price of 30, receiving a premium of 4.

If the option is exercised at its striking price of 30, the net loss in the stock will be $100; but your net profit in option premium would be $600, so your overall profit would be $500:

Striking price of shares	$3,000
Less original price of shares	−3,100
Loss on stock	−100
Profit on first call sold	200
Profit on second call sold	400
Net profit	$ 500

The roll down is an effective way to offset losses in stock positions in a declining market, as long as the price decline is not severe. Profits in the call premium offset losses to a degree, reducing your basis in the stock. This works as long as the point drop in stock does not exceed the offset level in call premium. You face a different problem in a rising market, where the likelihood of exercise motivates you to take steps to move from in-the-money to out-of-the-money status, or to reduce the degree of in-the-money. In that situation, you may use the *roll up*.

roll up
the replacement of one written call with another that has a higher striking price.

Example

Trading Losses for Profits: You originally paid $31 per share for 100 shares of stock, and later sold a call with a striking price of 35. The stock's current market value has risen to $39 per share. You cancel (buy) the call and accept a loss, offsetting that loss by selling another call with a striking price of 40 and more time to go until expiration.

With this technique, the loss in the original call can be replaced by the premium in the new call. With more time to go until expiration, the net cash difference is in your favor. This technique depends on time value to make it profitable. In some cases, the net difference will be minimal or may even cost money. However, considering you will be picking up an extra five points in the striking price by avoiding exercise, you can afford a loss in the roll up as long as it does not exceed that five-point difference.

Smart Investor Tip

Rolling techniques can help you to maximize option returns without going through exercise, most of the time. But the wise seller is always prepared to give up shares. That is the nature of selling options.

It is conceivable that the various rolling techniques can be used indefinitely to avoid exercise, while continuing to produce profits. Figure 5.4 provides one example of how this could occur.

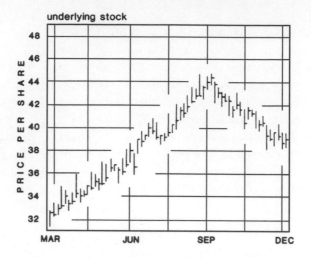

DATE	DESCRIPTION	RECEIVED	PAID
Mar 15	sell 2 Jun 30 calls at 5	$1,000	
Jun 11	buy 2 Jun 30 calls at 8		$1,600
	sell 5 Sep 35 calls at 6	$3,000	
Sep 8	buy 5 Sep 35 calls at 9		$4,500
	sell 8 Dec 40 calls at 6	$4,800	
Dec 22	Dec 40 calls expire worthless	–	–
	totals	$8,800	$6,100
	profit	$2,700	

FIGURE 5.4 Using the rolling technique to avoid exercise.

Example

Staying Ahead of the Curve: You own 800 shares of stock that you bought at $30 per share; your basis is $24,000. You expect the value of the stock to rise, but you also want to write covered calls and increase profits while providing yourself with downside protection. So on March 15, you sell two June 30 contracts for 5 apiece, and receive payment of $1,000.

On June 11, the stock's market value is at $38 per share. To avoid exercise, you close the two calls by buying them, paying a premium of 8 each (total paid, $1,600). You replace these calls with five September 35 calls and receive 6 for each, getting a total of $3,000.

On September 8, the stock's market value has risen again, and now is valued at $44 per share. You want to avoid exercise again, so you cancel your open positions and pay a premium of 9 each, or $4,500 total. You sell eight December 40 calls in replacement at 6 each, and you receive a total of $4,800.

By December 22, the day of expiration, the stock has fallen to $39 per share. Your eight outstanding calls expire worthless. Your total profit on this series of transactions is $2,700 in net call premium. In addition, you still own 800 shares of stock, now worth $39 per share, which is nine points or a total of $7,200 above your original basis. If you wish, you can begin selling calls again, now that all short positions have expired.

For the volume of transactions, you might wonder if the exposure to exercise was worth the $2,700 in profit. It certainly was, considering that the strategy here was dictated by rising stock prices. While you received a profit on call options premium, you also avoided exercise as prices rose. Upon expiration of the calls, you are free to repeat the process. The incremental return combining roll up and roll forward demonstrates how you can avoid exercise while still generating a profit. You cannot depend on this pattern to continue or to repeat, but strategies can be devised based on the situation. It helps, too, that the example involves multiple lots of stock, providing flexibility in writing calls.

This example is based on the premise that you would have been happy to accept exercise at any point along the way. Certainly, exercise would always have been profitable, considering original cost of shares, option premium, and striking prices. If you were to sell the 800 shares at the ending market value of $39 per share, total profit would have been substantial using covered calls, with 41.25 percent profit based on original cost of the stock:

Stock	
Sell 800 shares at $39	$31,200
Less original cost	−24,000
Profit on stock	$7,200
Options	
Sell 2 June contracts	$1,000
Buy 2 June contracts	−1,600
Sell 5 September contracts	3,000
Buy 5 September contracts	−4,500
Sell 8 December contracts	4,800
Profit on options	$2,700
Total profit	$9,900
Yield	41.25%

Whenever you roll forward, higher time value is a benefit. Greater premium value is found in calls with the same striking price but more time before expiration. The longer the time involved, the higher your potential future income from selling the call. In exchange for the higher income, you agree to remain exposed to the risk of exercise for a longer period of time. You are locked into the striking price until you close the position, go through exercise, or wait out expiration.

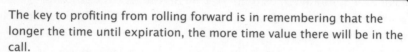

Smart Investor Tip

The key to profiting from rolling forward is in remembering that the longer the time until expiration, the more time value there will be in the call.

Example

Rolling Along: You own 200 shares of stock originally purchased at $40 per share. You are open on a short June 40 call, which you sold for 3. The stock currently is worth $45 per share, and you want to avoid being exercised at $40. Table 5.2 shows current values of calls that are available on this stock. A review of this table provides you several alternatives for using rolling techniques.

Your strategies to defer or avoid exercise combine two dissimilar goals: increasing your option income while also holding on to the stock, even when market value is above striking price. This can be achieved through profiting from higher time value, in recognition of the probability that options will not be exercised until closer to expiration date. Most exercise occurs at or near expiration.

TABLE 5.2 Current Call Option Values

	Expiration Month		
Striking Price	June	Sept.	Dec.
35	11	13	15
40	6	8	10
45	1	2	5

Strategy 1: Rolling up and forward. Sell one December 45 call at 5 while closing out the original June 40 call at 6. This produces a net cash payout of $100, but puts you at the money, removing the immediate risk of exercise. Because the striking price of the new short position is five points higher, you will earn $500 more in profit if the new call is eventually exercised.

Strategy 2: Rolling with incremental return. Sell two September 45 calls while closing the June 40 call at 6, producing $200 cash difference. You receive $400 for the two new short calls, versus the $600 you pay to close the original call. Now you are at the money on two calls, instead of being in the money on one.

Strategy 3: Rolling forward only. Sell one September 40 call at 8 while closing the June 40 call at 6, resulting in net cash received of $200. You're still in the money, but you increase premium income by two points.

Note in these strategies that we refer to the *loss* on the June call. Because that call currently is valued at 6, it requires a cash outlay of $600 to close the position. You received $300 when you sold, so your net loss is $300.

The loss of $300 is acceptable in all of these strategies because either the call with striking price of 40 is replaced with a call with a striking price of 45, which is 5 points higher, or additional income is produced to offset that loss by replacing the call with others that will expire later.

If the underlying stock is reasonably stable—for example, if its market value tends to stay within a five-point range during a typical three-month period—it is possible to employ rolling techniques and avoid exercise indefinitely, as long as no early exercise occurs. As stated before, however, you have to remember that when your short positions are in the money, exercise can occur at any time. Rolling techniques are especially useful when stocks break out of their short-term trading ranges and you want to take advantage of increased market value while also profiting from selling calls—while also avoiding exercise.

To demonstrate how such a strategy can work, refer to Table 5.3. This shows a series of trades over a period of $2^{1}/_{2}$ years, and is a summary of a series of trades taken from actual confirmation receipts. The investor owned 400 shares of stock. Sale and purchase price show actual amounts of cash transacted including brokerage fees, rounded to the nearest dollar. The total net profit of $2,628 involved $722 in brokerage charges, so that profits before those charges were $3,350.

The information in Table 5.3 shows each type of rolling trade and summarizes how an effective use of incremental return helps avoid exercise as the underlying stock's market value increases. This investor was willing to increase the number of short calls to avoid exercise, as long as all were covered by shares of stock. When the stock's market value fell, the investor rolled down but did not write calls below the original striking price of 35.

TABLE 5.3 Selling Calls with Rolling Techniques

Calls Traded	Type	Sold		Bought		Profit	Notes
		Date	Amount	Date	Amount		
1	Jul 35	3/20	$328	4/30	$221	$107	
1	Oct 35	6/27	235	10/8	78	157	
1	Apr 35	1/15	247	4/14	434	−187	
1	Oct 35	4/14	604	6/24	228	376	1
1	Oct 35	7/31	353	9/12	971	−618	
2	Jan 45	9/12	915	12/16	172	743	2
2	Apr 45	12/16	379	2/24	184	195	
4	Jul 40	3/9	1,357	5/26	385	972	3
4	Oct 40	6/5	1,553	7/22	1,036	517	
4	Jan 40	8/5	1,504	9/15	138	366	
	Totals		$7,475		$4,847	$2,628	

[1] A roll forward: The loss on the April 35 call was acceptable to avoid exercise, since the October 35 was profitable.

[2] A combination roll forward and roll up: The loss on the October 35 call was acceptable to avoid exercise at a low striking price. The number of calls was incrementally increased from one to two.

[3] A roll down combined with an incremental return: The number of calls changed from two to four, and the striking price of 45 was replaced with one for 40.

If you purchase shares primarily to write options—a common practice—chances are that you will pick issues more volatile than average, since these tend to be associated with higher-premium options. The strategy makes sense in one regard: You will have ample opportunity to take advantage of momentary price swings and their corrections by timing option trades. Volatile issues are attractive to option sellers because of their tendency to have higher time value; however, that is also a symptom of the stock's greater market volatility and thus lower safety as an investment.

Smart Investor Tip

Stocks whose options offer greater time value do so for a reason. As a general rule, those stocks are higher-risk investments.

You will be less likely to succeed if you buy overpriced stocks that later fall below your basis. No call seller wants to be exercised at a level below the basis in the stock. A comparison of risks between uncovered and covered calls

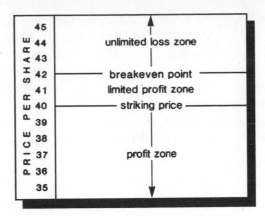

FIGURE 5.5 Example of uncovered call write with profit and loss zones.

is instructive. Check Figure 5.5. This shows the profit and loss zones for an uncovered call write. In this case, a single May 40 call was sold for 2. This strategy exposes the investor to unlimited risk. If the stock rises above the striking price and then exceeds the two points equal to the amount received in premium, losses rise point-for-point with the stock. Upon exercise, this investor will have to deliver 100 shares of stock at $40 per share, regardless of the current market value at that time.

The example of a covered call write shown in Figure 5.6 demonstrates that the loss zone exists only on the downside, so the covered strategy has a much different profile than the uncovered call strategy. In this example, the investor owned 100 shares of stock that originally were purchased at $38 per share. The

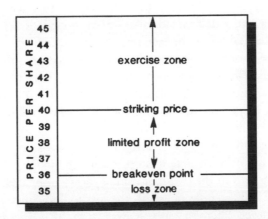

FIGURE 5.6 Example of covered call write with profit and loss zones.

investor then sold a May 40 call for 2. This discounts the basis in stock by $2 per share, down to $36. As long as the stock's market value is at or below the striking price of 40, exercise will not occur. If the stock's market value rises above $40 per share, the call will be exercised and the 100 shares called away at $40 per share. In the event of exercise, profit would be $400—$200 in profit on the stock plus $200 for call premium.

Rolling up, forward, or down makes sense as long as you (1) create a net credit in the exchange of cash and (2) defer or avoid exercise. Two important points to remember, however, about rolling:

1. *You can create a tax problem if you don't keep the rules in mind.* The idea of rolling forward makes sense as long as the striking price of the new option is close to the current market value of the stock. But the federal tax rules include an oddity, and rolling can create unintended consequences if you are not aware of it. Rolling involves two separate transactions, closing out a previous short option and opening up a new one. Under the federal rules, if the covered call you open today (even if it is part of a rolling strategy) is in the money by more than one increment (usually five points, sometimes less), you could lose the long-term capital gains treatment on your stock. (In a later chapter, this is explained in more detail.) So in rolling forward, make sure you don't jeopardize the status of your long-term capital gains if and when stock is called away.

2. *It sometimes makes sense to lose a little now to avoid exercise.* The concept of cutting your losses applies to covered calls as well as to any other kind of investment strategy. For example, if you sold a covered call with a striking price of 30 when the stock was at $28 per share, that was a sensible move. But if the stock has since moved up to $34 per share, your covered call is likely to be exercised. At the time you entered the strategy, you were aware of this possibility, and you accepted the risk. But now, you would like to avoid exercise by rolling up. For example, you may be willing to close your 30 call and replace it with a 35 call expiring later. In some cases, you will not be able to achieve this exchange without spending a little more (to close the previous call) than you receive (to open the new call). So you have to make a decision. Considering that the roll-up increases potential exercise price by five points ($500), is it worth the loss in the two-part rolling transaction? If the net difference is only $100, it could be worth the loss to "buy" five points in future exercise level. This also gets you away from the in-the-money exposure, if only by a single point.

If you do decide to exchange one option for another and take a small net loss, remember to track the net difference for the net call. Its net basis will not be what you sold it for, but the net between its sale price and the loss you took on the previous call. For example, if you sold the first call and received 2 ($200) and later closed it at 3 ($300), you have a net loss on $100. But you then open a new covered call at 1.50 ($150) with a strike price five points higher and exercise three months later. Your net basis in the new covered call is 0.50 ($50). The premium you received of $150 has to be reduced by the net loss on the previous call of $100. In this situation, you have reduced the overall option premium to $50 in exchange for a five-point increase in the strike price.

This example makes the point that timing and selection of the best striking price are crucial to the long-term success of your covered call program. If you pick stocks based on richness of time value premium, you should know ahead of time that you are exposing yourself to greater volatility; if you pick stocks with very narrow trading ranges, option premiums will be low as well. Either strategy has its good points; but it's crucial to know ahead of time what level of risk you will face. The next chapter examines methods for picking stocks with a call-writing strategy in mind.

Chapter 6

Choosing Stocks: Finding the Right Ingredients

The easiest job I have ever tackled in this world is that of making money. It is, in fact, almost as easy as losing it. Almost, but not quite.
—H. L. Mencken, in *Baltimore Sun*, June 12, 1922

How do you pick a stock? With about 8,000 to choose from, you need to narrow down the list. When picking stocks with options in mind, you will need to combine fundamental and technical tests to ensure that you pick those stocks with the greatest potential for growth *and* that offer you the very best options positions.

As a starting premise, be sure to observe some basic rules for picking stocks:

1. *Always pick stocks that are strong on their own merits.* A common error is to pick stocks based only on the option premium levels offered. This is a mistake because richer options are a symptom of higher than average stock volatility. So if you pick stocks based only on high option values, you will pick the highest-risk stocks. You will do better selecting stocks with strong fundamental and technical indicators.

2. *Combine a very short list of key indicators for stock selection.* You could spend all day applying endless tests to stock selection. But in fact, you should be able to use six fundamental indicators and confirm these with an equally short list of technical tests.

3. *Avoid stocks of companies that have never reported a profit, or whose stock price has been falling over many years.* As obvious as these guidelines might seem, they are often ignored. If a company is losing money each year or has never reported a profit, there is no rationale for expecting market value to grow. On the technical side, stock price trends tell the whole story. If a company has been experiencing a declining range of stock prices over many years, stay away. It usually means the company has lost its competitive edge and is on the way out.

4. *Look beyond option values; use past history of basic outcome.* The "basics" are usually the most dependable indicators. You should check revenues, profits, capitalization, and cash flow to make sure management is operating the company wisely. The history of fundamental trends is the strongest collective indicator for picking strong companies.

In this chapter, you have a short course on the fundamental and technical indicators you need to pick strong, well-managed, and competitive companies. This is achieved with an explanation of both fundamental and technical indicators that will give you the most reliable guidance for narrowing down a list of likely stocks to buy, whether you trade options on those stocks or simply hold them for the long term. Research is the starting point.

Careful, well-researched selection is the key to consistent investing success. This is true for all forms of investing and applies to all strategies. If your stock portfolio is not performing as you expected, you might be tempted to augment lackluster profits by using options. Short-term income could close a gap to offset small losses, improve overall yields, and even recapture a paper loss. However, short-term income is not guaranteed, and poorly selected stocks cannot be converted into high performers with options. Your best chance for success in the options market comes from first selecting stocks wisely, and from establishing rules for selection and strategy that suit your individual risk tolerance. A suitable options strategy has to be a sensible match for an individual stock based on its volatility, your goal in owning it, and its original basis versus current market value.

Deciding which stocks to buy should be based on your goals and risk tolerance levels, which are part of the process of setting an investment *policy* for yourself. That includes defining acceptable risks and focusing on how options can and should be used in your portfolio: to speculate, enhance income, or hedge equity positions. One danger of stock market investment is the tendency among investors to follow fads. It is invariably a mistake to begin buying shares of stock *after* prices have risen significantly. This brings up a number of problems, however, all dealing with timing. How do you know when a price run-up is about to begin in a particular stock or sector, and once invested, how do you know when to get out?

Both of these questions involve timing and risk. When you put capital at risk, and when you decide whether to sell, you are making risk-oriented decisions. The difficulty in these core questions can be mitigated, and risks reduced, with the use of options. Options are not purely speculative; they can also be useful for reducing risk of loss as well as risk of lost opportunity.

For example, instead of buying shares today, you might consider buying calls. Even though they will expire, they require far less capital and risk exposure. On the other end— when you own stocks whose market value has risen significantly—you can buy puts to insure against unexpected losses, or sell covered calls to (a) discount your basis and (b) increase income without selling your shares.

Options can be coordinated with long-term goals as well. A portfolio of well-chosen stocks should be treated as a long-term investment and, as a general rule, stocks will hold their value over the long term whether or not you write options.

Smart Investor Tip

Value in your portfolio of stocks exists whether you sell options or not. You cannot expect to bail out poorly selected stocks by offsetting stock losses with option profits.

One of the great advantages in selling covered calls is that a minimum profit level is likely as long as you also remember that the first step always should be proper selection of the stock.

Example

A Safe Decision: You bought 100 shares of IBM on the last trading day of 2006 and paid $97.61 per share. At the time, you believed it would be a safe investment with excellent prospects for long-term price appreciation; all of the ratings services made strong buy recommendations. At the same time, you considered selling a covered call. You looked at three calls with striking prices of 100, expiring in 4, 7, and 13 months. Premium values of these three calls were 3.20, 4.80, and 7.60. Quarterly dividends were about $125 at the time. In comparing the likely outcomes for both expiration and exercise, you need to annualize returns.

If the call expires:

	4-month	7-month	13-month
Call premium	$320	$480	$760
Dividend	125	250	500
Total profit	$445	$730	$1,260

Annualized yield
  if the call expires:
  ($445 ÷ $9,761) ÷ 4 × 12 = 13.7%
  ($730 ÷ $9,761) ÷ 7 × 12 = 13.3%
  ($1,260 ÷ $9,761) ÷ 13 × 12 = 11.9%

If the call is exercised:

	4-month	7-month	13-month
Call premium	$320	$480	$760
Dividend	125	250	500
Total profit on options	$445	$730	$1,260
Capital gain ($10,000 − $9,761)	239	239	239
Total profit, options and stock	$684	$969	$1,499
Yield	7.0%	9.9%	15.4%

Annualized yield if the call expires:
  ($684 ÷ $9,761) ÷ 4 × 12 = 21.0%
  ($969 ÷ $9,761) ÷ 7 × 12 = 17.0%
  ($1,499 ÷ $9,761) ÷ 13 × 12 = 14.2%

These returns—both impressive—are typical in situations where (a) you own appreciated stock, (b) exercise would be viewed as an acceptable outcome, and (c) you are interested in improving current return on stock you own without necessarily selling.

Developing an Action Plan

Earning a consistently high yield from writing calls is not always possible, even for covered call writers. In addition to picking the right options at the right time, a covered strategy has to be structured around well-selected stocks, preferably those that have appreciated since purchase. In addition, even with the right stocks in your portfolio, you might need to wait out the market. Timing refers not only to the richness of option premiums, but also to the tendencies in the stock and in the market as a whole. You could be able to sell a call rich in time value and profit from the combination of capital gains, dividends, and call premium. But the opportunity is not always going to be available, depending on a combination of factors:

- The price of the underlying stock has to be at the right level in two respects. First, the relationship between current market value and your basis in the stock has to justify the exposure to exercise, to ensure that in the event of exercise, you will have a profit and not a loss. If this is not possible, then there is no justification in writing the call. Second, the current market value of the underlying stock also has to be correct in relation to the striking price of the call. Otherwise, the time value will not be high enough to justify the transaction.

- The volume of investor interest in the stock and related options has to be high enough to provide adequate time value to build in a profit.

- The time between the point of sale of a call and expiration should fit with your personal goals. As with all other investment decisions, no strategy is appropriate unless it represents an intelligent fit.

In evaluating various strategies you could employ as a call writer, avoid the mistake of assuming that today's market conditions are permanent. Markets change constantly, resulting in unpredictable stock price levels. The ideal call write will be undertaken when the following conditions are present:

- *The striking price of the option is higher than your original basis in the stock.* Thus, exercise would produce a profit both in the stock *and* in the option. If the striking price of the option is lower than your basis in the stock, the option premium should be higher than the difference, while also covering transaction fees in both stock and option trades.

- *The call is in the money, but not deep in the money.* This means it will contain a degree of intrinsic value, so stock movements will be paralleled with dollar-for-dollar price changes in option premium, maximizing the opportunity to close the call at a profit with relatively minor stock price movement.

- *The call is out of the money, but not deep out of the money.* In this situation, all of the premium represents time value. As long as the stock's market value stays at or below the call's striking price, it will expire worthless. In the alternative, you can wait for time value to decline enough to close out the position at a profit.

- *There is enough time remaining until expiration that most of the premium is time value*. Even with minimal or no price movement in the stock, time value evaporates by expiration. As an option writer, you are compensated by being exposed to risk for a longer period, through higher time value.

- *Expiration will occur in six months or less*. You might not want to be locked in to a striking price for too long, and the identification of six months as a cutoff is arbitrary. The point is, the longer the time until expiration, the higher the time value; and that time value tends to fall most rapidly during the last two to three months. As an alternative, you can employ longer-term LEAPS options, accepting the extended exposure for higher time value premium.

- *Premium is high enough to justify the risk*. You will be locked in until expiration unless you later close the short option position with an offsetting purchase. In that sense, you risk price increases in the underlying stock and corresponding lost opportunity.

Example

Ideal Circumstances: You own 100 shares of stock that you bought at $53 per share. Current market value is $57. You write a 55 call with five months to go until expiration that has a premium of 6. The circumstances are ideal. Striking price is 2 points higher than your basis in the stock; the call is two points in the money, so that the options premium value will be responsive to price changes in the stock; two-thirds of current option premium is time value; expiration takes place in less than six months; and the premium is $600, a rich level considering your basis in the stock. It is equal to 11.3 percent of your original stock investment, an exceptional return ($600 ÷ $5,300).

In this example, you would earn a substantial return whether the option is exercised or expires worthless. If the stock's market value falls, the $600 call premium provides significant downside protection, discounting your basis to $47 per share. A worst-case analysis shows that if the stock's market value fell to $47 per share and the option then expired worthless, the net result would be breakeven.

Selecting Stocks for Call Writing

If you pick stocks based primarily on the potential yield to be gained from writing calls, it is a mistake—assuming you are a moderate or conservative investor. While a larger call premium discounts the stock's basis, it is not enough of a reason to buy shares. The best-yielding call premium most often is available on the highest-risk, most volatile stocks. So if you apply the sole criterion of premium yield to stock selection, you also accept far greater risks in your stock portfolio. Such a strategy could easily result in a portfolio of stocks with paper loss positions—all capital is committed in the purchase of overvalued stocks and you would then have to wait out a reversal in market value.

Smart Investor Tip

Using high-volatility stocks as a vehicle for producing current income from call writing is an appropriate strategy—as long as you accept the higher than average risks that go along with this strategy.

Example

Judging the Return: You decide to buy stock based on the relationship between current call premium and the price of the stock. You have only $4,000 to invest, so you limit your review to stocks selling at $40 per share or less. Your objective is to locate stocks on which call premium is at least 10 percent of current market value of the stock, with calls at the money or out of the money. You prepare a chart summarizing available stocks and options:

Current Value	Call Premium
$36	$3
28	3.50
25	1
39	4
27	1.75

You eliminate the first, third, and last choices because call premium is under 10 percent, and decide to buy the second stock on the list. It is selling at $28 per share and call premium is 3.50, a yield of 12.5 percent. This is the highest yield available from the list. On the surface, this study and conclusion appear reasonable. The selection of the call premium discounts the stock's basis by 12.5 percent. However, there are a number of problems in this approach. Most significant is the fact that no distinction is made among the stocks other than call price and yield. The selected issue was not judged on its individual fundamental nor technical merits. Also, by limiting the selection to stocks selling at $40 per share or lower, the range of potential choices is too restricted. It may be that with only $4,000 available, you would do better to select a stock on its own merits and wait until you are able to build up your portfolio.

The method in the preceding case also failed to consider time until expiration. You receive higher premiums when expiration dates are further away, in exchange for which you lock in your position for more time—meaning more change in the underlying stock's market value will be possible. Another flaw is that these calls were not judged in regard to the distance between striking price and current market value of the stock. The yield, by itself, is a misleading method for selecting options.

Smart Investor Tip

Picking options based on yield alone is a popular but flawed method. It fails to recognize far more important considerations, such as the quality of the underlying stock, time until expiration, and the point distance between current market value and striking price. All of these variables affect the comparison.

Covered call writing is a conservative strategy, assuming that you first understand how to pick high-quality stocks. First and foremost should be a stock's investment value, meaning that option yield should not be the primary factor in the selection of stocks in your portfolio. On the contrary, if you are led by the attractiveness of option premium levels, you are likely to pick highly volatile stocks. If you first analyze the stock for investment value, timeliness, and safety, the option value may then be brought into the picture as an additional method for selecting between otherwise viable investment candidates.

Benefiting from Price Appreciation

You will profit from covered call writing when the underlying stock's current market value is higher than the price you paid for the stock. In that case, you protect your position against a price decline and also lock in a profit in the event of exercise.

Example

Price Appreciation: You bought 100 shares of stock last year when the value was $27 per share. Today, the stock is worth $38.

In this case, you can afford to write calls with striking prices above your original basis, even if they are in the money; or you can write out-of-the-money calls as long as time value is high enough. Remembering that your original cost was $27 per share, you have at least four choices in methods for writing covered calls:

1. Write a call with a striking price of 25. The premium will include 13 points of intrinsic value plus time value, which will be higher for longer-out calls. If the call is exercised you lose two points in the stock, but gain 13 points in the call, for an overall profit of $1,100. If the stock's market value falls before exercise, or when time value disappears, you can cancel with a purchase and profit on the option trade, which frees you up to write another call. Any decline in stock market value is offset dollar-for-dollar by call profit in this case. The change in capital gain status and consequential tax liability on the stock should also be factored in to this calculation. (See Chapter 12.)

2. Write a call with a striking price of 30. In this case, intrinsic value is 8 points, and you can apply the same strategies as in number 1, above. However, because your position is not as deep in the money, chances for early exercise are reduced somewhat; in the event of exercise, you would keep the entire option premium, plus gaining $300 in profit on the stock.

3. Write a call with a striking price of 35. With only 3 points in the money, chances for early exercise are considerably lower than in the first two cases. Any decline in the stock's market value will be matched point-for-point by a decline in the call's intrinsic value, protecting your stock investment position. Because this call's striking price is close to current market value, there may be more time value than in the other alternatives.

4. Write a call with a striking price of 40 or 45. Since both of these are out of the money, the entire premium represents time value. The premium level will be lower since there is no intrinsic value; but the strategy provides you with three distinct advantages. First, it will be easier for you to cancel this position at a profit because time value will decline even if the stock's market value rises. Second, if the option is eventually exercised, you will gain a profit in the option *and* in the stock. Third, your long-term capital gain status in the stock will not be lost because the call is out of the money.

If you own stock with an appreciated market value, you face a dilemma that every stockholder has to resolve. If you sell and take a profit now, that is a sure thing but you lose out in the event that further profits could also be earned by keeping those shares. You also face the risk of a decline in market value, meaning some of today's appreciated value will be lost. As a long-term investor, you may be less concerned with short-term price changes; however, anyone would like to protect their paper profits.

Covered call writing is the best way to maximize your profits while providing downside protection. As long as your call is in the money, every point lost in the stock is matched by a lost point in the call; a paper loss in the stock is replaced with profits in the call position. The time value premium is potentially all profit, since it will disappear even if the stock's market value goes up, an important point that too many options traders overlook (especially buyers). When your basis is far below striking price of the call, you lock in a capital gain in the event of exercise.

Smart Investor Tip

Time value declines over time, even when the stocks's market value goes up. This is a problem for buyers, but a great advantage for sellers.

Example

Discounted Basis: You bought 100 shares of stock several years ago at $28 per share. Today it is worth $45. You sell a 45 call with four months to go until expiration. The premium was 4, all of which is time value. This discounts your original basis down to $24. If the stock were to fall 4 points or less, the call premium protects the paper profit based on current stock price. If the market value rises and the call is exercised, your shares would be called away at $45 per share, a profit of $2,100 ($1,700 on the stock plus $400 on the call).

In this example, you gain two levels of downside protection. First, the original basis is protected to the extent of the call premium; second, paper profits in the current market value also gain downside protection. When stock has appreciated beyond its original cost, it makes sense to protect current value levels, and call writing is a sensible alternative to selling shares you would not otherwise want to give up. You would probably view a decline in market value as a loss off the stock's high, even when the current stock price remains above your original cost. Call writing solves that dilemma.

Averaging Your Cost

You increase your profit potential with call writing using a strategy known as *average up*. When the price of stock has risen since your purchase date, this strategy allows you to sell in-the-money calls when the average basis in that stock is always lower than the average price you paid.

If you buy 100 shares and the market value increases, buying another 100 shares reduces your overall cost so that your basis is lower than current market value. The effect of averaging up is summarized by examples in Table 6.1.

> **average up**
>
> a strategy involving the purchase of stock when its market value is increasing. The average cost of shares bought in this manner is consistently lower than current market value, enabling covered call writers to sell calls in the money when the basis is below the striking price.

How does averaging up help you as a call writer? When you write calls on several-hundred-share lots of stock, you are concerned about the possibility of falling stock prices. While price decline means you will profit from writing calls, it also means your stock loses value. Covered call writing provides downside protection, but that is limited; if price decline extends beyond the discounted basis of stock, then you have a problem. The more shares you own of a single stock, the higher this risk. For example, if you are thinking about buying 600 shares of stock, you can take two approaches. First, you can buy 600 shares at today's price; second, you can buy 100 shares and wait to see how market values change, buying additional lots in the future. This means you will pay higher transaction costs, but it could also protect your stock's overall market value. By averaging your investment basis, you spread your risk.

	Shares	Price per	Average
Date	Purchased	Share	Price
January 10	100	$26	$26
February 10	100	28	27
March 10	100	30	28
April 10	100	30	28.50
May 10	100	31	29
June 10	100	32	29.50

TABLE 6.1 Averaging Up

A Law of Averages: You buy 100 shares on the 10th of each month, beginning in January. The price of the stock changes over six months so that by June 10, your average basis is $29.50.

This example, as illustrated in Table 6.1, allows you to reduce stock invest-ment risk. The average price is always lower than current market value as long as the stock's price continues moving in an upward trend. Buying 600 shares at the beginning would have produced greater profits. But how do you know in advance that the stock's market value will rise?

Averaging up is a smart alternative to placing all of your capital at risk in one move. The benefits to this approach are shown in Figure 6.1.

By acquiring 600 shares over time, you can also write six calls. Because your average basis at the end of the period is $29.50 and current market value is $32 per share, you can sell calls and with a striking price of 30 win in two ways:

1. When the average price of stock is lower than striking price of the call, you will gain a profit in the event of exercise.
2. When the call is in the money, movement in the stock's price is matched by movement in the call's intrinsic value.

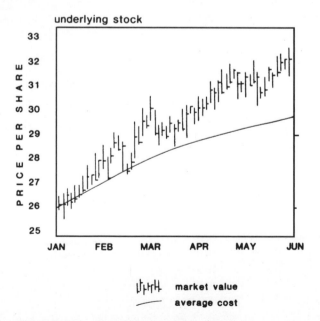

FIGURE 6.1 Example of averaging up.

What happens, though, if the stock's market value falls? You also reduce your risks in writing calls if you *average down* over time. An example of this strategy is summarized in Table 6.2.

When a stock's market value falls, selling calls may no longer be profitable; you may need to wait for the stock's price to rebound. This does not mean that selling calls on currently owned stock is a bad idea; a decline would affect portfolio value whether you wrote calls or not. In fact, if you do write calls, you discount the basis of stock, mitigating the effect of a decline in market price of stock. A decline that is only temporary has to be waited out because it makes no sense to set up a losing situation. You should never sell covered calls if exercise would produce an overall loss.

average down

a strategy involving the purchase of stock when its market value is decreasing. The average cost of shares bought in this manner is consistently higher than current market value, so a portion of the paper loss on declining stock value is absorbed, enabling covered call writers to sell calls and profit even when the stock's market value has declined.

Smart Investor Tip

When the stock's market value declines, selling covered calls is less likely to produce profits. Never write calls when exercise will produce a net loss.

In this situation, selling calls out of the money may also fail to produce the premium level needed to justify the strategy. When stock has lost value,

	TABLE 6.2 Averaging Down		
Date	*Shares Purchased*	*Price per Share*	*Average Price*
July 10	100	$32	$32
August 10	100	31	31.50
September 10	100	30	31
October 10	100	30	30.75
November 10	100	27	30
December 10	100	24	29

wait for its price to recover; meanwhile, if you continue to believe the stock is a worthwhile long-term hold, acquire more shares through averaging down.

Example

Reducing the Basis: You buy 100 shares of stock each month, beginning on July 10, when market value is $32 per share. By December, after periodic price movement, the current market value has fallen to $24 per share. Average cost per share is $29.

Your average cost is always higher than current market value in this illustration using the average down technique, but not as high as it would have been if you had bought 600 shares in the beginning. The dramatic difference made through averaging down is summarized in Figure 6.2.

When you own 600 shares, you can write up to six covered calls. In the preceding example, average basis is $29 per share. By writing calls with striking price of 30, you gain one point of capital gain on the total of 600 shares in the event of exercise. This demonstrates how averaging down can be beneficial to call writers in the event that the stock's market value falls.

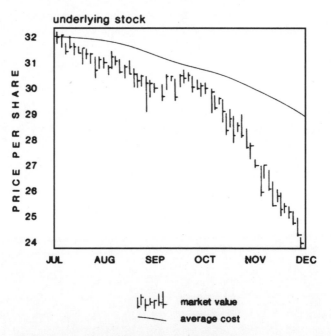

FIGURE 6.2 Example of averaging down.

Averaging up and down are important tools that help you to mitigate the effects of quickly changing stock prices. In a fast-moving market, price changes represent a problem to the call writer, since locked-in positions cannot be sold without exposing yourself to greater risks in the short call position. Both techniques are forms of *dollar cost averaging*. Regardless of price movement, averaging protects capital. A variation of dollar cost averaging is the investment of a fixed dollar amount over time, regardless of per-share value. This is a popular method for buying mutual fund shares. However, in the stock market, direct purchase of stock makes more sense when buying in round lot increments.

> **dollar cost averaging**
> a strategy for investing over time, either buying a fixed number of shares or investing a fixed dollar amount, in regular intervals. The result is an averaging of overall price. If market value increases, average cost is always lower than current market value; if market value decreases, average cost is always higher than current market value.

By averaging out the cost of stock, you reduce exposure to loss in paper value of the entire investment. For the purpose of combining stock and option strategies, owning several hundred shares is a significant advantage over owning only 100 shares. Transaction costs involving multiple option contracts are reduced; in addition, owning more shares enables you to use many more strategies involving options. For example, if you begin by selling one call, you can avoid exercise by rolling up and increasing the number of calls sold. This provides you with more premium income as well as avoiding exercise, even when the stock's market value is rising. By increasing the number of options sold with each subsequent roll up, you can increase profits over time. The technique is difficult if not impossible when you only own 100 shares of stock.

Analyzing Stocks

Stock selection is the starting point for covered call writing. Options are valued based upon market value of the stock in comparison to striking price and expiration date of the option. So options do not contain any fundamental or technical features of their own.

> **Smart Investor Tip**
>
> Don't look for fundamental or technical indicators in option; instead, study the attributes of the underlying stock.

Avoid the mistake of failing to question whether the particular stock is a good match for you, given your risk tolerance level, long-term investing goals, and available capital. Options traders are especially vulnerable to the temptation to buy stocks for the wrong reason—namely, to take advantage of high-priced option opportunities.

Risks are unavoidable attributes of investing. To spot excessive risks, follow these general rules of thumb:

- *If the information provided by the company is too complicated to understand, you should not invest.* In the past, some of the explanations provided by management or disclosed in footnotes were so obscure that they could not be understood, even by expert analysts. This is a danger sign.

- *If a stock continues to rise beyond reasonable expectations, it could be a sign of trouble.* It is rarely a good idea to buy shares in a company just because the stock's price has risen to impressive levels. Are those levels justified by earnings?

- *You need to apply tests that look beyond personal recommendations, rosy estimates of future earnings, and other suspicious indicators.* Recommendations coming from analysts, stockbrokers, friends and relatives, and anyone else, should be reviewed with great suspicion. You are better off investigating companies on your own, remembering that free advice may be more expensive than the kind you pay for.

- *Methods for valuing companies have to go beyond the ,traditional—and overly optimistic—tests so common in the market.* Question traditional assumptions and methods for picking companies. Study ratios and trends in accounts receivable, bad debt reserves, inventory levels, current and long-term liabilities, and capital assets.

- *Intelligent analysis has to be based on valuing companies rather than identifying target price and earnings levels.* You might be comfortable with short-term forecasting, at the expense of longer-term analysis, which can be a problem. Analysts pick target trading ranges or prices for stocks as well as earnings per share, based on anything but fundamental information. Instead of predicting price-related value in the next three months, analysts should be studying and reporting on the value of companies over the next 5 to 10 years.

core earnings
as defined by Standard & Poor's, the aftertax earnings generated from a corporation's principal business.

Standard & Poor's has changed its method for valuing companies, and its revised definition of *core earnings* is helpful in getting around many of the creative methods used in the past to inflate earnings and mislead investors. The S&P definition of core earnings is "the aftertax earnings generated from a corporation's principal business."

Under this definition, many items are excluded from earnings, including nonrecurring gain or loss from the sale of capital assets, *pro forma earnings* such as gains on pension investments, and fees related to mergers and acquisitions. In the past, the inclusion of these items inflated reported profits, so that the market had unrealistic and inaccurate ideas of a company's operating results.

The definition includes many expenses and costs that have been excluded or capitalized in the past, such as restructuring charges, write-down of amortizable operating assets, pension costs, and purchased R&D costs. One of the most substantial and glaring flaws of the past has been leaving out

pro forma earnings
"as a matter of form" (Latin), a company's earnings based on estimates or forecasts with hypothetical numbers in place of known or actual revenues, costs, or earnings.

employee stock option expense, which can be a huge number; but that flaw is gradually changing as many corporations have begun expensing stock options granted each year. As long as corporations left these and similar items out of the picture, stockholders were given a very unrealistic view of operations.

The move by S&P to arrive at a standardized definition of the real earnings number is a positive trend. It enables like-kind comparisons between many different corporations, without the very real concern for inconsistent treatment and interpretation of revenues or costs and expenses. The S&P definition makes more sense than the more widely used *EBITDA*, which is "earnings

EBITDA
a popular measurement of cash flow, an acronym for *earnings before interest, taxes, depreciation,* and *amortization*.

before interest, taxes, depreciation, and amortization." EBITDA was originally intended to serve as a measurement of cash flow or cash-based earnings for a company; however, this measurement is flawed.

Under EBITDA, no provision is included to account for purchasing of capital assets or paying down debts. Rather than a clarifying calculation, EBITDA has been used more as a way to make things appear better than they are. For example, when accounts receivable levels are rising, EBITDA does not make a distinction between cash sales and credit sales—an area where revenues have been exaggerated in some cases and where it is all too easy to alter the true numbers to inflate earnings.

Smart Investor Tip

EBITDA, a well-intended calculation, has been widely misused to distort the numbers. For this reason, it should be rejected as a formula in your analytical study of a company.

quality of earnings
a measurement of the reliability of financial reports. A high quality of earnings means the report reflects the real and accurate operations of a corporation and may be used reliably to forecast likely future growth trends.

As a starting point in the analysis of corporate reports, identifying core earnings helps you to analyze many different companies on a truly comparative basis. Going beyond that, you also need to quantify what analysts call the *quality of earnings*. While this term has many definitions, it is supposed to mean earnings that are reliable and true, as opposed to those that are overly optimistic or inflated. For example, if a company reports income based on accounts receivable that might never be collected, that is not a good quality of earnings. The definition should include revenues that are likely to be collected and not created out of accruals, acquisitions, or accounting tricks.

In addition to the importance of selectively identifying companies based on quality of earnings, make use of specific fundamental tests. Fundamental analysis—the study of financial information, management, competitive position within a sector, and dividend history, for example—provides you with comparative analysis of value, safety, stability, and the potential for growth in the stock's long-term value. Financial and economic information, corporate management, sector and competitive position, and other indicators involving profit and loss, all are part of fundamental analysis. The fundamentalist studies a corporation's balance sheet and income statement to judge a stock's long-term prospects as an investment. Other economic indicators may influence your decision to invest or not.

The fundamentals should be reliable. If we cannot rely on what is being reported, what good is any form of analysis? Any study involving the fundamentals has to involve analysis on two levels. The traditional level includes trend analysis, for the purpose of identifying changes in financial strength and competitive position. Second is an equally important study of financial ratios, for the purpose of ensuring that a company is not artificially inflating earnings in order to deceive investors.

The fundamental analyst believes in the numbers. However, part of a scientific analysis has to include verification of the core data as a starting point. The fundamental analyst has to be able not only to interpret the information, but also to use some basic forensic accounting skills to make sure the numbers are real. Those skills include a study of the basic ratios in a search for suspicious or questionable changes. If such changes are discovered and not adequately explained, that discovery is a warning that something could be wrong.

The technician will be less interested in the forensic aspects of current or past information. Technical analysis involves a forward-looking study relating almost exclusively to price of the stock, market forces affecting that price, and anticipation of changes based on supply and demand, market perception, and trading ranges. The technician uses financial data only to the extent that it affects a current price trend, believing that this trend provides the key to anticipating the future price movement of stock. Market analysts believe that price change is random, especially short-term price movement; but some technicians, notably the *chartist*, prefer to believe that patterns of price movement can be used to predict the direction of change in the stock's price.

chartist
an analyst who studies charts of a stock's price movement in the belief that recent patterns can be used to predict upcoming price changes and directions.

The fundamental approach is based on the assumption that short-term price movement is entirely random and that long-term value is best identified through a thorough study of a corporation's financial status. The technical approach relies on patterns in price of the stock and other price-related indicators associated more with the market's perception of value and less with financial information. Obviously, a current report on the corporation's net income will affect the stock's market price, at least temporarily, and technicians acknowledge this. However, their primary interest is in studying pricing trends.

Both theories have value, so it makes sense to apply fundamental and technical analysis in your analytical program. You monitor the market to make the four important decisions: buy, hold, sell, or stay away. Analysis in all of its forms is a tool for decision making, and no analysis provides insights that dictate decisions exclusively. Common sense and judgment based on experience are the extra edge that you can bring to your investment decisions. Successful investing is the result of being right more often than being wrong.

Smart Investor Tip
There are no formulas that will make you right all of the time. Investing success comes from applying good judgment, increasing your chances of being right about market decisions.

Never overlook the need to continuously track your stocks. Call writers may be inclined to ignore signals relating to the stock when, if they were not involved with writing options, they might tend to watch their portfolio more diligently. Call writers are preoccupied with other matters: movement in the stock's price (but only insofar as it affects their option positions); chances of exercise and how to avoid or defer it; opportunities to roll forward; and other matters concerning immediate strategies. As important as all of these matters are for call writers, they do not address the important questions that every stockholder needs to ask continuously: Should I keep the stock or sell it? Should I buy more shares? What changes have occurred that could also change my opinion of this stock?

The time will come when, as a call writer, you will want to close an open call position and sell the stock. For example, if you own 100 shares of stock on which you have written several calls over many months or years, when should you sell the stock and get out? For a variety of reasons, you might conclude that the stock is not going to hold its value into the future as you once believed. Even if you buy stocks for the long term, you may need to rethink your positions through constant evaluation, whether you write calls or not. It would be a mistake to continue holding stock because it represents a good candidate for covered call selling, when in fact that stock no longer makes the grade based on the analytical tests that you use to pick stocks as a starting point.

Fundamental Tests

A number of fundamental indicators are useful in deciding when to buy or sell stock; these tests should always override the attributes in the options. Remember, options are always related to stock valuation, and trying to make profit through options on stocks that are not worthwhile investments is a losing strategy. A worthwhile investment has to be defined as one containing fundamental strength: revenues and earnings, dividend history, and capitalization.

One indicator that enjoys widespread popularity is the *price/earnings ratio* (P/E ratio). This is a measurement of current value that utilizes both fundamental and technical information. The technical side (price of a share of stock) is divided by the fundamental side (*earnings per share* of common stock) to arrive at P/E.

price/earnings ratio
a popular indicator used by stock market investors to rate and compare stocks. The current market value of the stock is divided by the most recent earnings per share to arrive at the P/E ratio.

Example

Calculating the P/E: A company's stock recently sold at $35 per share. Its latest annual income statement showed $220 million in profit; the company had 35 million shares outstanding. That works out to a net profit of $6.29 per share: $220 ÷ $35. The P/E ratio is

$$\$35 \div \$6.29 = 5.6$$

Example

A Second Calculation: A company earned $95 million and has 40 million shares outstanding, so its earnings per share is $2.38. The stock sells at $28 per share. The P/E is calculated as

$$\$28 \div \$2.38 = 11.8$$

The P/E ratio is a relative indicator of what the market believes about the particular stock. It reflects the current point of view about the company's prospects for future earnings. As a general observation, lower P/E ratio means your risks are lower. Any

earnings per share
a commonly used method for reporting profits. Net profits for a year or for the latest quarter are divided by the number of shares of common stock outstanding as of the ending date of the financial report. The result is expressed as a dollar value.

ratio is only useful when it is studied in comparative form. This means not only that a company's P/E ratio may be tracked and observed over time, but also that comparisons between different companies can be instructive, especially if they are otherwise similar (in the same sector or same product profile, for instance). In the preceding examples, the first company's 5.6 P/E would be considered a less risky investment than the second, whose P/E is 11.8. However, P/E ratio is not always a fair indicator of a stock's risk level, nor of its potential for future profits, for at least six reasons:

1. *Financial statements may themselves be distorted.* A company's financial statement may be far more complex than it first appears, in terms of what it includes and what it leaves out. Conventional rules for reporting revenues, costs, expenses, and earnings may not convey the whole picture, and a more in-depth analysis of core earnings is an important step to take.

2. *The financial statement might be unreliable for comparative purposes.* Companies and their auditors have considerable leeway in how they report income, costs, and expenses, even within the rules. This makes valid comparison between different companies problematical.

3. *The number of shares outstanding might have changed.* Because shares outstanding is part of the P/E ratio equation, its comparative value can be affected when the number of shares changes from one year to another.

4. *The ratio becomes inaccurate as earnings reports go out of date.* If the latest earnings report of the company was issued last week, then the P/E ratio is based on recent information. However, if that report was published three months ago, then the P/E is also outdated.

5. *The P/E itself involves dissimilar forms of information.* The P/E ratio compares a stock's price—a technical value based on perceptions about current and future value—with earnings, which is historical and fundamental in nature. This raises the question about whether a purely technical matter such as market price can even be compared to a purely historical and fundamental matter such as earnings, or how much weight this indicator should be given in evaluating a stock.

6. *Perceptions about P/E ratio are inconsistent.* This indicator is widely used and accepted as a means for evaluating and comparing stocks. However, not everyone agrees about how to interpret P/E itself.

How should you use the P/E ratio? It is a valuable indicator for measuring market perception about value of a stock, especially if you are tracking the P/E ratio for a single stock and watching how it changes over time. Comparing P/E between two different stocks may be more of a problem in terms of reliability. Companies in different industries, for example, may have widely different norms for judging profits. In one industry, a 3 percent or 4 percent return on sales might be considered average, and in another an 8 percent return is expected. So comparing P/E ratios between companies with dissimilar profit expectations is inaccurate.

The proper use of P/E can be based on comparisons between companies. Remember, the P/E represents a *multiple* that price resides above annual earnings. So when the P/E is at 10, that means current price is 10 times annual earnings per share. A P/E between 10 and 20 is usually considered "reasonable" by most investors' standards. But when P/E rises to 50 or 60 (or higher), it is clear that the current price has become unrealistic.

multiple
The P/E's outcome, the number of times current price per share is above annual earnings per share; for example, if the P/E is 10, then current price per share is 10 times higher than the latest reported earnings per share.

The P/E can provide useful information as long as you also recognize its limitations. A more practical and tangible indicator is *dividend yield*. This is expressed as percentage of the share price. As the stock's market price changes, so does the yield. Compare:

dividend yield
dividends paid per share of common stock, expressed as a percentage computed by dividing dividend paid per share by the current market value of the stock.

$$\$3.50 \div \$65 \text{ per share} = 5.4\%$$
$$\$3.50 \div \$55 \text{ per share} = 6.4\%$$
$$\$3.50 \div \$45 \text{ per share} = 6.8\%$$

A larger dividend yield could reflect a buying opportunity at the moment. That yield, added to capital gains as well as returns from selling covered calls, could add up to a very healthy overall return. Like comparisons between P/E ratios, the dividend yield is a useful indicator for narrowing the field when you are choosing stocks for investment.

profit margin
the most commonly used measurement of corporate operations, computed by dividing net profits by gross sales.

A corporation's profitability is another important test. Long-term price appreciation occurs as the result of the corporation's ability to generate profits year after year. Short-term stock price changes are less significant when you are thinking about long-term growth potential of the stock, and for that, you want to compare *profit margin* from one company to another. This is the most popular system for judging a company's performance. It is computed by dividing the dollar amount of net profit by the dollar amount of gross sales. The result is expressed as a percentage.

The profit margin, as useful as it is for comparative purposes between companies, and for year-to-year analysis, often is not fully understood by people invested in the market. As a consequence, many market analysts as well as investors develop unrealistic expectations about profit margin. Two points worth remembering:

1. *An "acceptable" level of profit varies between industries.* One industry may experience lower or higher average profit margin than another. This makes it impractical to arrive at a singular standard for measuring profitability; the unique aspects of each sector should be used to differentiate between corporations. Comparisons should be restricted to those between corporations in the same sector.

2. *It is not realistic to expect that a particular year's profit margin should always exceed that gained in the previous year.* Once a corporation reaches what is considered an acceptable and realistic profit margin, it is unrealistic to expect it to continuously grow in terms of higher percentage returns.

total capitalization
the combination of long-term debt (debt capital) and stockholders' equity (equity capital), which in combination represents the financing of corporate operations and long-term growth.

Another very important fundamental indicator is the test of *total capitalization*. Corporations pay for operations through equity (stock) and debt (bonds and notes). Stockholders are compensated through dividends and capital gains, whereas bondholders are paid interest and, eventually, get their entire investment repaid. An important point for stockholders to remember is that as debt capitalization increases, a growing portion of operating profit has to be paid out in interest. That means that, in turn, there remains less profit available for dividends. The *debt ratio* tracks long-term debt as a percentage of total capitalization. (This indicator may also be referred to as the debt-equity ratio or the debt-to-equity ratio.) If the debt portion of capitalization increases steadily over time, stockholders lose out as their dividend income is eroded. A secondary consequence is the erosion of market price resulting from ever-growing reliance on debt capitalization.

These examples of fundamental indicators are important, but they do not provide the entire picture. No single indicator should ever be used as the sole means for deciding what actions to take in the market. Fundamental analysis should be comprehensive. You can employ combinations of information, including a thorough study of all of the tests that reveal trends to you. They may confirm a previous opinion, or they may change your mind. Either way, the purpose in using the fundamentals is to gather information and then to act upon it.

debt ratio
a ratio used to follow trends in debt capitalization. To compute, divide long-term debt by total capitalization; the result is expressed as a percentage.

You should be able to judge a company based on its fundamentals by studying 10 years' history of P/E ratio ranges; earnings per share; dividend yield; profit margin; total capitalization; and debt ratio. With these six tests, you have a good grip on the company's financial strength and profitability.

Smart Investor Tip

You can find 10 years' history for most listed companies by referring to the *S&P Stock Reports*. Some online brokerage services provide this valuable service free of charge. For example, Charles Schwab & Company (www.schwab.com) allows investors to open free accounts and offers the *S&P Stock Reports* and other analytical reports, all free of charge.

Technical Tests

Using a combination of fundamental and technical tests helps you to review a stock from different points of view. While the fundamentals help you to gain insights into a company's overall financial and capital strength, technical indicators help you to judge market perception. The fundamentals look back at a company's history to estimate the future; technical indicators are used to forecast the future based on current market information.

Price—the primary technical indicator—is the most popular measurement used by technicians. It is an easy value to find, widely reported in the financial press and online. And while the short-term price movement of a stock is not valuable as a long-term indicator, it is of utmost importance to every options trader.

Smart Investor Tip

Long-term value of stocks is inconsistent with valuation methods for options, which are by nature short-term. You need to track and monitor both.

Often overlooked in this analysis is the study of volume in a stock. You may apply volume tests to the market as a whole; they can also be applied to individual stocks. When volume increases, it indicates increased market interest in the stock. High volume can have two opposite conclusions, which will be determined by the direction that the stock's price is moving on a particular day. You can track changes in volume and price in the financial press or on the Internet. Charting is widely available and free on many sites. The analysis of price and volume together improves your insight into the way that a stock acts in the market. You need to assess each stock based on historical price and volume patterns, as well as overall volatility in the stock's market price.

Smart Investor Tip

Free charts of stock price and volume are available on dozens of sites, free of charge. Check these web sites for a sampling:

Investor Guide	http://investorguide.com
StockMaster	http://www.stockmaster.com
Financial Times	http://ft.com

support level
the lowest trading price, under present conditions, below which the price of the stock is not likely to fall.

Among the things to watch for on the technical side is a stock's *support level*, which is the lowest likely price level, given current conditions. On the other side of the chart is the *resistance level*, the highest price a stock is likely to trade under current conditions. The concepts of support and resistance are not only keys to the technical approach to studying stock price movement; they also are revealing because they indicate a stock's *relative volatility*. The wider the range between support and resistance, the more volatile a stock; and of course, the thinner that trading range, the more stable the stock. So a stock with a wider than average trading range would contain higher relative volatility. This measurement is especially instructive when comparing stocks in the same sector or with options priced at similar levels. Even when not judging relative volatility, the visualization of a stock's trading pattern can help to identify a stock's overall volatility over time. The level of volatility is the best method for determining a stock's market risk.

The price range in between support and resistance price levels is called the *trading range*. Even when a stock's price is moving in an upward or downward direction, the trading range may remain unchanged. For example, a particular stock might consistently trade within a 15-point trading range, although the longer-term trend is upward. When price changes occur along with significant changes in the trading range, a related change in option premium is likely to occur at the same time.

The stock price is considered stable as long as it remains within the established trading range. When the price does move beyond the trading range, that is called a *breakout* pattern. The essence of charting is to try to identify in advance of the breakout when it is going to occur. The chartist believes that by studying the trading patterns, it is possible to predict price movement.

The support and resistance levels as well as breakout patterns are shown in Figure 6.3. In the illustration, an initial trading range is shown at the left, with a breakout on the upside; this establishes a new trading range and is then followed with a breakout on the downside. The breakout patterns are indicated by the arrows.

Options traders can make good use of support and resistance and other technical theories. By observing the pattern of recent trading ranges, you may better judge a stock's relative volatility. The chart reveals a pattern over time,

resistance level
the highest trading price, under present conditions, above which the price of the stock is not likely to rise.

relative volatility
the degree of volatility in comparative form, such as between portfolios or between a specific stock and other stocks or markets.

trading range
the price range between support and resistance; the current price area where stock purchase and sale levels occur.

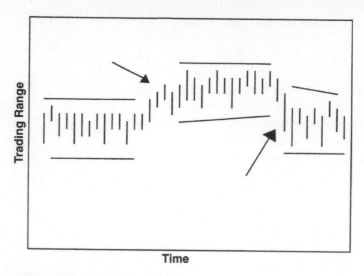

FIGURE 6.3 Chart patterns.

so that you can judge whether the trading range is broad or thin; whether it is changing and, if so, to what degree; and how often previously established trading ranges have been modified by breakouts. The length of time a trading range remains unchanged is also revealing, as it helps options traders to determine a stock's tendency to react to market changes in general, or to trade with its own timing pattern.

breakout
the movement of a stock's price below support level or above resistance level.

Accompanying an in-depth review of volatility, a sound analysis of a stock may include a further study of the high and low price ranges over time. This demonstrates several things. For example, the more volatile stocks—those with broader high and low ranges—may, in fact, be volatile at the beginning of the period but not at the end, or vice versa. A simple one-year summary is not reliable in terms of today's price trend.

The stock reports in the financial press present only the 52-week high and low price ranges. Given the many possible varieties of trading patterns that can result in the same high and low summary, this information is unreliable. A more detailed study is required.

Example

Side-by-Side Comparisons: Five different stocks have reported 52-week trading ranges as follows (based on one year ending May 2004):

Company	Low	High	Volatility %
IBM	82	99	21%
ChevronTexaco	72	94	31%
Avon	62	86	39%
Sears	35	55	57%
Allegheny	175	260	49%

If you were to select the least volatile stock from among this field, the first choice would be IBM. But is it the least volatile stock? A more detailed analysis shows that IBM's price varied during the year from a low of 82 to a high of 99, but in between moved up and down quite often. In comparison, Avon, ChevronTexaco, and Allegheny all moved steadily upward during the year; their trading ranges were consistently upward-trending, whereas IBM started and ended the year at virtually the same price. Sears did the same; it began the year at $35 per share and ended at $37, but in between surged up to $55.

Any study in which we look at how prices have moved within a 52-week high and low range is going to be far more revealing than a more limited study of outward price levels alone. In fact, with these variations in mind, the volatility percentage is meaningless. That percentage—computed by dividing the high/low price difference by the low for the year—only provides a range distinction; it does not tell us whether a stock's trend is up, down, or flat. It also does not demonstrate price spikes.

No single fundamental or technical test can be used reliably to identify good stock candidates. The high and low ranges might represent a fair starting point for stock selection, but the analysis should explore further into the timing and attributes of the stock and its trading range. You can evaluate stocks by tracking key indicators over time, looking not only for patterns but also for the emergence of *new* pricing trends. For example, you might decide to track a stock you are thinking of buying, combining dividend rate, P/E ratio, high and low range, and current price (close each day) of a stock. The worksheet in Table 6.3 can be used for this purpose. You might use the close each Friday to track a particular stock. After entering information on each line, you can begin to see how each piece of information changes or interacts with the others.

The problem with analysis is that it takes time. And the more time you spend on analysis, the more quickly it goes out of date. Having online charting services available free of charge makes your task much easier.

TABLE 6.3 Stock Evaluation Worksheet

stock name _____

DATE	DIVIDEND RATE	P/E RATIO	HIGH	LOW	CLOSE

Deciding Which Tests to Apply

How do you determine which of the many fundamental and technical tests are most useful for picking stocks, tracking them, and deciding when to sell? The answer depends on your own opinion. Before deciding on one form of analysis over another, be aware of these important points:

- *Many analysts love complex formulas.* A theory that is difficult to understand and that requires a lot of mathematical ability is probably useless in the real world. Avoid the complex, recognizing that useful information also tends to be straightforward and easily comprehended.

- *You can perform your own tests. You do not need to pay for analysis.* Even though some of the accounting-related ratios can be complex and difficult to follow, the actual tests leading to decisions to buy, hold, or sell are going to be very basic and straightforward. The process does not have to be complicated.

- *Price has nothing to do with the fundamentals.* The price of any stock reflects the market's perception about future potential value, whereas the financial condition of that company is historical. A study of fundamentals has nothing to do with today's price.

- *The net worth of a company has nothing to do with price.* Current market value is determined through auction between buyers and sellers, and not by accountants at the company's headquarters. The actual value of the stockholders' equity in a corporation is found in the *book value* of shares of stock.

  book value
  the actual value of a company, more accurately called *book value per share*; the value of a company's capital (assets less liabilities), divided by the number of outstanding shares of stock.

- *The past is not an infallible indicator.* When you attempt to predict price movement through studying the fundamentals, you face an elusive task, since the fundamentals do not affect short-term price movement as much as other factors, such as perception of the market as a whole. Remember the wisdom that the stock market has no past.

- *Predictions abound, but reliable predictions do not exist.* You can get lucky and make an accurate prediction once in a while. Doing so with any consistency is far more difficult. You can study any number of factors, either fundamental or technical, but none will enable you to accurately predict future price movement of stocks.

- *Common sense is your best tool.* You are more likely to succeed if you employ common sense, backed up with study, analysis, and comparison. Market success without hard work is no more likely in the stock market than anywhere else.

- *Stock prices, especially in the short term, are random.* Most predictive theories acknowledge that, while long-term analysis can accurately narrow down the guesswork, short-term price movement is completely random. In the stock market, where opinion and speculation are widespread, no one can control the way that stock prices change from one day to the next.

The two major theories directing opinions about stock prices are the *random walk* theory and the *Dow Theory*. The Dow Theory contends that certain signals are confirmed independently and indicate a change in market directions. The random walk hypothesis is based on the idea that market movements are not predictable based on specific tests, and that given the presumed efficiency of the auction marketplace, there is an equal chance that future prices of stocks will rise or that they will fall. The one point that both of these theories agree upon is that short-term indicators are of no value in determining whether to buy or sell in the market. For the options investor, this is an interesting observation. If short-term price movement is unpredictable, that means that stock selection has to be done on a long-term basis. However, at the same time, you have an exceptional opportunity when using options. You *know* in advance how time value premium is going to change. That change occurs only due to time and is not affected by changes in the stock's market price. So while you should select long position stocks with the long term in mind regardless of which theory you accept about how price is determined, the method used for selling short calls is going to involve two elements not affected by stock valuation: option premium richness (meaning time value) and the amount of time remaining until expiration.

Even though you know in advance how time value is going to change over time, the degree of time value is affected by the stock's volatility. More volatile stocks (higher-risk stocks) will tend to hold higher time value. So you will have greater profit potential due to higher time value in those cases, offset by higher market risk associated with owning the stock.

Options traders should be especially aware of the principles underlying both the random walk and the Dow Theory, since both agree on one key point: that short-term prices cannot be accurately predicted. This idea has ramifications for options traders and, if both theories agree on that point, it probably has merit.

A third idea about market pricing supports the pricing theories expressed in the random walk and the Dow Theory. That is the *efficient market hypothesis*. An efficient market is one in which

random walk

a theory about market pricing, stating that prices of stocks cannot be predicted because price movement is entirely random.

Dow Theory

a theory that market trends are predictable based on changes in market averages.

efficient market hypothesis

a theory stating that current stock prices reflect all information publicly known about a company.

current prices reflect all information known to the public. Thus prices are reasonable based upon perceptions about markets and the companies whose stock is listed publicly. If the efficient market hypothesis is correct, then all current prices are fair and reasonable. Again, this idea has ramifications for all options traders.

Anyone who has observed how the market works understands that the efficient market is a pure theory, because prices are not always applicable. For example, Value Line divides the stocks it studies into five groups, from the highest-rated for safety and timeliness, down to the lowest. The first two tiers beat market averages with consistency, proving that there is value in going through the analysis of prices, price movement, and the range of fundamentals. A reasonable approach is to believe that the market is efficient, but only to a degree. Market observers know that the public tends to overreact to news in the market. Prices rise beyond a reasonable level on good news, and decline beyond a reasonable degree on bad news. So in short-term trading, prices cannot be called efficient by any means. In fact, short-term market price movement is highly chaotic and unpredictable. The often unrealistic pricing swings present momentary opportunities for you, whether operating as a speculator or as an options trader.

Like the other two theories, the efficient market hypothesis points out both danger and opportunity for options traders. Short-term price changes cannot be predicted with any reliability whatsoever, even in the efficient market; however, the characteristics of the underlying stock can be used reliably to select a profitable portfolio. It is fair to surmise that a stock with strong fundamental and technical characteristics is not only a good long-term investment, but also a viable candidate for writing covered calls. The option buyer, on the other hand, undertakes considerable risks, remembering that none of the theories place any reliability on short-term price changes. Option buyers are speculating on the short-term. Their only edge is found in the ability to locate unusual price conditions in a particular stock, and to take advantage of overbought or oversold conditions by picking and timing option purchases wisely.

Smart Investor Tip

All theories agree that short-term price changes provide no useful information. This presents problems for option buyers; for option sellers, the volatility of short-term prices can inflate time value, meaning greater opportunities for profits.

Applying Analysis to Calls—the "Greeks"

Keep the major market theories in mind when you analyze stocks, and remember that exceptionally rich option premium is not a dependable standard for stock selection. Moderate volatility in a stock's price levels may work as a positive sign for options trading, as it demonstrates investor interest. A stock that has little or no volatility is, indeed, not a hot stock and such conditions will invariably be accompanied by very low volume, a consistently low P/E ratio and, of course, lower option premium levels. So some short-term volatility might demonstrate not only that investor interest is high, but also that option activity and pricing will be more promising as well. As a technical test of a stock's price stability, volatility should be analyzed in terms of both short-term and long-term levels. Ideally, your stocks will contain long-term stability but relatively volatile price movement in the short term.

With the distinctions in mind between different causes and patterns of volatility, the selection of stock may be based on a comparative study of the past 12 months. First, ensure that the stocks you are considering as prospects for purchase contain approximately the same causes for their volatility. Then apply volatility as a test for identifying relative degrees of safety.

Greeks

a series of analytical tests of option risk and volatility, so called because they are named for letters of the Greek alphabet.

A series of calculations are used by options analysts to study risk and volatility in options. These are collectively referred to as the *Greeks* because they are named after letters in the Greek alphabet. These calculations are for the most part useful for comparative purposes in options analysis. It is good to know *what* they reveal, but the calculations themselves are beyond the interests of most traders. However, if you subscribe to a service that compares options for you, then it makes perfect sense to know what the Greeks reveal.

beta

a measurement of relative volatility of a stock, made by comparing the degree of price movement to that of a larger index of stock prices.

Fundamental and technical tests are complemented with the use of another feature in a stock's price used to define volatility—that is the stock's *beta*. This is a test of relative volatility, in other words, the degree to which a stock tends to move with an entire market or index of stocks. A beta of 1 tells you that a particular stock tends to rise or fall in the same degree as the market as a whole. A beta of 0 implies that price changes of the stock tend to act independently when compared to price changes in the broader market; and a beta of 2 indicates that a stock's price tends to overreact to market trends, often by moving to a greater degree than the market as a whole.

Because time value tends to be higher than average for high-beta stocks, premium value, like the stock's market value, is less predictable. From the call writer's point of view, exceptionally high time value that declines rapidly is a clear advantage, but it would be shortsighted to trade only in such stocks, especially if you also want stability in your stock portfolio.

delta
the degree of change in option premium in relation to changes in the underlying stock. If the call option's degree of change exceeds the change in the underlying stock, it is called an *up delta*; when the change is less than in the underlying stock, it is called a *down delta*. The reverse terminology is applied to puts.

Another interesting indicator that is helpful in selecting options is called the *delta*. When the price of the underlying stock and the premium value of the option change exactly the same number of points, the delta is 1.00. As delta increases or decreases for an option, you are able to judge the responsiveness (volatility) of the option to the stock. This takes into consideration the distance between current market value of the stock and striking price of the call; fluctuations of time value; and changes in delta as expiration approaches. The delta provides you with the means to compare interaction between stock and option pricing for a particular stock.

The calculation of delta (the delta ratio) is a study of the relationship between the stock's price movement and value of the option. When this relationship does not move as you would expect, it indicates a change in market perception of value, probably resulting from adjustments in proximity between market price and striking price. This change is worth tracking through the delta, since it presents occasional opportunities to profit from unexpected price adjustments. The delta ratio is also called *hedge ratio*.

Delta measures aberrations in time value. If all delta levels were the same, then overall option price movement would be formulated strictly on time and stock price changes. Because this is not the case, we also need to use some means for comparative option volatility, apart from the volatility of the underlying stock. The inclination of a typical option is to behave predictably, tending to approach a delta of 1.00 as it goes in the money and as expiration approaches. So for every point of price movement in the underlying stock, you would

hedge ratio
alternate name for the delta, the measurement of changes in option value relative to changes in stock value.

expect a change in option premium very close to one point when in the money. Time value tends to not be a factor when options are deep in the money. Time value is more likely to change predictably based on time until expiration. For options further away from expiration, notably those close to the striking price, delta is going to be a more important feature. In fact, the comparison of delta between options that are otherwise the same in other attributes will indicate the option-specific risks and volatility not visible in a pure study of the stock itself. Time value can and does change for longer-term options close to the money. The delta can work as a useful device for studying such options. The relative volatility of the option is the key to identifying opportunities.

open interest
the number of open contracts of a particular option at any given time, which can be used to measure market interest.

Accompanying these indicators of relative volatility, you may also follow *open interest*. This is the number of open option contracts on a particular underlying stock. For example, one stock's current-month 40 calls had open interest last month of 22,000 contracts; today, only 500 contracts remain open. The number changes for several reasons. As the status of the call moves higher into the money, the number of open contracts tends to change as the result of closing sale transactions, rolling forward, or exercise. Sellers tend to buy out their positions as time value falls, and buyers tend to close out positions as intrinsic value rises. And as expiration approaches, fewer new contracts open. In addition to these factors, open interest changes when perceptions among buyers and sellers change for the stock. Unfortunately, the number of contracts does not tell you the reasons for the change, nor whether the change is being driven by buyers or by sellers.

Applying the Delta

The delta of a call should be 1.00 whenever it is deep in the money. As a general rule, expect the call to parallel the price movement of the stock on a point-for-point basis, especially when closer to expiration. In some instances, a call's delta may change unexpectedly. For example, if an in-the-money call increases by 3 points but the stock's price rises by only 2 points (a delta of 1.50), the aberration represents an *increase* in time value, which rarely occurs. It may be a sign that the market perceives the option to be worth more than its previous price, relative to movement in the stock. This can be caused by any number of changes in market perception. The deeper out of the money, the lower the delta will be. Figure 6.4 summarizes movement in option premium relative to the underlying stock, with corresponding delta.

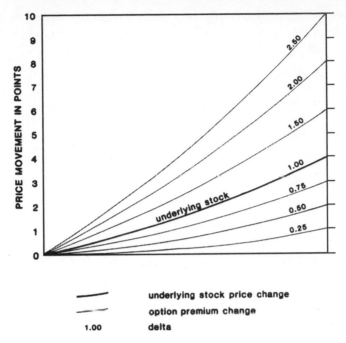

FIGURE 6.4 Changes in an option's delta.

Time value is reasonably predictable in the pattern of change, given looming expiration. It does not move in a *completely* predictable manner, since perceptions about the option are changing constantly.

Example

A Delta Increase: You bought 100 shares of stock at $48 per share. During yesterday's market, the stock rose from $51 to $53, based largely on rumors of higher quarterly profits than predicted by analysts. The 60 call rose from 4 to 8, an increase of 4 points (and a delta of 2.00).

In the preceding example, market overreaction to current news presents a call selling opportunity. Distortions in value often are momentary and require fast action. The covered call writer needs to be able to move quickly when opportunities are presented.

The same strategy can be applied when you already have an open covered call position and you are thinking of closing it. For example, your call is in the money and the stock falls 2 points. At the same time, option premium falls by 3 points, for a delta of 1.50. This could be a temporary distortion, so profits can be taken immediately on the theory that the overreaction will be corrected within a short time.

The Rest of the Greeks

Beta and delta are the most popularly used and cited of the Greeks; but there are more levels of analysis as well. Another is *gamma*, which is a test of how rapidly delta moves upward or downward in relation to the price of the underlying stock.

gamma

a measurement of the speed of change in delta, relative to price movement in the underlying stock.

The gamma changes as the stock's price moves away from the option's strike price. For example, when an option moves from out of the money and goes in the money, the delta tends to increase. How quickly that occurs is where gamma comes into play. You may also consider gamma a method for measuring extrinsic value. In other words, gamma will be at its greatest level when the stock's market value is at or near the option's striking price. When options are deep in the money or deep out of the money, gamma will be close to zero.

For example, if a stock is at $39, a call with a striking price of 50 may have a delta of 0.50 and a gamma of 0.05. When the stock moves up to $40 per share, the delta is going to grow by the same degree as the gamma (0.50 plus 0.05, or 0.55). Because delta can only by 1.00 at the most, this trend is limited and most meaningful when market value of the stock is very close to the option's striking price, which is always the most interesting price relationship where options are involved. Gamma is always expressed as a positive number, whether related to a call or a put; it is only a measurement of delta's trend. The delta will change to the degree of the gamma. In the example of a gamma of 0.05, if the stock moves one point, delta will change by 0.05, or 5 percent of the stock change; so if the stock moved up two points, delta would increase by 0.10 (5 percent of two points), from 0.50 to 0.60. Delta moves by the percentage of the gamma.

You can use delta and gamma in combination to test the relationship between a stock and its options, and to select one company over another because of levels in these price-responsive trends. You will also observe that as expiration nears, the gamma for at-the-money options is going to increase rapidly. It is quite likely that gamma will grow at about trice the price movement of the stock, because the delta is responding to the combined forces of pending expiration and in-the-money or at-the-money price changes. In comparison, out-of-the-money options near expiration are going to have very low gamma trends; and as expiration is closer, the gamma trend confirms the ever-lower expectation that the option will move in the money.

Another interesting Greek is the *tau*, which is also termed *vega* by some analysts. This measures the relationship between an option's price and changes in the underlying stock's volatility. Whether applied to a call or a put, tau is always a positive number.

tau
a measurement of an option's premium value in relation to the underlying stock's changes in volatility.

The less volatile a stock, the cheaper its options. So if and when volatility increases (especially if measured as an expansion of the stock's trading range), option values will rise as well. Defining "volatility" as the percentage of range off a stock's 52-week low, you can quantify vega in the same manner, on a percentage basis. This becomes very interesting because it assigns a percentage value to an option's premium; and it also places a numerical value on a stock's market risk. This is useful for comparisons between stocks and their options.

vega
a name sometimes applied to the calculation of tau.

On average, stocks are expected to show around 15 percent volatility. For example, if a stock has traded between $20 and $23 per share, the three-point spread represents 15 percent volatility ($3 \div 20 = 15$ percent); as a stock's value changes, vega tracks that change.

Another Greek, *theta*, reveals the strength or weakness of time value (exclusive of extrinsic value), also known as *sensitivity* of the price in relation to the time remaining until expiration. Many options traders consider theta the most important of the Greeks because time sensitivity defines value, notably near expiration.

theta
a measurement of an option's value based on time until expiration.

Theta is valuable as a comparative study between two or more options (and their underlying stocks). Based on a stock's specific volatility, time decay may be quite rapid or fairly slow; and identifying the degree of theta characteristic of a particular stock is a valuable analytical exercise.

The Greek *rho* is also a sensitivity measurement, but is far less directly involved in valuation than most other Greeks. Rho compares pricing of options to trends in interest rates, based on the theory that the higher market interest rates trend, the higher call pricing. This Greek is less useful than

sensitivity
the degree of change in an option's value based solely on the time remaining until expiration.

most others, however, because it is not easy to translate long-term trends such as interest rates, into action steps for fast-moving markets such as options. The general observation of rho is an oddity: As interest rates rise, call prices will follow, but put prices will tend to fall. In this regard, rho becomes an expression of market sentiments based on interest rates, with the results seen in option prices.

rho

a calculation of the effect of interest rate trends on option valuation; a long-term analytical tool rather than one of immediate value.

The Greeks are collectively an interesting series of observations concerning option trends and tendencies. All options traders are aware of changes in valuation based on the proximity issues: between striking price of options and market value of the underlying stock, and between today and expiration. The Greeks are useful for tracking the changes in all three forms of value (intrinsic, extrinsic, and time) but are also best used to make comparisons in option valuation between two different companies. Time, volatility, and chance all play roles in valuation; the Greeks are useful in observing how prices and values react to ever-changing market conditions.

Acting on Good Information

All market analysts depend on their best estimates in making decisions. You cannot time your decisions perfectly or consistently; so you have to depend on a combination of fundamental and technical indicators to provide yourself with an edge. That means you improve your percentages, but not that you will be right every time. Base your strategy on the thorough analysis and well-thought-out selection of stocks. Pick stocks on their fundamental merits as long-term investments and not merely to provide coverage for short option positions. Also keep in mind your long-term reasons for buying the stock; keep the stock in your portfolio as long as the company's attributes remain strong. Avoid making stock-related decisions as a response to option-specific conditions. Don't take advantage of the chance to earn a short-term profit if exercise of a covered call would contradict your long-term goals.

Example

Broker or More Broke: You bought 300 shares of stock last year as a long-term investment. You have no plans to sell and, as you hoped, the market price has been inching upward consistently. Your broker is encouraging you to write calls against your shares, pointing to the potential for additional profits as well as downside protection. Your broker also observes that if exercised, you will still earn a profit. However, remembering your reasons for buying the stock, you reject the advice. Call writing is contrary to your goal in buying the stock.

Even when writing covered calls is an appropriate strategy, never overlook the need for continued monitoring of the stock. By preparing a price performance chart like the one shown in Figure 6.5, you can track movement by week. A completed chart helps you to time decisions, especially for writing covered calls. If you have access to the Internet, you can also use free sites to produce price and volume charts. Three of the many sites that provide this free benefit were listed earlier in this chapter.

Track both the option and the underlying stock. If profits in one are offset by losses in the other, there is no point to a strategy except when you hedge a loss with the use of an option for insurance. By observing changes in the option and the stock, you will be able to spot opportunities and dangers as they emerge.

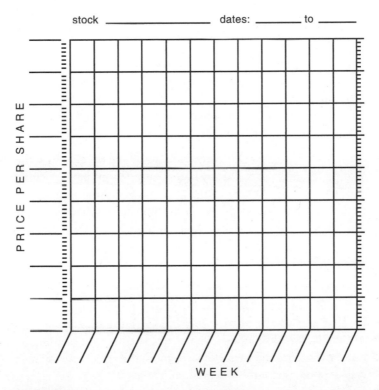

FIGURE 6.5 Stock performance chart.

Example

Programmed Portfolio Losses: You bought 100 shares in each of four companies last year. Within the following months, you wrote covered calls in all four. Today, three of the four have market values below your basis, even though the overall market is higher. You add up the total of call premium, dividends, and paper capital gains and losses, and realize that if you were to close out all of your positions today, you would lose money.

This example demonstrates that stocks were poorly chosen or purchases were poorly timed. While paper losses might have been greater had you not written calls, this situation also raises questions about why a particular mix of stocks was selected. A critical review of your selection criteria might reveal that you are picking stocks based on option premium value rather than on the stock's fundamental and technical indicators. Relatively safe stocks tend to have little options appeal, because time value is minimal in low-volatility stocks. So more volatile stocks are far more likely candidates for premium action. That does not mean they are worthwhile investments; it could mean that option profits will be offset by capital losses in your portfolio.

Perhaps the greatest risk in call writing is the tendency to buy stocks that are overly volatile because they also have higher time value premium in their options. You will do better if you look for moderate volatility as a secondary strategy. Three suggestions worth remembering:

1. *Select stocks with good growth potential* and hold them for a while without writing options. Give the stocks a chance to appreciate. This gives you much more flexibility in picking options. The combination of premium, dividends, and capital gains can be built into your strategy with ease, assuming that current market value is higher than your original cost per share.

2. *Time your decision to sell calls* on stock you already own, to maximize your potential for gains from the options.

3. *Remember the importance of patience.* You might need to wait out a market that seems to be moving too slowly. Your patience will be rewarded if you select stocks properly. Opportunity does come around eventually, but some novice call writers give in to their impatience, anxious to write calls as soon as possible. This is a mistake.

Putting Your Rules Down on Paper

Setting goals helps you to succeed in the options market. This is equally true if you buy stocks and do not write options. By defining your personal rules, you will have a better chance for success. Define several aspects of your investment plan, including:

- Long-term goals for your entire portfolio.
- Strategies you believe will help you reach those goals.
- Percentages of your portfolio that are to be placed in each type of investment.
- Definitions of risk in its many forms, and the degree of risk you are willing to assume.
- Purchase and sale levels you are willing and able to commit.
- Guidelines for review and possible modification of your goals.

Writing down your rules leads to success because it focuses your efforts. Guidelines can and should be modified as conditions change. Having self-imposed rules to follow provides you with a programmed response to evolving situations, and improves your performance and profits.

The next chapter explains how you need to change investing strategies in volatile markets.

Chapter

7

Strategies in Volatile Markets: Uncertainty as an Advantage

The market doesn't reward qualities that are not scarce.
—Mark A. Johnson, *The Random Walk and Beyond*, 1988

Volatility—the feature that stockholders are most concerned with—may serve as a big advantage to options traders. Stockholders like steadily rising markets because that makes profits. If you are like so many first-time investors, you probably began your investment program during bull markets; unfortunately, markets are cyclical and those uptrends can and do turn suddenly.

If you are a more experienced investor, you understand that success has to be defined in terms other than the absolute of winning or losing. You know that being right more often than wrong defines investing success. You also know how to diversify and limit risk even in a rising market, and you understand the old wisdom that stocks climb a wall of worry.

Smart Investor Tip

Success in the market may be defined as being right more often than being wrong. Expecting loss is realistic; if a loss takes you by surprise, then you need to take a second look at your expectations.

Hindsight always clarifies observations of upward and downward trends. When we look back, the signals appear obvious, as though they could have been anticipated easily. However, it is far more difficult to identify the type of market we are experiencing at this moment, and what is going to happen next. At any given time, some observers think the market is rising, others think it is falling, and a third group adopts a wait-and-see approach. Each of these groups can cite plenty of market data to support their points of view, but they cannot all be right. Your dilemma in this environment of uncertainty is finding a way to build your portfolio of stocks while also minimizing your risk of catastrophic losses. You want to take advantage of emerging rises in the price of stocks and, at the same time, limit your risk exposure. You may be tempted to flee the market in times of uncertainty, understandably. But fleeing is not the only prudent decision. You can also employ options in volatile markets to take advantage of that volatility, and to improve profits while protecting yourself against unexpected losses.

Avoiding 10 Common Mistakes

As a starting point in defining your market strategy, examine the basic assumptions that go into how and why you have made past decisions. How do you pick a company? Do you study its fundamentals, follow price chart patterns, or buy stocks on the basis of name recognition?

Some common errors characterize the way that some investment decisions are made. These include the following 10 mistakes:

insider information
any information about a company not known to the general public, but known only to people working in the company, or with nonpublic knowledge about matters that will affect a stock's price.

1. *Failing to follow your own rules.* So many people define themselves as believers in the fundamentals, and then contradict their own standards. Instead of monitoring trends in the important areas of statements, they find themselves tracking stock charts or making decisions based on index movements.

The market is full of temptations, promises of easy money, and artificial excitement. But it is also a dangerous place. With the benefit of history, it is easy for you to recognize the real situation at any given time. However, in the heat of the moment, many investors give way to an emotional response to information. If you hear a stock is about to "take off," the human tendency is to want to buy some before that happens. A logical, rational approach would tell you otherwise. If the person giving you this tip does actually have *insider information*, it is illegal to pass that information on to others—and it is illegal for others to act on the information. If the person does not have insider information, then it could be only a rumor, in which case you should not act on the information. It could also be a *pump-and-dump* move. This occurs when someone owns a stock whose price has fallen. They want to get the price up so they can sell their shares at a profit, so they promote (pump) the company, get others to buy, and then they sell (dump) inflated shares.

pump and dump
action by an individual holding shares of a company. It involves spreading false rumors in order to get people to buy shares and increase the price of stock, and then selling shares at a profit.

2. *Forgetting your risk tolerance limits.* More than anything else, continually examine and reexamine your limitations. *Risk tolerance* means just that: the amount of risk you can afford to take and are willing to take. If you cannot afford to lose, then you should not expose yourself to a high risk of loss.

Identifying risk tolerance levels should be thought of as the first step in beginning an investment program. When someone buys their first house, they identify how expensive a home they can afford, the level of down payment required, market trends, and other important factors. This is all part of risk tolerance. However, the same people may enter the market with little or no thought to the level of risk. Unfortunately, this approach has consequences. If you cannot afford to lose money, you need to question whether a particular strategy is appropriate. This applies not only to trading in options, but to every market and strategy. Knowing your risk tolerance is essential.

risk tolerance
the amount of risk that an investor is able and willing to take.

3. *Trying to make up for past losses with aggressive market decisions.* Losses can happen very suddenly, or they can accumulate over time, eroding your portfolio value. In either case, losses represent ill-timed decisions. Avoid the tendency to try to make up for big losses by taking unacceptable risks.

The reason it is so important to identify your risk tolerance is to avoid making big mistakes when your decisions don't go the way you planned. Many investors try to offset unexpected losses by taking ever-higher risks in the hope of getting their losses back. When those investor begin this practice, they cease being investors and become gamblers. And most gamblers lose. It makes more sense to accept losses as part of the outcome within your portfolio, learn from those losses, and take steps to decrease losses in the future. Those steps can include better stock selection, protective measures (including the use of options, for example), and diversification.

4. *Investing on the basis of rumor or questionable advice.* The Internet chat room is not a good place to get market information. Unsolicited phone calls, pop-up advertisements, or mail solicitations for investment solutions, promising fast and easy profits, are not going to make anyone rich. Advice from friends, relatives, coworkers, or people you talk to on the bus or train, should be discarded.

mutual funds
investment programs in which money from a large pool of investors is placed under professional management. For a fee, management invests in stocks and bonds. Mutual funds may be set up to pay a sales load to salespeople, often called *financial advisers*; or they may be no-load, meaning investors can buy shares directly and not pay commissions.

If you are intent on getting advice from someone else, think carefully before you pay for that advice. The history of analytical services offered by the big brokerage firms has been quite poor. Not only have these firms given historically poor advice; it would often have been more profitable to do the exact opposite. The big firms have also been fined millions of dollars for knowingly giving poor advice to clients. With today's Internet-based market, a lot of free advice is available from many different places. You can also act based on advice from friends, relatives or co-workers. But the truth is, no one is going to give you free *good* advice. Making smart investment decisions invariably requires that you perform your own research, apply your own standards based on clearly identified risk standards, and do your homework directly.

5. *Trusting the wrong people with your money.* As a group, analysts' advice has led to net losses for their clients. The problem is not limited to analysts' conflicts of interest. As a group, analysts tend to pick earnings and price targets rather than try to find solid fundamental strength in companies. This makes analysts a poor source for market information; you are better off on your own.

If you do intend to hire someone to advise you, make sure they base their investment advice on sound fundamentals. If you check, you will discover that the majority of financial advisers and analysts know little or nothing about accounting standards and rules and do not base decisions on tried-and-true fundamental principles. It is more likely that a financial adviser will try to steer you into *mutual funds* rather than stocks because funds pay more than 8 percent commission to salespeople; and of course, investors pay this through a *sales load*. For example, if commission is 8.25 percent, that means that out of every $100 you invest, only $91.75 goes into the investment; the rest goes to the salesperson (financial adviser). You do not need to pay commissions to find sound investments; and by definition, anyone buying stocks and trading options should be making their own decisions and not relying on expensive advice.

6. *Adopting beliefs that simply are not true about the markets.* The market thrives on beliefs that, although strongly held, are simply not true. Widespread beliefs are difficult to overcome, but it is wise to question convention, especially when you see time and again that those beliefs are invariably misleading.

sales load
a commission charged when a financial adviser places a client's capital into a load mutual fund.

For example, many investors insist on believing that there are secret, magic formulas that guarantee success in the stock market. Even though the facts clearly dispute this belief, thousands of people send away money every year to learn these "insider secrets" to market wealth. You will never meet anyone who has become rich in the market by following any formula that they paid to find out about.

7. *Becoming inflexible even when conditions have changed.* You may find a method that works for you, so you stick with it, even when conditions have changed and the strategies are no longer working. You need to maintain your flexibility, because markets are in a continual state of change.

The market is constantly evolving and changing. Very little remains true for long, so even today's favorite stock or market sector could easily be out of favor next month. You only need to look back over history to realize how easily an industry can become obsolete. Before 1900, auto and airline stocks did not exist, and before 2000, digital cameras were not widely known, so companies such as Polaroid and Kodak dominated the film markets. A review of the fundamentals for any company out of favor today reveals falling stock prices, lower profits, and a relentless decline in all of the fundamental indicators. There are good lessons to be learned from history, and the market reflects change as a constant element.

8. *Taking profits at the wrong time.* The temptation to take profits when available is a strong one. However, the timing of profit taking should depend more on your overall strategy than on a momentary opportunity. If you always take profits when available, you will end up with a portfolio full of stocks whose current market value is lower than your original cost.

Using options as a secondary strategy in your stock portfolio enables you to take profits without needing to sell stock. This can be accomplished in several ways. For example, when stock values climb high, you can sell covered calls or buy puts. If and when market values fall back to previous levels, the short call or long put positions can be closed at a profit—but you continue to hold your long-term stock. When stock values fall, you can also take advantage of the temporary panic, by buying calls (you can also sell puts in this situation, a topic covered in the next chapter). When the stock price rises back to previous levels, the option positions can be closed at a profit.

9. *Selling low and buying high.* The advice to buy low and sell high is easily given but harder to follow. It is all too easy to make investment decisions on the basis of panic (at the bottom) or greed (at the top). A worthwhile piece of market wisdom states that bulls and bears are often overruled by pigs and chickens.

contrarian
an investor who recognizes the tendency for the majority to be wrong more often than right, who invests opposite popular opinion.

It is not easy to resist the emotions of greed and panic; but you need to think long term when you invest in stock. If you select companies based on sound criteria, you do not need to be concerned about short-term price movement, not to mention rumor and speculation about what will happen tomorrow. Options can also be useful in overcoming the paradoxical temptation of long-term investors, which is to act like short-term speculators and against their own best interests. Options are excellent instruments for hedging other positions, riding short-term price movement, and taking profits, all without having to sell stock before you really want to (on the upside) or because prices fall temporarily (on the downside).

10. *Following the trend instead of thinking independently.* Crowd mentality is most likely to be wrong. Crowds don't think; they react. So mistakes are likely to occur when you follow the crowd instead of thinking for yourself.

Successful investors learn to think for themselves and to avoid crowd thinking. This means not only resisting the temptation to follow the majority, but also to recognize that the majority is usually wrong. This *contrarian* approach to investing has proven to be successful historically because crowd mentality is a misguided way to think.

Modifying Your Risk Tolerance

Recognizing common mistakes in approaches to investing is a good starting point in determining how *not* to approach stock and options investing. All of the mistakes involve perceptions or misperceptions about the markets, but they all share a common element: a perception about risk. If you can identify risk levels to a particular strategy and quickly decide whether they are good matches for your own risk tolerance, you will be far ahead of most other investors and traders. Risk exposure is the central determining test for every investing strategy you will consider.

Your ability and willingness to be exposed to risk is a matter of degree. Risk tolerance is defined by capital resources and income, investing experience, family status, condition of the market, and your personal attitude. It is everchanging because as your own circumstances evolve, all of these areas evolve as well.

Smart Investor Tip
Risk tolerance is an everchanging matter, reflecting your attitude, experience, knowledge, and resources at the moment. It will be different next year and the year after, so you need to review risk tolerance constantly.

Capital resources and income define your ability to undertake certain risks. If you have a large amount of capital to invest, you will be able to consider a wider array of possible investments than if your assets are more limited. Of course, that also means that you will likely be unaware of the risks associated with some decisions. Having a large amount of capital available might contain risk of its own in that regard; so if you inherit a large sum of money, sell your house, or take other actions that bring you a large nest egg to invest, you need to still pay attention to risk. The same arguments apply to income levels. An individual with a comfortable level of income will be more inclined to diversify in terms of investment products *and* risks. As a strategy, it makes sense to vary the risk levels of your portfolio as long as it is part of a plan. The danger arises when risks come about unexpectedly.

Investing experience has a lot to do with the risks you take on and how you evolve as an investor. As you become familiar with options, for example, you will be willing to try advanced strategies, use options in different ways within your portfolio, and diversify risks with option positions. Experience has another side: Those who have lost money in the market learn about risk the expensive way. Many people walk away from the market permanently, which is a risk decision. They conclude that the market is simply not a safe investing environment. In fact, it can be, if you learn how to mitigate specific risks.

Family status has a lot to do with the types of investments you choose. If you are a young single person making good money, you will be inclined to take greater risks; if you are married, buying a home, and raising young children, you will by necessity think about security, college education expenses, and retirement savings. Major events, like marriage, birth of a child, divorce, losing a job or starting a new career, relocating, health problems, or the death of a loved one, will understandably have a major impact on how you invest, because such events change your risk tolerance profile.

Condition of the market will also change your risk tolerance. When the market is going through a broad-based bull period, it is easy to feel confident about investing. As a result, there is a tendency to lower your observation. In these conditions, it makes sense to buy and hold securities as long as the good times last; but at the same time, be aware of risks. Markets can turn around quickly.

> ### Smart Investor Tip
>
> Even recognizing the fact that markets change continually, it is easy to make the mistake of fixing your definition of risk and never changing. As a consequence, your profile can become outdated.

Personal attitude will have more to do than anything else with your definition of risk tolerance. If you consider yourself ultraconservative, you will prefer to leave the majority of your portfolio in low-yielding, insured money market accounts. Others can tolerate high risk and seek the best possible returns and will speculate in long-shot investments. Most people are somewhere in between.

The Nature of Market Volatility

Risk comes in many forms and, as a result, your definition of risk tolerance has to take the different forms of risk into account. A study of price volatility is a good place to start. Volatility can and should be applied to individual issues. This does not mean that overall volatility trends should be ignored; however, because listed options are specific to a single stock, the study of volatility can be used to measure risk, to identify market conditions, and to find option opportunities.

Market volatility follows cyclical patterns just as prices do. When prices for specific stocks, sectors, or the overall market rise rapidly, we usually also see increases in the volume of shares traded. A short-term rally is characterized by a corresponding short-term volatility, meaning prices can change in both high and low directions within a single day or week. A longer-term rally—lasting several weeks, for example—will tend to be broader based. Market volatility will slow down as the rally begins to lose its momentum, which is one way to identify the top of the market—not always, but often.

Being aware of the patterns and tendencies of market volatility does not necessarily provide you with a key to the timing of option decisions. In fact, in the most volatile of markets, it is the uncertainty of the timing of events that makes the market the most interesting, and the most dangerous.

Smart Investor Tip

Volatility introduces both risk and opportunity. The very uncertainty associated with big price swings provides options traders with the best environment for profits—if properly understood.

Volatility is an expression of conflicting investor interests converging at the same moment. A high demand or a high supply resulting from greater than usual volume has an immediate effect on stock share prices and on option premium levels. When time value is distorted during high volume periods, it creates a momentary advantage for options traders. Distortions occur most often during highly volatile periods for a specific stock, but the offsetting market reaction tends to correct the condition within the same trading day. So to take advantage of time value price distortions, you will need to track the market throughout the day.

Smart Investor Tip

Options traders who plan to take advantage of short-term price aberrations have to be prepared to track prices closely, and to act quickly.

Market Volatility Risk

Understanding the nature of volatility is essential. When you use options to accompany open stock positions, you eventually realize that volatility is going to affect your equity position, and is not just a short-term profit opportunity in options. The risk feature of volatility is going to determine the safety of your portfolio.

This danger—market volatility risk—is especially important if you write covered calls. Selecting stocks for long-term growth as the primary means for finding investment candidates is a fundamental strategy. However, picking stocks primarily based on the richness of option premium levels is a shortsighted strategy that may lead to losses. There is no sense in exchanging short-term option profits for losses in stock value. Richer option premiums are associated with more volatile stocks. The higher premium levels exist because the stock itself is higher risk.

This is a trap for options traders. When you think about buying stock without considering the related options, you will tend to look at financial information, long-term competitive stance, the sector, management, dividend yield, and price history, among other indicators. However, when you are looking for covered call writing opportunities, it is tempting to buy 100 shares and sell an option at the same time, using the discounting effect (return from the option) as your primary consideration. If you ignore other risk elements of the stock, you invite greater risk. The more volatile stock is, the more likely it will be to lose market value in a market decline.

Smart Investor Tip

Beware the tempting rates of return available from buying stock and selling covered calls at the same time. Don't overlook the importance of analyzing the stock as a starting point, not as a subordinate point to the option's value.

The question should be, does the option discount the share price adequately to justify the higher risk? If the option profit only serves to equalize the market risk of the stock, are there more sensible alternatives? It makes more sense to purchase the stock of less volatile companies and wait out price movement, and then sell covered calls with striking prices well above your purchase price, ensuring higher profits even in the event of exercise. While this strategy is more conservative and requires time to build profits, it also avoids the problems of market volatility. Because the federal tax rules affecting capital gains also affect aftertax profits, it makes more sense to sell out-of-the-money calls than in-the-money calls, or to accept short-term gains in exchange for higher premium income.

fundamental volatility

the tendency for a company's sales and profits to change from one period to the next, with more erratic change representing higher volatility.

The comparative analysis of market volatility emphasizes a stock's share price and trading range, which are technical indicators. An equally important form of volatility involves a study of trends in the financial results of the company. An analysis of *fundamental volatility* is a valuable method for picking stocks wisely.

Investors like predictability. You may take comfort when a company's sales increase gradually and predictably from one year to the next, and when profits remain within an expected and predictable range. This preference has led to pressure on companies to equalize earnings through accounting decisions. You will also take comfort in the low volatility of financial reports, even when this results from creative accounting treatment of a less certain reality. You may feel safe with predictable outcomes, when fundamental volatility is low.

In the real world, however, sales and profits do not materialize consistently and steadily. Actual outcome is far more chaotic. How do companies even out their results, and isn't that fraud? The Generally Accepted Accounting Principles (*GAAP*) rules give corporations a lot of flexibility to interpret and report their numbers.

The GAAP guidelines exist in no one place, but consist of a series of published opinions, guidelines, and regulations developed by many groups, with the American Institute of Certified Public Accountants (AICPA) serving as central authority for GAAP standards. The Financial Accounting Standards Board (FASB) develops new guidelines and also serves as a clearinghouse for rules within the auditing profession.

Smart Investor Tip
Check the AICPA and FASB web sites to learn more about these organizations and the role they play in developing GAAP standards: www.aicpa.org and www.fasb.org.

GAAP rules are broad enough that corporations can bank earnings one year and recognize them in the next, so that the results are less volatile. This is called *cookie jar accounting* and, as long as the justification appears to make sense, it is allowed under GAAP. In fact, because earnings are being deferred, the bending of the rules is far more acceptable than the opposite—booking nonexistent revenues and hoping to absorb them in better sales periods of the future.

In the typical cookie jar entry, some of this year's revenues, along with corresponding costs, are deferred and set up in a liability account. These are not true liabilities, just credit-balance accounts. So the *deferred credit* is reversed the following year and recognized as income. This is only one of many techniques used to reduce fundamental volatility. The existence of a deferred credit does not necessarily mean manipulation has taken place. In some

GAAP
acronym for Generally Accepted Accounting Principles, the rules by which auditing firms analyze operations, and by which corporations report their financial results.

cookie jar accounting
the practice of banking revenue or earnings in exceptionally high-volume years and booking them in later periods, to even out results consistently and to reduce fundamental volatility.

deferred credit
an account listed under the liabilities section of a balance sheet, representing income to be recognized in future years.

instances, revenue is received in advance of being earned and it is appropriate to defer it; but the account is also used at times to control reported revenues and earnings.

Inflating current results to improve an otherwise dismal operating result requires a different type of manipulation. For example, current-year expenses may be capitalized and then amortized over several years, increasing the current year's profits. Depreciation can be spread out over a longer period than normal by making an election under Internal Revenue Code rules. Or reserves set up during acquisitions can be reversed to inflate current profits.

All of these types of entries *might* be allowed under GAAP; but whether accountants can justify questionable interpretations or not, the fact remains that these practices are deceptive. They give you a distorted and inaccurate picture of operations. If you make investment decisions based on inaccurate or unreliable information, you are being deceived. And to the extent that stock prices are distorted by misleading accounting decisions, option values are distorted as well.

Full disclosure and application of a universal reporting standard would be desirable. Full disclosure might also mean higher fundamental volatility. While this might be unsettling, it is always better to see an accurate result than to settle for the short-term comfort you gain from low fundamental volatility. Remember, higher volatility could have a positive effect on premium levels.

Smart Investor Tip

More accurate, consistent reporting probably would also mean greater fundamental volatility. Ironically, the more honest financial statements could reflect higher than average year-to-year volatility; this could require the market to change widely held opinions about the nature of volatility and risk.

Options in the Volatile Environment

The more uncertain a trading environment, the greater your concern for the safety of your capital. When prices are very low, you may be fearful about placing capital at risk, especially if you have already lost money in the market. At the same time, such moments are buying opportunities.

If you have cash to invest but you are concerned about market volatility, limited speculation could be a wise strategy. While buying calls is highly speculative due to the unavoidable expiration factor, the decision can work as an alternative strategy. Instead of putting all of your capital at risk in purchasing shares, you can buy calls as a method for controlling stock. If and when those shares climb in value, the calls can be exercised and you can purchase shares at the fixed striking price. But if stock prices decline, you are not obligated to exercise and you will lose only the money invested in call premium.

Considering that time works against the buyer, is it wise to buy calls as an alternative to simply buying stock? It can be. Using LEAPS calls with long-term life spans can make a lot of sense in volatile markets. Because LEAPS options last up to 36 months, they are more interesting than shorter-term listed options. In the market, 36 months is a very long time. If you select stocks that you believe have a better than average chance to appreciate in value, going long on LEAPS calls could be a profitable form of speculation.

When you buy long-term LEAPS calls, you will have to expect to pay extra premium for more time value. So LEAPS calls are going to be far more expensive than shorter-term calls; but with the time element in mind, the longer-term speculation can work to your advantage. There are ways to reduce the cost of long-term LEAPS positions as well. In Chapter 9, advanced strategies employing LEAPS calls are explained in detail. For example, you can purchase a call and then sell earlier-expiring calls with higher striking prices. This strategy reduces the cost of the long call. It is a relatively safe strategy, because the long position covers the short. Because you will have up to 36 months before the long LEAPS call expires, you can sell a series of short calls and allow them to expire during the holding period.

Another possible strategy for those who already own shares and want to acquire more is to sell a covered call and an uncovered put at the same time. (Selling puts is discussed in Chapter 9.) Using LEAPS options, this can create a substantial rate of return. So there are numerous LEAPS strategies, both long and short, that provide you with alternatives to the popular stock-specific strategies: dollar cost averaging, hold-and-wait strategies, profit taking, or simply getting out of the market. The use of options, especially longer-term LEAPS options, allows you to remain in the market and to create new opportunities with minimum risk.

The problem of investing more capital in a down market is well known. Typically, when prices are down, there are numerous buying opportunities available; but it is also common for people to hesitate, fearing further declines. In this condition, it requires a cool head and calm nerves to go against the crowd mentality of the market, and to recognize the opportunity. Using LEAPS options, you can take advantage of depressed prices, without risking capital in long positions.

Example

Solving the Capital Problem: You have approximately $10,000 to invest. You have been following five stocks that you believe will increase in value over the next two to three years; but you cannot buy 100 shares of all of these with your limited capital. And because the market has been very volatile lately, you are not even sure that the timing is right for committing money right now. You don't want to miss an opportunity, and you remain uncertain about short-term volatility.

In the circumstances just described, there are three problems: (1) limited capital, (2) uncertainty about short-term price volatility, and (3) the desire to profit from longer-term change. Everyone faces these conditions from time to time, and many face them continually. LEAPS options address all three concerns. With a $10,000 capital base as described, it is possible to buy calls for all five of the stocks. As long as options are picked out of the money, the premium cost will be lower than it would be for an in-the-money option on the same 100 shares. This diversifies the $10,000 capital into five different 100-share lots; but because these are options and not shares, the risk of loss is limited. The entire $10,000 could be lost if none of the stocks rises in value. But if they are selected well, that is a remote possibility at best. Three years is a very long time and in the cyclical market, today's depressed conditions are likely to reverse and price will advance.

Smart Investor Tip

The LEAPS option removes the most inhibiting factor of the options market, the short-term nature of contracts and ever-looming expiration. A three-year lifespan is an eternity in the stock market.

Is it prudent to buy calls, given the risks of long positions as a general rule? It could make more sense than buying shorter-expiring standardized calls, which will expire in a few months. Remembers, a LEAPS contract has a life up to three years, and a lot can happen in that time. If you believe that stocks will rise in value during those months, then buying long-term options represents a smart strategic choice. If the market value does not rise, you lose the option premium. However, since you will be spreading a limited amount of capital among options on several different stocks, you stand a good chance of profiting overall as long as the market direction is upward during the lifetime of the LEAPS.

There are three possible outcomes in this strategy:

1. The LEAPS expires worthless. If the stock fails to rise above the LEAPS striking price, the strategy produces a loss.

2. The LEAPS increases in value and you close it at a profit. You might decide later on that you would rather take the option profit when available, and give up the opportunity to buy shares later.

3. The stock value rises and you exercise the LEAPS option, purchasing shares at the fixed striking price. This is the strategy to aim for; LEAPS are used to own the right to buy 100 shares at a fixed price, with the idea that you will want to make the purchase as long as fundamental conditions do not change.

LEAPS can be used in all of the ways that short-term options can be used. LEAPS calls can be bought to insure against losses in short stock positions; and LEAPS puts can be used to insure against losses in long stock positions. You can also sell LEAPS, either naked or covered. The covered call strategy will produce far higher premium income because of higher time value. In exchange, you will also be required to keep your stock tied up to cover the short option for a longer period of time. The typical time value pattern for LEAPS is that it remains fairly stable and then rapidly falls off during the last four to six months. Thus covered call writing on very long-term periods should be analyzed and compared with shorter-term alternatives. When comparing likely rates of return, remember to annualize the outcomes to make them comparable; a 10 percent return on a one-year covered call is twice as profitable as a 15 percent return on a three-year covered call.

Smart Investor Tip

The risk-reward question for LEAPS covered call writers has to be analyzed carefully. The question of time is one aspect only, and the other aspect—exposure to exercise—is much longer-term than for standard short-term options.

The potential uses of LEAPS beyond expected purchase (or sale) of shares in the future can become quite interesting. When you combine the longer expiration of LEAPS options with the features of shorter-term expirations, some of the typical trading techniques become more advantageous, especially on the short side. Remember, time works for the seller and against the buyer. As a seller of a LEAPS option, you are going to have more time value to work with, and a longer time until expiration. As a buyer of a LEAPS option, you still work against time; but because expiration is so far away, the potential for profit—or at least the uncertainty of what will happen—makes buying options far more feasible.

The same arguments favoring buying calls in anticipation of an upward-moving market apply just as well when you expect market values to fall. You can buy LEAPS puts when you have seen a big run-up in value and you anticipate a reversal. This strategy makes sense whether you own stock or not.

When you own shares and the market value has risen substantially, you face a dilemma. Do you take your profits now, while you can, and risk missing out on even more appreciation? Or do you wait, risking losses when prices fall? You may continue to think of the company as a sound long-term investment, so you don't want to sell; but you are worried about short-term corrections to market price. If you buy a LEAPS put in this situation, the downward price movement in the stock will be matched point-for-point by increasing value in the in-the-money LEAPS put. You also discount your basis by selling calls with rich time value premium, an alternative to profit taking that allows you to continue owning shares.

American-style option an option that can be exercised at any time before expiration. All equity options and some index options are American-style.

When you don't own shares and market value has run up, buying a put is a speculative move. You anticipate a correction; when prices fall, you will experience a corresponding increase in value of the LEAPS put. Without taking a short position or selling uncovered calls—both high-risk strategies—you can profit if you are right when stock market prices fall, by owning the put. And because expiration is further out, you have as much as three years to be proven right.

When you want to buy more shares and you believe the price is too high today, selling puts may work well for you. The premium you receive lowers your basis and risk, and as long as you consider the striking price a good price for shares, exercise would not be devastating. If share prices continue to rise, you keep the premium from selling the put. This strategy mitigates the dilemma for every stock investor: If you buy more shares today and prices then fall, you have a paper loss position. If you don't buy more shares and the stock's price rises, you miss the opportunity. Look at short puts as a possible solution to this dilemma.

Smart Investor Tip

Using LEAPS to time market swings or insure other positions is more practical than with short-term options. The longer time until expiration provides better value, enabling you to protect paper profits more economically.

The advantage of longer expiration overcomes the option buyer's ongoing struggle with time, at least to a degree. In long positions, you will pay more for time value but you have more time. In a volatile market, your chances of profiting with LEAPS calls and puts are greater because expiration is not immediate.

In addition to trading in LEAPS on individual stocks, you can also buy or sell index LEAPS. These are somewhat more complex because the relationship between striking price and index value is not the same as for individual stocks. In addition, index LEAPS may be set up in one of three ways. An *American-style option* can be exercised at any time prior to expiration. All short-term options and LEAPS in stocks are exercised as American-style options. However, some index options are *European-style options*, which means that exercise is allowed only during a shorter period of time immediately before expiration. A third variation is the *capped-style option*. This gives the owner the right to exercise, but only during a specific time period before expiration. If the option reaches its cap value before expiration, it is exercised automatically.

The next chapter explains an often overlooked but powerful strategy: selling puts. This strategy is often overlooked because puts cannot be covered in the same way as calls. However, upon analysis, it becomes evident that exposure to short put risk is not the same as that for short calls; in fact, the short put offers great potential for short-term profits with *acceptable* levels of risk.

European-style option

an option that can be exercised only during a specified period of time immediately preceding expiration. Some index options are European-style.

capped-style option

an option that can be exercised only during a specified period of time; if the option's value reaches the cap level prior to expiration, it is exercised automatically.

Chapter

Selling Puts:
The Overlooked Strategy

The place where optimism most flourishes is the lunatic asylum.
—Havelock Ellis, *The Dance of Life*, 1923

Selling puts is an optimistic strategy. You will profit if and when the stock's market value rises; even so, it is easy to forget this because so much emphasis is placed on calls. The incredible feature of options trading is that strategies can be devised to suit any type of market and any level of risk. Evaluate puts for their potential, and compare short put risks to the risk of long calls. Their profile is identical; the risks are far different.

Comparing short puts to long calls is only one of the comparisons worth making. You may be well aware of the special risks involved in selling calls, and may consider short puts to fit into the same risk category; this is a mistake. When you sell uncovered calls, a number of things can occur: The underlying stock could rise indefinitely, so that, in theory, risk is unlimited. Even when you write covered calls, you still face the risk of lost future profits because striking prices lock in the option seller to a fixed price in the event of exercise.

The situation is completely different when you sell puts. The put is the opposite of a call, so as a put seller, you hope that the value of the underlying stock will rise. As the stock rises, the value of the put falls, creating a profit. You also face the risk that the stock's market value will fall. In that case, you experience a loss; however, this loss is finite. The greatest loss possible, in theory, is zero, but a stock is unlikely to fall that far. A well-selected company's stock will have a limited likely range of market price; for example, while market value could fall below a company's tangible book value per share, it does not stand to reason that market price would decline far below that level.

Smart Investor Tip

Selling calls cannot be compared to selling covered calls. Short puts are always uncovered. However, risk is quite limited compared to uncovered calls, because stock can decline only so far.

---

tangible book value per share
the net value of a company, computed by subtracting all liabilities from all assets, and further reducing the net by all intangible assets. The net of tangible assets is then divided by the number of outstanding shares of common stock.

value investing
an approach to picking stocks based on actual value of the company rather than on price or price targets.

Even a drastic decline in a stock's market value has limited consequences for the put seller. The risk of loss is confined, realistically, to the price range between striking price and book value; that is the lowest reasonable price level. There is no guarantee, however, and the market has shown time and again that price levels are relatively oblivious to the intrinsic value of stock. In other words, the fundamentals serve as a valuable means for evaluating a company's long-term growth potential, but short-term price changes are unreliable; the fundamentals mean little in terms of pricing over the next few months. Short-term indicators are unstable for any purpose of analysis. The market can be viewed as having reliable intermediate and long-term trends showing up through indicators; but the short-term trends are highly chaotic and unreliable, and this is where option risks reside.

Tangible book value per share—book value minus all intangible assets such as goodwill—is a fundamental support level for the valuation of stock. It is today's financial worth, without considering any prospects for future growth. A popular investing concept, *value investing*, means just that. You will do better buying a company's value, not a stock's price. So when analysts publish a target range for a stock, it makes sense to question (1) how the target range was arrived at; (2) whether price targeting is based on fundamentals; and (3) how price equates to the company's long-term investment value.

The primary question a value investor asks is, "What could this company be sold for today, if it were on the market?" Another might be, "If I owned this company, what would it be worth per share?" Upon analysis, you arrive at a reasonable value for a company; and by comparing this to the market value of the stock, you can gain a sense of whether it is undervalued or overvalued.

A put seller takes a reasonable position in assuming that book value per share is a fair support level for stock price, and that the stock's price will not be likely to fall below that level. So a stock selling at $50 per share with book value of $20 per share could be assessed at having a maximum risk range of 30 points.

Example

A Finite Risk Strategy: You bought 100 shares of Xerox Corporation (XRX) and paid $14 per share. When the stock had risen to $17 per share, you sold a three-month put in the belief that the stock would continue to rise in value. Striking price was 19 and you received a premium of 2 ($200). Tangible book value per share at the time was $4.68 per share. Given these facts, your maximum risk was $732:

Purchase price of stock	$1,400
Less: premium received for put	−200
Net basis in stock	$1,200
Tangible book value	−468
Net risk	$732

You sold this put because you believe that $19 per share is a reasonable price; given the premium of $200, the price upon exercise would be reduced to $17 per share, the value of the stock on the day you sold the put. This is one of several ways to use options as a form of purchasing additional shares of stock at a discount.

In this example, the "net risk" represents the risk if and when the company were to be completely liquidated. In other words, Xerox Corporation would have to sell all of its assets and settle up with its creditors, leaving stockholders with $4.68 per share. A put seller evaluates this as the maximum risk, but, realistically, the exposure is far less. The $200 return on a $1,400 investment (before annualizing) is 14.3 percent. Because the put expires in three months (meaning risk exposure only lasts that long), annualized return should be four times greater, or 57.2 percent.

A put is an option to *sell* 100 shares of the underlying stock, at a fixed price by a specific date in the future. So when you sell a put, you grant the buyer the right to "put" 100 shares of stock to you at the striking price, to sell you 100 shares. In exchange for receiving a premium at the time of your opening sale transaction, you accept the risk of exercise. You are willing, as a put seller, to buy 100 shares of the underlying stock even though at the time of exercise, current value of the shares will be lower than the fixed striking price.

Smart Investor Tip

It makes sense to sell puts as long as you believe that the striking price is a fair value for that company's stock.

As a put seller, you reduce your exposure to risk by selecting stocks within a limited price range. For example, if you sell puts with striking prices of 50 or less, your maximum loss is 50 points, or $5,000; that, of course, would occur only if a stock were to become worthless by expiration date. If you sell puts with striking price of 25 or lower, the maximum exposure is cut in half, to $2,500 per contract. However, the more realistic way to assess maximum risk is to identify book value per share in comparison to striking price. That gap represents a more likely range of risk, regardless of the stock's current market value.

Analyzing Stock Values

If you consider the striking price to be fair and reasonable for 100 shares of the underlying stock, selling puts has two advantages:

1. You receive cash at the point that you sell a put.
2. The premium you receive discounts your basis in the stock in the event of exercise.

If you are willing to purchase shares of stock at the striking price, then selling puts is a smart strategy. You may even argue that there is no actual risk because you believe the stock price is reasonable. If, as an alternative, you were to purchase 100 shares of stock today, you would pay the current price without receiving a premium for selling a put; and the market value is just as likely to decline as if you were to sell the put.

Buying shares above market value may be acceptable if you plan to keep those shares as a long-term investment, considering (a) the discounting effect from selling puts and (b) the possibility of generating profits from selling puts that are not exercised. If the difference between striking price and current market value at the time of exercise is greater than the amount you received in premium, you have a paper loss at the point of exercise. In that outcome, you will need to wait out the time required for the stock's price to rebound before you can recapture that loss. You may be able to offset this loss by selling covered calls against stock acquired in this manner.

Acquiring stock through writing puts has to be done with the stock's value as the essential element in the decision. Remember, *value* does not mean the current market value of the stock; it means the price you are willing to pay per share. Put sellers, like call sellers, usually prefer to avoid exercise, so they use rolling techniques, such as rolling forward and down, for example, to either defer exercise or reduce the eventual exercise price. Once you identify the degree of risk involved with exercise, you need to compare that to the premium income in order to determine whether placing yourself in a short position is worth that risk exposure. If you embark on a program of put writing, you will need to have available adequate capital to purchase the shares of stock involved, an important factor that limits the degree of put writing you are likely to undertake. In fact, you will be required to have adequate funds on hand in your brokerage account. If you experience a high volume of exercise, you will use up your available capital and fill your portfolio with shares of stock acquired above current market value. So you naturally need to limit put writing to those stocks you would like to own whether you wrote puts or not.

Example

Calculating the Put Advantage: You sold a put with a striking price of 55 and received 6 (discounting the net price per share to $49). You considered $49 per share a reasonable price for those shares. Before expiration, the stock's market value fell to $48 and your put was exercised.

Two observations need to be made concerning this transaction:

1. The outcome is acceptable as long as you believe that $49 per share is a fair price for the stock. You would then also believe that current market value—only one point lower than your basis—is likely to rebound in the future. If your assumption is correct, the loss is a paper loss only and it will turn out to be a worthwhile investment.

2. If the stock's market value had risen, you would have profited from selling the put. It would not have been exercised and would have expired worthless; or time value would have evaporated, enabling you to buy to close at a profit. In those outcomes, the put premium would have been all profit. So selling puts in a rising market can produce profits when you are unwilling to tie up capital to buy 100 shares; this can be achieved with limited risk exposure.

Put sellers who seek only the income from premiums need to select stocks that they consider to be good prospects for price increase. Premium value is only half the test of a viable put sale; the other half is careful selection of stocks. As a put seller, you have to be willing to acquire 100 shares of stock for each short put written. If risks are too great, or if you do not want to acquire shares, then you cannot justify the strategy.

Evaluating Risks

Comparisons between selling calls and selling puts provide good insights about risk. Stock selection contains specific risks for call sellers. More attractive option premiums are associated with more volatile stocks. So covered call writers may be prone to selecting higher-risk stocks in order to sell higher-than-average time value.

The same risks apply to put sellers. Higher time value premiums for puts are going to be found on stocks with higher-than-average volatility. The direction of price movement you desire is different with puts than with calls, but the risks in the underlying stock are the same. Put sellers face the risk that the underlying stock's market value will fall. The more drastic the price falls, the greater the risk of exercise. However, a put seller's perception of risk has to be different from that of the call seller. The key to selecting puts should not be the size of the premium, but your willingness to buy the stock at the striking price in the event of exercise.

margin requirement
the maximum amount of outstanding risk investors are allowed to hold in their portfolio, or the maximum unfunded dollar level allowed when trading on margin.

Depending solely on premium dollar value can be deceiving as well. For example, a put premium of 4 on a $30 stock with a striking price of 30 provides four points of downside protection and, in the event of exercise, a return of 13.3 percent. A premium of 8—twice as much—on a $90 stock with a striking price of 90 represents a return if the put is exercised of 8.9 percent. Exercise in the first example would require you to purchase stock at $30, and in the second example you would be required to invest $90 per share. So your exercise cost would be three times higher ($9,000 versus $3,000) but your if-exercised rate of return would be about two-thirds as good. This demonstrates that depending solely on premium levels can be very deceiving. A more realistic evaluation of risk is required to make a logical decision.

However, selling puts does require planning and risk evaluation in the same manner as selling calls. For example, the *margin requirement* a brokerage firm imposes as a hard-and-fast rule means you have to plan ahead and have equity on hand before you begin selling puts. This naturally limits the transaction volume, since no one has unlimited equity in their portfolio.

Smart Investor Tip

Whenever you sell puts, your brokerage firm is going to require that you have at least 50 percent of the exercise price left on deposit. In this way, in the case of exercise, your margin requirement will be met.

The evaluation of risk for put sellers is different than for call selling. The put seller needs to apply those fundamental and technical tests to a stock in the same way as call sellers. The difference, however, is that while covered call writers own shares of the stock when they sell a call, the put writer has to be willing to buy the stock if exercise does occur. Your risk is limited to the degree of short position risk you can assume at one time and, of course, the risk exposure your brokerage firm will allow you to carry. You will need to be able to demonstrate that you have equity available to pay for shares in the event of exercise. A short position always carries a degree of risk, and if the market trend turns downward, your short puts could be exercised within a short period of time.

Given the possibility of gaining shares at or slightly below current market value, why bother to sell puts at all? In the examples in the previous section, the net result of selling a put was acquisition of stock at a net cost of $49 when market value was $48. Remember, however, that exercise is only one possible result. The put seller should be happy to acquire the stock for an adjusted basis of $49, given what the analysis of the company revealed. A value analysis should indicate that $49 per share is a good bargain. At the same time, put sellers will also profit if the stock rises. As this occurs, puts lose value and will expire worthless or can be closed at a profit. So rather than simply buying shares (placing more capital at risk), the put seller has a two-part strategy. If exercised, the net cost is considered a fair value, in spite of potentially lower current market value. And if the put falls in value as a result of rising market value in the stock, then the put sale is profitable. As a form of leverage, put selling produces profits from market movement without the requirement of investing in 100 shares of the stock.

Put Strategies

There are five popular strategies for selling puts: to produce short-term income, to make use of idle cash deposits in a brokerage account, to buy stocks, to cover short stock positions, or to create a tax put.

Strategy 1: Producing Income

The most popular reason for selling puts is also the most apparent: the purely speculative idea of earning short-term profits from put premiums. The ideal outcome would be a decline in put value from falling time and intrinsic value, enabling you to purchase and close the short position at a profit. Time is on your side when you sell, so the more time value in the total premium, the better your chances for profit.

> ### Example
>
> **The Put Time Strategy:** Last January, you sold a June 45 put for 4. At that time, the underlying stock's market value was $46 per share. Because market value was higher than the striking price, the entire premium was time value. (For puts, in-the-money is opposite than for calls.) If the stock's market value remained at or above $45 per share, the put would eventually expire worthless. If by exercise date stock is valued between $41 and $45 per share, you would earn a limited profit or break even in the event of exercise (before trading costs). The $41 per share level is 4 points below striking price, and you received $400 for selling the put.

A short position can be canceled at any time. As a seller, you can close the position by buying the put at the current premium level. However, the buyer has the right to exercise the put at any time. So when you sell a put, you are exposed to exercise if that put is in the money (when the stock's market value is lower than striking price). For the premium you receive, you willingly expose yourself to this risk.

You can make an informed decision about short puts by being aware of the profit and loss zones in any open positions. From this analysis, you are able to decide in advance at what point to close the positions or how long to keep them open. This self-imposed goal is related to premium level, the status of current market value in relation to striking price, and the degree of time value premium remaining. If a profit becomes unlikely or impossible, you have the choice of closing the position and accepting a limited loss.

> ### Smart Investor Tip
>
> Options traders recognize that they cannot be right all of the time. It often is wisest to accept a small loss rather than continue to be exposed to potentially greater losses.

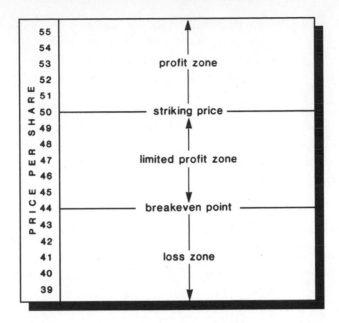

FIGURE 8.1 Put selling profit and loss zones.

An example of profit and loss zones for selling a put is shown in Figure 8.1. This is based on a striking price of 50 with put premium of 6. The premium creates a six-point limited profit zone between $44 and $50 per share and a profit zone above striking price. Below the breakeven point of $44, you will experience a loss. This visual range analysis helps you to define when and where you will close a position, based on proximity between a stock's current market value and loss zone.

It is possible to close the put at a profit even when the stock's market value falls below striking price. This relies on time value decline. The analysis of profit and loss zones in Figure 8.1 is based on the worst-case assumption about where a stock's price will end up at the point of expiration. If the premium contains a good amount of time value, you can profit merely by trading in the put, even when considerable price movement occurs. Of course, whenever it moves to an in-the-money range, you also risk exercise.

Conceivably, you could select stocks that will remain at or above the striking price and earn premium profits repeatedly, without ever experiencing exercise. However, foresight about which stocks will achieve such consistent price support is difficult. It takes only a single, temporary dip in price to be exposed to exercise, a risk that cannot be overlooked. Exercise is not necessarily a drastic outcome; but it does tie up your capital because it requires that you buy stock above current market value. While you wait for the stock's price to rebound, you will miss other market opportunities.

Remember the basic guideline for selling puts: You need to be willing to buy 100 shares of the underlying stock at the striking price, which you consider a fair price for that stock. If current market value is lower than striking price, you should believe that the price is going to rebound, justifying the purchase you will be required to make upon exercise. In other words, work with stocks you consider worthwhile long-term investments.

This does not mean you would necessarily welcome exercise. It only means that you would not mind buying those shares at the striking price. You might still want to avoid exercise whenever possible by rolling positions, remembering that exercise of many puts means you may end up with a portfolio of overpriced stocks.

Example

Poor Programming: You sold several puts in the past few months. This month the entire market fell several hundred points. Five of your puts were exercised at the same time, requiring you to purchase 500 shares of stock. All of your available capital now is tied up in these shares. Consequently, your portfolio's basis is higher than current market value for *all* of the shares you own. The market is recovering, but very slowly. Even considering your premium income, you are in a large paper loss position. You have no choice but to sit out the market and hope for a rebound in the future.

The net cost level for stock acquired through exercise of puts is the striking price, minus premiums you received when you sold the puts. Allowing for transaction fees paid (both when you sold the put and when you bought the shares), your basis will be higher still. You should not overlook the potential paper loss position you could experience in the event of a broad down-trending market. You may recover this paper loss position by selling calls on the stock you have acquired; but you also have to be careful with that strategy. Be sure that if the calls are exercised, you will not go out of the long position with a net loss. Chances are that in the event of a large market decline, you will need to wait out a recovery before making any further decisions.

Strategy 2: Using Idle Cash

When you sell options, your broker requires deposits of cash or securities. With puts, the maximum risk is identified easily. It is equal to the striking price of the put. If the short put is exercised and you are required to buy 100 shares, the firm needs to ensure that you have cash or securities available to honor the purchase.

You may hold your capital on the sidelines, believing that stocks you want to buy are overpriced and will be more attractively priced in the future. The dilemma is that the longer cash is held in reserve, the more you miss opportunities to put that money to work. Idle cash does not earn money, and there is no way to know how long it will take for conditions to present themselves, making the desired move practical.

One way to deal with this problem is by selling puts on the targeted stock. In this way, capital is still kept in reserve, yet you earn money from put premiums *and* you discount the basis in the stock in the event of exercise. You will profit from selling the put if the stock's price rises; and you will end up buying shares at the striking price (less premium discount) if the stock's market value falls. In either event, the premium you receive will be yours to keep.

Example

Planning for a Correction: You are interested in buying stock as a long-term investment. However, you believe that the current market price is too high, and that a correction is likely to occur in the near future. One possible solution: Sell one put for every 100 shares you want to buy, instead of buying the stock. Place your capital on deposit with the brokerage firm as security against your short position in the puts. If the current market value of the stock rises, your short puts will fall in value and can be closed at a profit or allowed to expire worthless. In this way, you benefit from rising market value without placing all of your capital at risk.

If market value of the stock declines, you will purchase the shares at the striking price. Your basis will be discounted by the amount of premium you received for selling the puts. As a long-term investor, you will be confident that the share price will grow over time, and the current paper loss will be partially offset by the premium.

One aspect of this approach that is troubling is the possibility of lost opportunity. If you are wrong in your belief about a stock and its market value continues to rise, selling puts brings some income, but you pass up the chance to buy stock. So when you sell puts as an alternative to buying shares outright, you also need to accept this risk, or to mitigate the risk in other ways. For example, many combination strategies provide the chance to reduce lost opportunity risk while continuing to sell short options. Chapter 9 explores combination techniques in more detail.

Strategy 3: Buying Stock

The third reason for selling puts is to intentionally seek exercise. Selling a put discounts the basis in stock in the event of exercise, and when seeking exercise, you will not be concerned with price drops in the stock.

Example

Putting It Another Way: You have been tracking a stock for several months, and you have decided that you are willing to buy 100 shares at or below $40 per share. The current price is $45. You could wait for the stock to drop to your level, which might or might not happen. However, an alternative is to sell a November 45 put, which has a current premium value of 6. This is all time value. If the market value of stock rises, the put will become worthless and the $600 you received is yours to keep. You could then repeat the transaction on the same argument as before, at a higher price increment. If the stock's market value falls below striking price, the put will be exercised. Your basis would be $39—striking price of 45 minus six points received in put premium—or $1 per share below your target purchase price.

In this example, the put was sold at the money and the premium—all time value—was high enough to create a net basis below your target price. Even if the stock's market value were to fall below $40 per share, your long-term plans would not be affected. You considered $40 per share a reasonable purchase level for the shares. As a long-term investor, you are not concerned with short-term price changes. Simply waiting for the right price to come along means you expose yourself to the risk of losing the opportunity to get the stock at your price. Selling puts discounts current market value and makes it worthwhile to wait for exercise, especially if you believe the current market price is inflated. For example, if a broad-based market rise has resulted in the stock's price rising quickly, the timing for the option position could be good. If time value is high in the put you're thinking of selling, it is a better alternative than buying shares of stock.

Example

Reduced Basis, Nicely Put: You are interested in buying stock at $40 per share. Current market value is $45. You sell a put with a striking price of 45 and receive 6. Willing to take exercise, you reduced your potential basis to $39 per share by selling the put. However, instead of falling, the stock's market value rose 14 points.

In this scenario, the put will expire worthless and you keep the $600 as profit. But if you had bought shares instead of selling the put, you would have earned $1,400 in profit. However, once your put expires, you are free to sell another one, offsetting the lost opportunity and perhaps exceeding that potential profit over time. The lost $1,400 is easy to recognize after the fact; however, at the time of making the decision to sell a put, you have no way of knowing whether the price will rise or fall. If share price were too high, you could risk *losing* $1,400 just as easily as you miss the opportunity for profiting by the same degree. This is why selling puts sometimes presents an attractive alternative to buying shares outright.

You risk losing future profits in two ways as a put seller, so you need to be willing to assume these risks in exchange for the premium income:

1. If the price of the underlying stock rises beyond the point value you received in premium, you lose the opportunity to realize profits by owning the stock. You settle for premium income only. However, when this occurs, your put expires worthless and you are free to sell another and receive additional premium.

2. If the price of the underlying stock falls significantly, you are required to buy 100 shares at the striking price, which will be above current market value. It might take considerable time for the stock's market value to rebound to the striking price level. Meanwhile, your capital is tied up in stock you bought above current market value.

Selling puts as a means for buying stock (or exposing yourself to the possibility of buying) makes sense as long as you believe the striking price is a reasonable price for that stock. So if the put expires or falls in value, you profit from the short put. If it is exercised, you purchase stock at a price higher than current market value. This *contingent purchase* strategy makes sense because you can also recover the difference between striking price and market value by selling covered calls.

contingent purchase
a strategy involving the sale of a put and willingness to accept exercise, which will result in purchasing 100 shares of stock. The strategy makes sense when the individual believes the striking price is a reasonable price for the stock.

Example

From Put to Call: You sold a put on a stock that you would purchase at the striking price, based on today's values. That strike price was 30 and you received 2 ($200) for selling the put. However, after you sold the put, the stock's value fell to $26 per share and the put was exercised. You purchased 100 shares at $30 per share. Your net basis is $28 per share ($30 minus $2 you received for selling the put). You check options listings and discover that you can sell a covered call expiring in eight months for 3 ($300) and with a striking price of 27.50. If exercised, your overall profit will be $750 before calculating trading costs. The $300 received for selling the call reduces your basis to $25 per share. If the call is exercised at $27.50, you lose 2.5 points ($250), but you also gain $500 received for selling a put ($200) and a call ($300):

Purchase price of stock upon exercise of short put	$3,000
Sale price of stock upon exercise of covered call	−2,750
Net loss on stock	$ −250
Premium from sale of put	200
Premium from sale of call	300
Net profit	$250

While the risks of put selling are far more limited than those associated with uncovered call selling, you can also miss opportunities for profits in the event of stock price movement in either direction.

Strategy 4: Writing a Covered Put on Short Stock

While covered puts are not the same as covered calls, there is a corresponding position. If you are short 100 shares of stock, you cover that position by selling one put. (Your put is also defined as covered as long as you have cash in your brokerage account adequate to purchase shares at the striking price).

In the case of a short put accompanied by a short position in stock, profit is limited to the net difference between striking price of the put and the original price per share in the short position. However, the potential loss is a far more serious problem. If the price of stock were to increase substantially, profits in the put would not be enough to match the resulting loss in the stock. Thus the covered put does not provide the same definition of "cover" as does the covered call.

Alternative option strategies—such as buying calls—provide better protection for those with short stock positions. In the event the stock rises in value, in-the-money calls will match the loss with dollar-for-dollar profits. In comparison, the covered put is too limited to offer any true protection against the worst-case outcome.

Strategy 5: Creating a Tax Put

A fifth reason to sell puts is to create an advantage for tax purposes, which is known as a *tax put*. However, before employing this strategy, you should consult with your tax adviser to determine that you time the transaction properly and legally, and to ensure that the tax rules have not changed. (See Chapter 12 for more information on taxation of options.) You also need to be able to identify the risks and potential liabilities involved with the tax put.

An investor who has a paper loss position on stock has the right to sell and create a capital loss at any time, even if the timing is intended to reduce income tax liability. Such losses are limited to annual maximums. You can deduct capital losses only up to those maximums; the excess is carried over to future years. By selling puts at the same time that you take a tax loss, you offset part of that loss. The tax put is maximized when the put expiration occurs in the following tax year. (For example, expiration will occur in January or later, but you sell the put in December or earlier.) If your net stock loss is greater than the maximum allowed, the profit on the put is absorbed by that over-the-limit loss. By selling a put when you also sell stock at a loss, one of three possible outcomes will occur:

tax put
a strategy combining the sale of stock at a loss—taken for tax purposes—and the sale of a put at the same time. The premium received on the put offsets the stock loss; if the put is exercised, the stock is purchased at the striking price.

1. The stock's market value rises and the option expires worthless. The stock loss is deducted in the year stock is sold, but profit on the short put is taxed in the following year, when it expires. This has the effect of enabling you to take stock losses in the current year but defer put premium gains until the following year.

2. The stock's market value rises and you close the position in the put, profiting by the premium difference. This creates a short-term capital gain in the year the position is closed.

3. The stock's market value falls below the striking price, and you are assigned the stock. In this case, your basis in the stock is discounted by the amount received for selling the put.

A potential problem arises in the event that the put is exercised within 30 days from the date you sold the shares of stock. Under the *wash sale rule*,

wash sale rule
a provision in the tax code prohibiting the deduction of a loss if the security position is reopened within 30 days from the date of the sale.

DATE	ACTION	RECEIVED	PAID
Aug. 15	buy 100 shares at $50		$5,000
Dec. 15	sell 100 shares at $47	$4,700	
Dec. 15	sell 1 Feb 50 put at 6	$ 600	
	total	$5,300	$5,000
	net cash	$ 300	

PRICE MOVEMENT	RESULT
stock rises above striking price	$300 profit
	put is bought at a profit
stock falls below striking price	put is exercised at $50, net cost $47 (with $300 profit from tax put)

FIGURE 8.2   Example of tax put.

you cannot claim a loss in stock if you repurchase the same stock within 30 days.

The tax put provides you with a twofold advantage. First, you take a current-year loss on stock, reducing your overall tax liability, while deferring tax on the put sale until the following tax year. Second, you profit from selling the put, as shown in Figure 8.2, in the following two ways:

1. The premium income offsets the loss in stock.
2. In the event of exercise, your basis in the stock is discounted by the put premium.

Example

A Strategy with Several Aspects: You bought stock at $38 per share, and it is currently valued at $34. You sell shares in December and take a

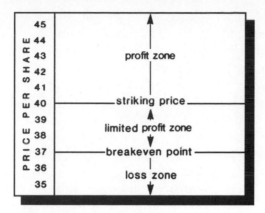

FIGURE 8.3 Example of put write with profit and loss zones.

$400 loss. At the same time, you sell a March 35 put at 6. The $400 loss in stock is offset by a $600 premium from selling the put. If exercised, adjusted basis in the stock is discounted by the put premium. The put is not taxed until exercised, closed, or expired, so this also creates a tax deferral on the option side and a current write-off for loss on the stock side. (If the buyer were to exercise the put within 30 days from the date you sold stock, you would not be able to claim the loss on stock, under the wash sale rule.)

Put sellers enjoy an important advantage over call sellers: Put risk is not unlimited because the stock's market value can only fall so far. An example of a put write is described next and illustrated with profit and loss zones in Figure 8.3.

Example

Finite Loss Potential: You sold one May 40 put at 3. The outcome of taking this short position will be profitable as long as the stock's market value remains at or above the striking price of $40. If, at expiration, the market value is below $40, the put will be exercised and you will buy 100 shares at $40 per share. Losses are limited between striking price and $37 due to the put premium received. If the stock's market value falls below $37, you will have a net loss at the point of exercise.

While the premium you receive for the put is yours to keep, you acquire stock above market value and you can then wait until the price rebounds. You could also absorb the paper loss on acquired stock by selling covered calls against it, further discounting your basis in the stock.

The most undesirable outcome you face as a put seller is that stock may become worthless. This is a remote possibility, but it remains within the realm of possible outcomes. You mitigate the risk by selecting stocks critically and applying fundamental tests aimed at identifying tangible value, rather than depending on popularity measures and technical indicators. The possibility only emphasizes the importance of selecting stock carefully before writing puts. In the event a stock became worthless, your put would be exercised and you would buy 100 shares at the striking price. Current market value would be zero. The more likely risk level is book value. It is always possible for a stock's market value to fall below book value. The fundamental value of a company's equity has little to do with market pricing, especially in the short term. Additionally, it is possible that reported book value has been inflated by reporting of exaggerated earnings, improper capitalizing of expenses, or underreporting of liabilities. All of these potential causes for loss have to be considered as possible risks when selling puts, not to mention as risks of purchasing stock even without involving options.

Tangible net worth—assuming it is an accurate value—often is overlooked in the more important factor affecting value. The *perception* of future investment value, which might be positive or negative, directly and immediately affects current share price. Even when the fundamental strength of a company has been established, the market might discount that value to some degree. Market pricing is far from rational, and you need to keep that reality in mind. Having this knowledge gives you an advantage, because you can judge a stock's value before deciding how or whether you employ calls or puts.

You need to be willing, as a put seller, to buy 100 shares at the short put's striking price, recognizing that exercise is possible when the put is in the money. In the event of exercise, the exercise price will always be above current market value. As long as you believe that striking price is reasonable, exercise is acceptable, because short-term price movement does not affect the stock's long-term growth potential. If you believe in the company's prospects as a long-term investment, selling puts can be a smart way to increase current income while discounting your basis in the stock.

In the next chapter, we examine various buying and selling strategies in combination, to decrease (or increase) risks and returns.

Chapter

9

Combined Techniques: Creative Risk Management

One of the greatest pieces of economic wisdom is to know what you do not know.
— John Kenneth Galbraith, in *Time*, March 3, 1961

The strategies of options are among the most intriguing tools available. You can be highly speculative or very conservative, or create a personally tailored plan anywhere in between. In this chapter, we explore various combinations that can be put to work in creative and profitable ways.

Options traders can employ only four basic strategies: buying calls, selling calls, buying puts, and selling puts. But these four basics can be combined in numerous strategies; for example, you can modify risks in long positions with offsetting short positions in options.

Your reasons for buying or selling options define the level and degree of risk that you are willing to assume. The utilization of options defines your risk profile as a stock investor. Any strategy has to be secondary to the more important phase in your investment program: the selection of stock. A lot of emphasis is placed on option risk or reward, but the stock risk is easily overlooked. Before even considering how or whether to employ options, you need to first identify a strategy that helps you select stocks with several important investing rules in mind, including the following:

- Protect your capital from catastrophic losses due to stock market volatility.
- Avoid long positions in stocks with severe liquidity or solvency problems.
- Select companies whose industry position is strong and growing.

This short list only defines the overall importance of selecting stocks as a starting point in your program, and that may or may not include options. The big mistake is to pick stocks to cover rich-premium options and, in the process, unintentionally fill your portfolio with highly volatile issues such that any downturn in the market is likely to cause a severe loss of value in the stock. In that situation, a limited short-term option profit is accompanied by a larger loss in stock value and, potentially, problems recapturing value through a reversal in direction of price movement.

You have the right to decide individually how much risk exposure is appropriate. Applied to the options market, defining risk levels also helps you to decide whether a particular strategy is right for you. Consider the difference between one investor who wants only to profit from buying and selling options, and another who covers calls with shares of stock in order to maximize returns. The risks are on opposite sides of the spectrum, and the different uses of options by each person define and distinguish their perceptions of risk and opportunity, their desired outcomes, and even their basic ideas about how to operate within the market.

spread
the simultaneous purchase and sale of options on the same underlying stock, with different striking prices or expiration dates, or both.

In moving beyond the four basic options strategies, you may discover value in a variety of combinations, which can be put into action for many different reasons. For example, long and short option positions can be engaged in at the same time, so that risks offset one another. Some combined strategies are designed to create profits in the event that the underlying stock moves in either direction; others are designed to create profits if the stock price remains within a specific range.

Overview of Advanced Strategies

There are three major classifications of advanced strategies.

The Spread

The first advanced strategy is called a *spread*. This is the simultaneous opening of both a long position and a short position in options on the same underlying stock. The spread increases potential profits while also reducing risks in the event that the underlying stock behaves in a particular manner, as illustrated shortly.

vertical spread
a spread involving different striking prices but identical expiration dates.

In order to meet the definition of a spread, the options should have different expiration dates, different striking prices, or both. When the striking prices are different but the expiration dates are the same, it is called a *vertical spread*. This is also referred to as a *money spread*.

money spread
alternate name for the *vertical spread*.

Example

Vertical Spread, More than Margarine: You buy a 45 call and, at the same time, sell a 40 call. Both expire in February. Because expiration dates are identical, this is a vertical spread.

Example

A Second Vertical Situation: You buy a 30 put and, at the same time, sell a 35 put. Both expire in December. This is also a vertical spread.

The vertical spread is created using either calls or puts. The spread can have different expiration dates or a *combination* of different striking prices and expiration dates. Spreads can be put together in numerous formations.

combination
any purchase or sale of options on one underlying stock, with terms that are not identical.

Spread strategies using short-term options—expiring in six months or less—are, of course, limited in value to that time range. However, spread strategies are far more complex when you combine short-term options with LEAPS. These longer-term options may have a life up to three years, so the offsetting possibilities can be far more complex. Knowing, for example, that time value declines the most during the last two to three months, you can "cover" a short-position option with a longer-term LEAPS option. We qualify the term *cover* in this strategy. Although it is widely referred to in that manner, it is in fact more accurately a form of spread.

Example

Thinking Ahead: You purchase a LEAPS 40 call that expires in 30 months. The stock is currently selling at $36 per share. You pay 11 ($1,100). Although time value premium is high due to the long-term nature of this option, you believe that the stock will rise in price during this period and that this will justify your investment. A month later, the stock's market value has risen to $41 per share. You sell a 45 call expiring in four months and receive a premium of 3. Three months later, the stock is selling at $44 per share and the short call is valued at 1. You close the position and take a profit of $200 (minus trading fees). You now are free to sell another call against the LEAPS, and you can repeat the process as many times as you wish.

The preceding transaction should be evaluated with several points in mind. The LEAPS cost $1,100 and you have already recovered $200 of that cost. The LEAPS is now in the money, so the price movement direction is favorable. This transaction took four months, so you have 26 more months before the long LEAPS call expires. You could repeat the short-term call sell again and again during this period. It is possible that you could recover the entire premium invested in the long position through well-timed short-term call sales—and potentially still profit from the long position as well. This would be an ideal outcome, and you have two and a half years for it to materialize. In comparison to using only short-term calls, you have far greater flexibility using short-term options in combination with long-term LEAPS options.

A variation of the spread offers potential double-digit returns, especially using the high time value of LEAPS options. For example, you can combine a covered call and an uncovered put on the same stock and receive premium income on both. This strategy is appropriate if and when:

- You are willing to write a covered call, recognizing that if exercised, your stock can be called away.

- You are also willing to write an uncovered put, in full knowledge that if exercised, you will have to purchase 100 shares of stock above current market value. This is appropriate when the striking price, less put premium you receive, is a good price for the stock.

- You structure the short call and put so that exercise may be avoidable through rolling techniques if and when the stock moves close to either striking price.

Example

Double-Digit Returns: You own 100 shares of stock that you purchased at $26 per share. Today, market value is $30. You write 29-month LEAPS options on this stock. You sell a 35 call and a 25 put at the same time. Your total premium on these two LEAPS options is 11 points, or $1,100. That represents a net return, based on your purchase price of $26 per share, of 42.3 percent.

In this example, you would experience one of four outcomes:

1. One or both of the LEAPS options may expire worthless. In that outcome, the premium is 100 percent profit.

2. One or both of the LEAPS options may be exercised. If the call is exercised, you will give up shares at $35 per share. Your basis was $26 so your capital gain is $900, plus the call premium. If the put is exercised, you will buy 100 shares at the striking price of 25, so that your average basis would be 25.50 in this stock.

3. One or both of the LEAPS options can be rolled forward to avoid exercise. The call can be rolled forward and up; and the put can be rolled forward and down. With each change in striking price, you change the eventual exercise value, so that upon exercise you would be more points ahead. If the call is exercised, you will gain five points more with a five-point roll. If the put is exercised, you will buy stock at five points less than before.

4. One or both LEAPS options can be closed. As long as time value falls, you may be able to close these short positions at a profit. However, they can also be closed to reduce losses if the stock's price movement is significant.

One interesting variation on the spread is the *collar*. This strategy involves three positions: buying the stock; selling an out-of-the-money call; and buying an out-of-the-money put. It is designed to limit both potential profits and potential losses. While trading costs may be high when collars are used for single-contract transactions, they are viable in some situations. The further out of the money the call and put, the more bullish your point of view. This strategy combines the

collar
a spread strategy combining long stock, a covered call, and a long put, with both options out of the money. The collar limits potential gains and potential losses.

most optimistic points of view and, when the short call pays for the cost of the long put, the potential loss is limited as well. Potential outcomes include exercise of the short call, in which the stock will be called away; inadequate movement on either side, resulting in little or no net loss; or your exercise or sale of the long put in the event of a decline in the stock's price.

Given the overall returns possible from selling long-term LEAPS calls and puts, the combined sale of a call and a put can produce very attractive returns; and exercise can be either avoided or accepted as a profitable outcome.

The Hedge

The second advanced strategy is the *hedge*, which has been discussed many times throughout this book in specific applications. For example, you hedge a short sale in stock by purchasing a call. In the event the stock rises, the short seller's losses will be offset by a point-for-point rise in the call. A put also protects a long stock position against a decline in price. So using options for insurance is another type of hedge. Both spreads and straddles contain hedging features, since two dissimilar positions are opened at the same time; price movement reducing the value on one side of the transaction tends to be offset by price movement increasing value on the other side.

hedge

a strategy involving the use of one position to protect another. For example, stock is purchased in the belief it will rise in value, and a put is purchased on the same stock to protect against the risk that market value will decline.

Advanced strategies often produce minimal profits for each option contract, given the need to pay trading fees upon opening and closing. Such marginal outcomes do not necessarily justify the associated risks, so advanced options traders apply these strategies with large multiples of option contracts. When you deal in multiples, the brokerage deposit requirements are increased as well.

In the advanced strategy, what appears simple and logical on paper does not always work out the way you expect. Changes in option premium are not always logical or predictable, and short-term variations occur unexpectedly. This is what makes option investing so interesting; such experiences also test your true risk tolerance level. You may find that your risk tolerance is different than you thought, once you employ advanced option strategies. Being at risk is daunting, so think of the *range* of risks and costs before embarking on any advanced strategies.

The Straddle

The third combination strategy is called a *straddle*. This is defined as the simultaneous purchase and sale of an identical number of calls and puts with the same striking price and expiration date. While the spread requires a difference in one or more of the terms, the straddle is distinguished by the fact that the terms of each side are identical. The difference is that a straddle consists of combining calls on one side with puts on the other.

straddle

the simultaneous purchase and sale of the same number of calls and puts with identical striking prices and expiration dates.

The spread example involving short covered calls with uncovered short puts can also be applied in the straddle. Instead of spreading with the use of higher call striking prices and lower put striking prices, both can be sold at or near the money. In this situation, premium income will be far greater, consisting of high time value on both sides. The chances of exercise are greater as well, and if you wish to avoid exercise, you will have to roll at least one of the straddle positions, and possibly both. If the stock's direction reverses itself, it could result in the need to roll the call forward and up *and* to roll the put forward and down.

If you enter an at-the-money straddle using short covered calls and short uncovered puts, you need to be prepared to accept exercise if it does occur. Because you keep the premium for selling these options, it can be a very profitable strategy.

strangle

a strategy in which an equal number of long calls and puts are bought (long strangle) or sold (short strangle). Thee terms include different striking prices but the same expiration date, and it will be profitable only if there is a large price movement in the underlying stock.

The Strangle

A strategy combining features of both the spread and the straddle is the *strangle*. In this strategy, you will make a profit only if the stock has a significant move. A strangle consists of a long call and a long put with different striking prices but the same expiration date, and it is affordable primarily because both options are out-of-the-money.

Example

Strangle, Not Choke: You have been tracking a stock that has traded in a narrow range for many months. You expect a large price movement, but you don't know which direction it is likely to take. The stock currently trades at $43 per share. You enter a strangle, consisting of a 45 call and a 40 put, both expiring in seven months. The total cost of these two options is 4 ($400). As long as the stock's price remains between $36 and $49 per share, the strangle cannot be profitable (striking prices expanded by cost of both options). But if the price moves above or below that range, one side or the other will be profitable. In a short strangle, potential profits exist as long as options remain out-of-the-money, and that profit range is expanded by the receipt of option premium.

iron condor

the combination of a long strangle and a short strangle on the same underlying stock. The cost is reduced due to offsetting premium payments and receipts; and it is practical as long as short position exercise costs do not exceed long position profits.

The strangle is a strategy based on the belief that the stock will move substantially. Of course, because it requires the purchase of two options, the chances for success in this strategy are less than those for purchasing a single option. To enter a strangle, you should be confident that substantial price movement is likely to occur before expiration.

A related strategy partially solves the problem. As shown in the previous example, the cost of long options makes it difficult to reach and exceed a breakeven point. The *iron condor* is a variation on the strangle. It consists of four different options: long and short calls and long and short puts, all on the same underlying stock.

Vertical Spread Strategies

You can use spreads to exploit time value premium. These changes are predictable because everyone knows what happens to time value as expiration approaches. And when options are in the money, it is reasonable to expect intrinsic value premium to react dollar-for-dollar with movement in the price of the underlying stock. Time value premium can change in predictable ways, which presents opportunities for short-term profits. The relationship between intrinsic value and time value is what makes the spread an interesting and challenging strategic tool.

Smart Investor Tip

As with most option strategies, time value spells the difference between profit and loss in most spreads.

You have an advantage when offsetting long and short positions. The spread employing short-term options is likely to involve one side in the money and the other side out of the money. The in-the-money side will tend to change in value at a different rate from the out-of-the-money side, because it contains intrinsic value. By observing the differences on either side of the striking price, you can anticipate advantages that you can gain through the spread strategy, whether the market moves up or down.

> **bull spread**
> a strategy involving the purchase and sale of calls or puts that will produce maximum profits when the value of the underlying stock rises.

Bull Spreads

A *bull spread* provides the greatest profit potential when the underlying stock's market value rises. With the bull spread, you buy an option with a lower striking price and sell another with a higher striking price. You can employ either puts or calls in the bull spread.

Example

Bull Spread, Not a Bad Thing: You open a bull spread using calls. You sell one December 55 call and buy one December 50 call, as shown in Figure 9.1. At the time of this transaction, the underlying stock's market value is $49 per share. After you open the spread, the stock's market value rises to $54 per share. When that occurs, the 50 call increases in value point-for-point once it is in the money. The short 55 call does not change in value as it remains out of the money and, in fact, will drop in value as its time until expiration nears. Because of the advantage the spread creates at the time the stock has reached the $54 per share level, both sides of the spread will be profitable. The long 50 call rises in value and the short 55 call remains out of the money.

This example describes the ideal situation, in which both sides of the spread are profitable, because the stock's price behaves perfectly to suit the spread. Of course, you have no control over price movement, so this outcome will not always occur. Even when only one side is profitable, however, the strategy works as long as you achieve an overall net profit.

Smart Investor Tip

The spread is most profitable when the stock's price changes in the desired direction, timing, and pattern. Both sides of the spread can work out well. This would be much easier if stock price movement could be controlled or predicted—which it cannot.

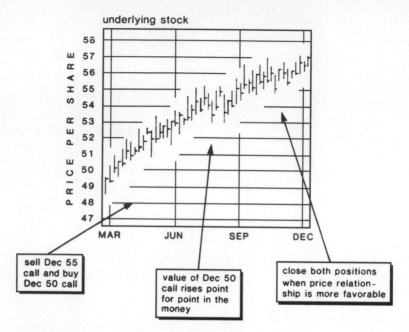

underlying stock

sell Dec 55 call and buy Dec 50 call

value of Dec 50 call rises point for point in the money

close both positions when price relationship is more favorable

FIGURE 9.1 Example of bull spread.

A bull vertical spread is profitable when the underlying stock's price moves in the anticipated direction. For example, a lower-priced call will be profitable if the stock rises in value, whereas the higher-priced short call will not be exercised as long as it remains out of the money, as previously illustrated.

A bull vertical spread with defined profit and loss zones is shown in Figure 9.2.

Example

Defining the Zones: You sell one September 45 call for 2, and buy one September 40 call for 5. The net cost is $300. When the stock rises between $40 and $45 per share, the September 40 call rises dollar-for-dollar with the stock, while the short September 45 call remains out of the money. Its premium value will decline as time value disappears. As long as the stock remains within this five-point range, both sides can be closed at a profit (as long as closing the positions would produce net income higher than your initial cost of $300). If the stock's price rises above $45 per share, the five-point spread in striking prices will be offset by the long and short positions. Both calls will be in the money. So this strategy limits both profits as well as losses.

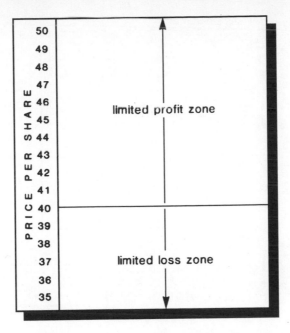

FIGURE 9.2 Bull vertical spread profit and loss zones.

Bear Spreads

While the bull spread seeks increases in market value, the *bear spread* will produce profits if the stock's market value falls. In this variety of the spread, the higher-value option is always bought, and the lower-value option is always sold.

bear spread

a strategy involving the purchase and sale of calls or puts that will produce maximum profits when the value of the underlying stock falls.

Example

A Bearish Idea: You open a bear spread using calls. You sell one March 35 call and buy one March 40 call. The stock's market value is $37 per share. The premium value of the lower call, which is in the money, will decline point-for-point as the stock's market value falls; if the stock's value does fall, the position can be closed at a profit.

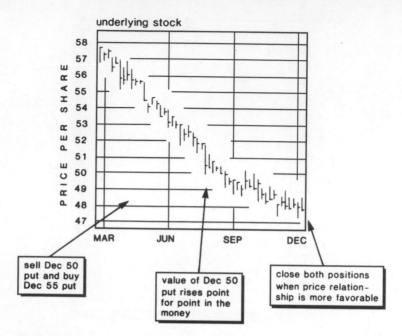

underlying stock

sell Dec 50
put and buy
Dec 55 put

value of Dec 50
put rises point
for point in the
money

close both positions
when price relation-
ship is more favorable

FIGURE 9.3 Example of bear spread.

Example

Going Pessimistic with Puts: You open a bear spread using puts. As shown in the example in Figure 9.3, you sell one December 50 put and buy one December 55 put. The underlying stock's market value is $55 per share. As the price of the stock moves down, the long 55 put will increase in value point-for-point with the change in stock price. By the time the stock's price moves down to $51, both puts will be profitable—the long put from increased intrinsic value, and the short put from lower time value.

This scenario assumes ideal conditions in which the stock's price moves the desired number of points in the perfect time frame, which enables the bear spread writer to profit. The example illustrates the ideal outcome using a bear spread. You gain more flexibility when going long using LEAPS options in the bear spread; this enables you to write several short-term puts against the "covered" longer position. The cost for the long position will be greater due to the time factor, but the potential for profit makes the entire strategy far more flexible as well.

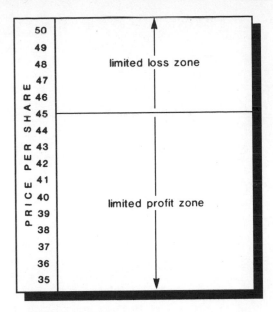

FIGURE 9.4 Bear vertical spread profit and loss zones.

Smart Investor Tip

Bear strategies often are overlooked, because people tend to be optimists. Look at *all* of the possibilities. You can make money when the stock goes down in value, too.

A detailed bear spread with defined profit and loss zones is illustrated in Figure 9.4.

Example

Profits on Both Sides: You sell one September 40 call for 5 and buy one September 45 call for 2; your net proceeds are $300. As the stock's market value falls below the level of $45 per share, the short 40 call will lose point value matching the stock's decline; the long call will not react in the same way, as it remains out of the money. As the $40 per share price level is approached, the spread can be closed with profits on both sides.

TABLE 9.1 Spread Risk Table		
Number of	*Striking Price Interval*	
Option Spreads	*5 Points*	*10 Points*
1	$500	$1,000
2	1,000	2,000
3	1,500	3,000
4	2,000	4,000
5	2,500	5,000
6	3,000	6,000
7	3,500	7,000
8	4,000	8,000
9	4,500	9,000
10	5,000	10,000

Consider how the above example would work with puts instead of calls. In that scenario, the long put would *increase* point-for-point with a decline in the stock's market value.

When the bear spread employs calls, profits are frozen once both sides are in the money, at least to the degree that intrinsic value changes; one side's increase will be offset by the other side's decrease. The only remaining opportunity to increase profits at that point would lie in time value premium left in the short position.

In all of these examples, the most significant risk is that the stock will move in the direction opposite that desired. Be prepared to cut losses by closing a spread in that event before the short position increases to value. You risk exercise on the short side at any time that option is in the money, and you might need to close to avoid exercise. Your maximum risk other than that of exercise is limited to the point difference between the two striking prices (minus net premium received when the position was opened, or plus net premium paid). In the preceding examples, a five-point spread was used, so that maximum point-spread risk is $500. The point-spread risk increases as the gap between striking prices changes, as shown in Table 9.1.

Example

Limiting the Risk Zone: You open a spread. The difference between striking prices on either side is five points. Your maximum risk is $500 plus trading fees, plus net premium paid when you opened the position (or minus net premium received).

A Four-Part Position: You open a spread buying and selling four options on either side. The difference between striking prices is five points. Your maximum risk is $2,000 (modified as in the previous example), because four positions are involved, each with a five-point difference between striking prices.

Box Spreads

When you open a bull spread *and* a bear spread at the same time, using options on the same underlying stock, it is called a *box spread*. This limits risks as well as potential profits, and is designed to produce a profit in one side or the other, regardless of which direction the stock moves.

box spread

the combination of a bull spread and a bear spread, opened at the same time on the same underlying stock.

Boxed in with Options: As illustrated in Figure 9.5, you create a box spread by buying and selling the following option contracts:

Bull spread: Sell one September 40 put and buy one September 35 put.

Bear spread: Buy one September 45 call and sell one September 40 call.

In this example, if the underlying stock's price moves significantly in either direction, portions of the box spread can be closed at a profit. One important reminder: It makes sense to close corresponding long and short positions in the event of a profit opportunity, to avoid the risk of leaving yourself exposed with an uncovered short option. In the ideal situation, the stock's price will move first in one direction (enabling half the box spread to be closed at a profit) and then in the other (enabling the close of the other half, also at a profit).

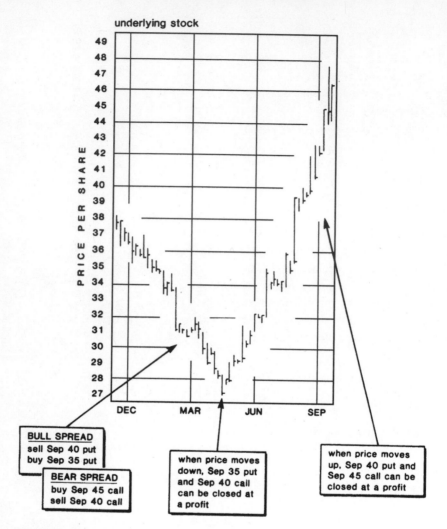

underlying stock

BULL SPREAD
sell Sep 40 put
buy Sep 35 put

BEAR SPREAD
buy Sep 45 call
sell Sep 40 call

when price moves
down, Sep 35 put
and Sep 40 call
can be closed at
a profit

when price moves
up, Sep 40 put and
Sep 45 call can be
closed at a profit

FIGURE 9.5 Example of box spread.

Smart Investor Tip

When one side of the box spread expires, you might be left exposed on the other side. Keep an eye on the changing situation to avoid unacceptable risks.

The detailed profit and loss zones of a box spread are summarized in Figure 9.6. The net proceeds from this box spread result from the following

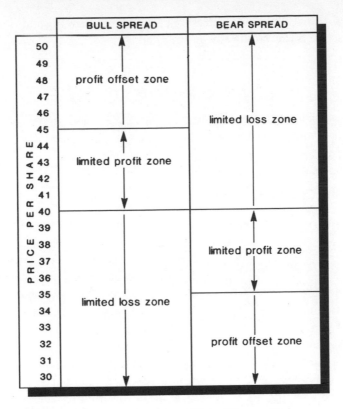

FIGURE 9.6 Box spread profit and loss zones.

outcomes:

Bull spread: Sell one September 45 put for 6 (+$600) and buy one September 40 put for 2 (−$200)

Bear spread: Sell one December 35 put for 1 (+$100) and buy one December 40 put for 4 (−$400)

If the stock's market price rises to between $40 and $45 per share, the bull spread can be closed at a profit. Above that level, the difference in bull spread values will move to the same degree in the money, offsetting one another. At that level, you can wait out time value decline, but it could also make sense to close the position when profits are available, if only to avoid exercise.

If the stock falls to between $35 and $40 per share, the bear spread can be closed at a profit. The long December 40 will be in the money and will change point-for-point with change in the stock's price. Below the level of $35 per share, the long and short position will change in intrinsic value levels, offsetting one another. Closing in-the-money positions makes sense to avoid exercise, remembering that time value offsets are likely to minimize any additional profits you could earn from waiting any longer.

Smart Investor Tip
When you close part of a box spread, close related long and short positions to avoid leaving open uncovered short positions.

Debit and Credit Spreads

The simultaneous opening of long and short positions involves receipt *and* payment of money. When you go short, you receive a premium, and when you go long you are required to pay. When you receive more than you pay, that also extends your profit range in a combination strategy. While it is always desirable to receive more money than you pay out, it is not always possible. Some strategies will involve making a net payment. When you make a payment to open the position, more profit is required in changed value levels to offset the amount paid and produce a net profit.

credit spread

any spread in which receipts from short positions are higher than premiums paid for long positions, net of transaction fees.

Smart Investor Tip
When a spread involves a net receipt, that broadens your profit potential; a net payment is accompanied by the requirement for greater profits in changed option premium to make up the difference.

A spread in which more cash is received than paid is called a *credit spread*. When you are required to make a payment, that is called a *debit spread*.

debit spread

any spread in which receipts from short positions are lower than premiums paid for long positions, net of transaction fees.

Horizontal and Diagonal Spread Strategies

Vertical spreads involve options with identical expiration dates but different striking prices. Another variation of the spread involves simultaneous option transactions with different expiration months. This strategy is called a *calendar spread*, or *time spread*.

The calendar spread can be broken down into two specific variations:

Horizontal spread—in this strategy, options have identical striking prices but different expiration dates.

Diagonal spread—in this strategy, options have different striking prices *and* different expiration dates.

calendar spread

(also called *time spread*) a spread involving the simultaneous purchase or sale of options on the same underlying stock, with different expirations.

horizontal spread

a calendar spread in which offsetting long and short positions have identical striking prices but different expiration dates.

diagonal spread

a calendar spread in which offsetting long and short positions have both different striking prices and different expiration dates.

Example

Going Horizontal: You create a horizontal calendar spread. You sell one March 40 call for 2, and you buy one June 40 call for 5. Your net cost is $300. Two different expiration months are involved. The earlier, short call expires in March, while the long call does not expire until June. Your loss is limited in two ways: by amount and by time. This strategy is illustrated in Figure 9.7. If, by March expiration, the first call expires worthless, you have a profit in that position and the second phase goes into effect. The short position no longer exists. If the stock rises at least 3 points above striking price before expiration, the overall position is at breakeven; above that, it will be profitable.

Example

The Diagonal View: You create a diagonal calendar spread. You sell one March 40 call for 2, and you buy one June 45 call for 3. Your net cost is $100. This transaction has different striking prices *and* expiration months. If the earlier-expiring short position is exercised, the long call can be used to cover the short call. In other words, as owner of the long position, you can exercise the call when your short position call is exercised. If the earlier call is not exercised, the overall risk is restricted to the net cost of $100. After expiration of the short call, breakeven is equal to the long call's striking price plus the cost of the overall transaction. In this case, the net cost was $100, so the breakeven price (not allowing for trading costs) is $46 per share. This is illustrated in Figure 9.8.

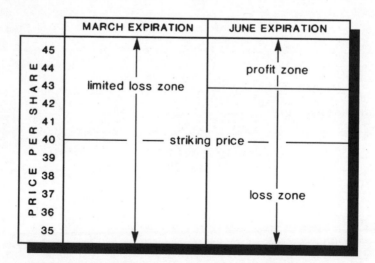

FIGURE 9.7 Profit and loss zones for an example of horizontal calendar spread.

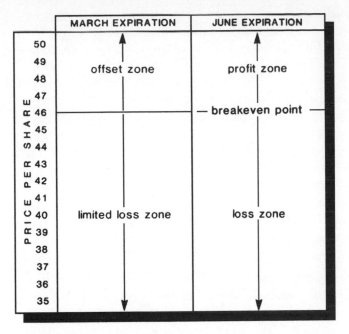

FIGURE 9.8 Profit and loss zones for an example of diagonal calendar spread.

Giving different spread strategies the names *vertical*, *horizontal*, and *diagonal* helps distinguish them from one another, and makes it easier to visualize the relationships between expiration and striking prices. These distinctions are summarized in Figure 9.9.

A horizontal spread is an attractive strategy when the premium value between two related options is temporarily distorted, or when the later option's features cover the risks of the earlier-expiring short position.

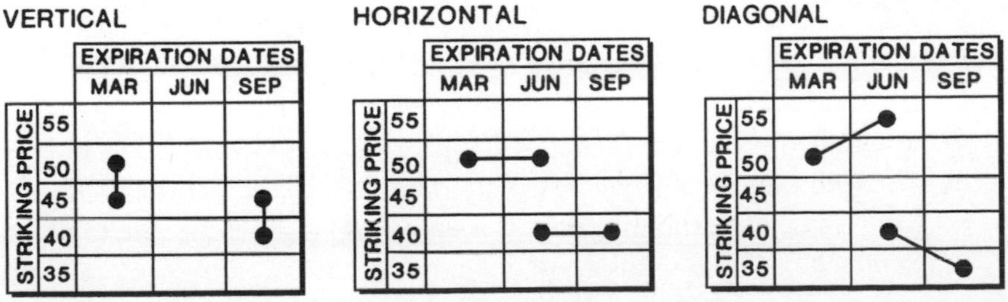

FIGURE 9.9 Comparison of spread strategies.

Example

Unlimited Risk, Horizontally Speaking: You open a horizontal spread using calls. You sell a March 40 call for 4, and you buy a June 40 call for 6. Your net cost is $200. If the market value of the underlying stock rises, the long position covers the short position. The risk is no longer unlimited. The maximum risk in this situation is the $200 paid to open the spread. If the stock remains at or below striking price, the short call will lose value and expire worthless; or it can be bought and closed at a profit. For example, if the short call's value fell to 1, you could buy and realize a profit of $300. Compared to the net cost of opening the spread, this puts you $100 ahead overall, but you still own the long call. If the premium value were to rise above the $600 paid for this call, it could be sold at a profit.

A horizontal spread is also effective in reducing risks when a position is already open. For example, if you previously sold a call and the stock begins to change in value so that you are at risk of exercise, you can reduce that risk by buying an option with a later expiration, which offsets the short position. This may be a less expensive alternative than buying the short position at a loss, because the long position has the potential to increase in value. If you own stock and do not want to go through exercise, the horizontal spread provides an alternative: You can use the long call to satisfy exercise instead of giving up stock.

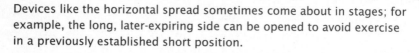

Smart Investor Tip

Devices like the horizontal spread sometimes come about in stages; for example, the long, later-expiring side can be opened to avoid exercise in a previously established short position.

Example

Avoiding Exercise Horizontally: You sold a covered June 45 call last month. The stock's market value is above striking price. You do not want to close the position because that will create a loss, and you also would like to avoid exercise. By buying a September 45 call, you create a horizontal spread. If the June 45 call is exercised, you will be able to use the September 45 call to fulfill the assignment. However, if the call is not exercised, you own a later-expiring call that has its own potential for profit within a time span of an additional three months.

A diagonal spread combines vertical and horizontal features. Long and short positions are opened with different striking prices and expiration dates.

> **Example**
>
> **Reduced Risk with Diagonal Strategies:** You create a diagonal spread. You sell a March 50 call for 4, and you buy a June 55 call for 1. You receive $300 net for these transactions. If the stock's market value falls, you will earn a profit from the decline in premium value on the short position. If the stock's market value rises, the long position call's value rises as well, offsetting increases in the short call. Maximum risk in this situation is 5 points; however, because you received net premium of $300, the real exposure is limited to two points (five points between striking prices, less three points net premium). If the earlier, short call expires worthless, you continue to own the long call. With its later expiration, you have potential profit for three more months.

This variety of spread becomes far more interesting when combining LEAPS options for the long side and shorter-term options for the short side. Because so much time is involved in the LEAPS option—up to three years—you have far more flexibility in designing, modifying, and developing strategies for horizontal and diagonal spreads.

For example, it is likely that by selling short-term options against the longer-term LEAPS, the strategy can be repeated many times. Enough premium income could be generated by selling calls to offset the cost of the long-position LEAPS. As the stock price changes over time, the corresponding horizontal or diagonal differences can be adjusted as well. The result could be to maximize premium income without risking exercise. Remember, the greatest decline in time value occurs in the last quarter of an option's life span. So you maximize this strategy by timing to offset long positions: You would seek short positions with higher striking prices (for calls) or lower striking prices (for puts).

The box spread adds complexity but opens the possibility for variations on this theme. A box spread employing long-position LEAPS and a series of offsetting shorter-term option short sales enables you to modify the range as the stock's price moves in either direction.

Altering Spread Patterns

The vertical, horizontal, and diagonal patterns of the spread can be employed to reduce risks, especially if you keep an eye on relative price patterns and

ratio calendar spread

a strategy involving a different number of options on the long side of a transaction from the number on the short side, when the expiration dates for each side are also different. This strategy creates two separate profit and loss zone ranges, one of which disappears upon the earlier expiration.

you recognize a temporary price distortion. Going beyond reduction of risk, some techniques can be employed to make the spread even more interesting. Combining LEAPS options with shorter-expiring options also increases the flexibility in spread strategies. In the best possible outcome, you will be able to profit both from spreads *and* on the underlying stock.

Varying the Number of Options

The *ratio calendar spread* involves the use of a different number of options on each side of the spread, plus different expiration dates. The strategy is interesting because it creates two separate profit and loss zone ranges, broadening the opportunity for interim profits.

Example

The Geometric Approach: You enter into a ratio calendar spread by selling four May 50 calls at 5, and buying two August 50 calls at 6. You receive $800 net ($2,000 received less $1,200 paid) before transaction fees are deducted. You hope that between the time you open these positions and expiration, the underlying stock's market value will remain below striking price; that would produce a profit on the short side. Your breakeven is $54 per share.

If the stock is at $54 at the point of expiration, you break even due to the ratio of four short calls and two long calls. Upon exercise, the two short calls will cost $800—the same amount that you received upon opening the ratio calendar spread. If the price of stock is higher than $54 per share, the loss occurs at the ratio of 4 to 2 (since you sold four calls and bought only two). If the May expiration date were to pass without exercise, the four short positions would be profitable, and you would still own the two August 50 calls.

The profit and loss zones in this example are summarized in Figure 9.10. Note that no consideration is given to transaction costs, time value of the longer-expiration premiums, or the outcome in the event of early exercise.

sell 4 May 50 calls for 5,
buy 2 Aug 50 calls for 6:
net proceeds $800

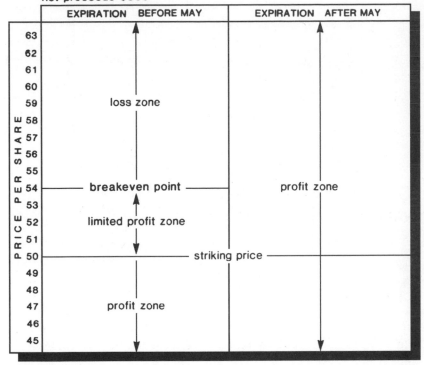

FIGURE 9.10 Example of ratio calendar spread.

Another complete ratio calendar spread strategy with defined profit and loss zones is summarized in Figure 9.11 and explained in the following example.

Example

A Complexity of Zones: You sell five June 40 calls at 5, and buy three September 40 calls at 7. Net proceeds are $400. The short position risk is limited to the first expiration period, with potential losses partially covered by the longer-expiration long calls. If the stock's market value does not rise above the striking price of 40, the short calls will expire worthless.

Once the June expiration passes, the $400 net represents pure profit, regardless of stock price movement after that date. However, if the stock's market value were to rise above the long calls' striking price, they

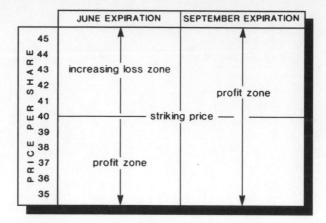

FIGURE 9.11 Ratio calendar spread profit and loss zones.

would increase in value three points for each point of increase in the stock. The calls can also be sold at any point prior to expiration, to create additional profit.

Table 9.2 shows a summary of the values for this strategy at various stock price levels as of expiration. No time value is considered in this summary. If the stock remains at or below the $40 per share level, the ratio calendar spread will be profitable. However, that profit will be limited as long as all positions remain open.

TABLE 9.2 Profits/Losses for Ratio Calendar Spread Example

Price	June 40	Sept. 40	Total
$50	−$5,000	+$3,000	−$2,000
49	− 4,500	+ 2,700	− 1,800
48	− 4,000	+ 2,400	− 1,600
47	− 3,500	+ 2,100	− 1,400
46	− 3,000	+ 1,800	− 1,200
45	− 2,500	+ 1,500	− 1,000
44	− 2,000	+ 1,200	− 800
43	− 1,500	+ 900	− 600
42	− 1,000	+ 600	− 400
41	− 500	+ 300	− 200
40	+ 2,500	− 2,100	+ 400
39	+ 2,500	− 2,100	+ 400
38	+ 2,500	− 2,100	+ 400
Lower	+ 2,500	− 2,100	+ 400

Expanding the Ratio

The ratio calendar spread can be expanded into an even more complex strategy through employment of the *ratio calendar combination spread*. This strategy places another dimension to the ratio calendar spread by adding a box spread to it.

Example

Doubling Up Calls *and* Puts: As illustrated in Figure 9.12, you open the following option positions:

Buy one June 30 call at 3 (pay $300).

Sell two March 30 calls at 1.75 (receive $350).

Buy one September 25 put at 0.75 (pay $75).

Sell two June 25 puts at 0.625 (receive $125).

The net result of these transactions is a receipt of $100, before calculation of trading charges. This complex combination involves 2 to 1 ratios between

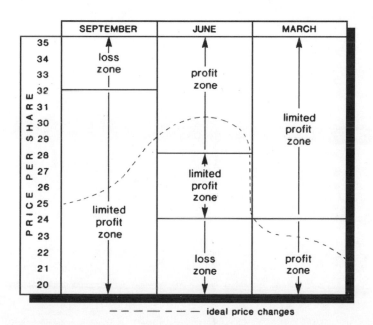

FIGURE 9.12   Example of ratio calendar combination spread.

ratio calendar combination spread
a strategy involving both a ratio between purchases and sales and a box spread. Long and short positions are opened on options with the same underlying stock, in varying numbers of contracts and with expiration dates extending over two or more periods. This strategy is designed to produce profits in the event of either price increases or decreases in the market value of the underlying stock.

short and long positions on both sides (two short option positions for each long option position). In the event of unfavorable price movements in either direction, you risk exercise on at least a segment of this overall strategy. The ideal price change pattern would enable you to close parts of the total combination at a profit, while leaving other parts open. Short positions should be closed in advance of long positions, given their least partial coverage against exercise. When prices move in one direction and then reverse and go the other way, it is called a price *whipsaw*. For the more complex options strategies, whipsaws can create ideal profit opportunities, or cause complete chaos—all depending on the timing, duration, and direction of the whipsaw.

Smart Investor Tip

You will want to close short positions in advance of long positions to avoid unacceptable risk—a point worth remembering when you open the positions in the first place.

whipsaw
a price trend in stocks when the price moves in one direction and then reverses and moves in the opposite direction.

Because trading fees add up quickly, any combination using only a small number of options is a costly strategy. Considering the risk exposure, potential profits would not justify the action in many cases; the previous example is a case in point. However, for the purpose of illustration, this shows how the strategy works. In practice, such strategies would be more likely to involve much larger numbers of option contracts, thus more money—and more risk exposure.

Exercise risk is reduced when you own shares in the underlying stock, providing full or partial coverage against short call exercise. For example, when writing two calls and buying one, the risk of a price increase is eliminated if you also own 100 shares. Those shares cover one call, and the other short call is covered by the long call.

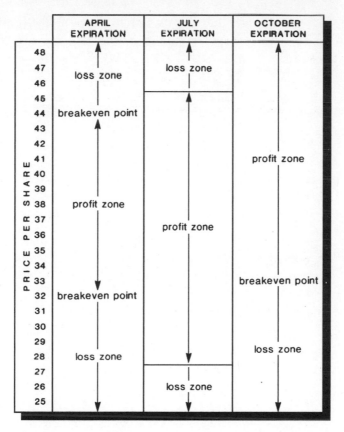

FIGURE 9.13 Ratio calendar combination spread profit and loss zones.

Example

Watching the Clock: A complete ratio calendar combination spread with defined profit and loss zones is shown in Figure 9.13. In this example, you open the following positions:

Buy one July 40 call for 6 (−$600).

Sell two April 40 calls for 3 (+$600).

Buy one October 35 put for 1 (−$100).

Sell two July 35 puts for 2 (+$400).

Net proceeds in this example are $300.

TABLE 9.3 Profits/Losses for Ratio Calendar Combination Spread Example

Price	April 40 Call	July 40 Call	July 35 Put	Oct. 35 Put	Total
$47	+$100	−$800	$ 0	+$400	−$300
46	0	− 600	0	+ 400	− 200
45	− 100	− 400	0	+ 400	− 100
44	− 200	− 200	0	+ 400	0
43	− 300	0	0	+ 400	+ 100
42	− 400	+ 200	0	+ 400	+ 200
41	− 500	+ 400	0	+ 400	+ 300
40	− 600	+ 600	0	+ 400	+ 400
39	− 600	+ 600	0	+ 400	+ 400
38	− 600	+ 600	0	+ 400	+ 400
37	− 600	+ 600	0	+ 400	+ 400
36	− 600	+ 600	0	+ 400	+ 400
35	− 600	+ 600	0	+ 400	+ 400
34	− 600	+ 600	0	+ 200	+ 200
33	− 600	+ 600	+ 100	0	+ 100
32	− 600	+ 600	+ 200	− 200	0
31	− 600	+ 600	+ 300	− 400	− 100
30	− 600	+ 600	+ 400	− 600	− 200
29	− 600	+ 600	+ 500	− 800	− 300
28	− 600	+ 600	+ 500	−1,000	− 500
27	− 600	+ 600	+ 500	−1,200	− 700
26	− 600	+ 600	+ 500	−1,400	− 900

This example consists of two separate ratio calendar spreads, boxed together. Profits would result if the stock's market value were to move in either direction, whereas losses are limited. Three separate expiration dates are involved. One danger in this elaborate strategy is that, as earlier options expire, later open positions become exposed to uncovered option exercise, so risks are increased. This situation can be reversed—so that chances for profits are greater—by building a combination using later-expiring long positions instead of short positions. Table 9.3 provides a breakdown of profit and loss produced at various price levels based on the example.

Strategies with a Middle Range

Another technique calls for the opening of offsetting options in middle striking price ranges, with opposing positions above *and* below. When options strategies are designed to create maximum advantages in periods of price consolidation for the stock, they are referred to as *sideways strategies*. The most popular of these is known as the *butterfly spread*. It can involve long and short positions in calls or puts. There are several possible variations of the butterfly spread. For example:

> **sideways strategies**
> option strategies designed to produce maximum gains when the underlying stock is expected to exhibit lower than average volatility.

- Sell two middle-range calls and buy two calls, one with a striking price above that level and one with a striking price below that level.

> **butterfly spread**
> a strategy involving open options in one striking price range, offset by open positions at higher and lower ranges at the same time.

- Sell two middle-range puts and buy two puts, one with a striking price above that level and one with a striking price below that level.

- Buy two middle-range calls and sell two puts, one with a striking price above that level and one with a striking price below that level.

- Buy two middle-range puts and sell two puts, one with a striking price above that level and one with a striking price below that level.

Example

The Butterfly in Flight: You sell two September 50 calls at 5, receiving $1,000. You also buy one September 55 call at 1 and one September 45 call at 7, paying a total of $800. Net proceeds are $200. This is a credit spread, since you receive more than you pay. You will profit if the underlying stock's price falls. And no matter how high the stock's price rises, the combined long positions' value will always exceed the values in the two short positions.

Smart Investor Tip

Exotic combinations are more often good for studying strategy than for actual use in the market. Trading costs are likely to offset potential limited profits in such strategies.

Butterfly spreads often are created when a single open position is expanded by the addition of other calls or puts, most often to protect a short position when a stock moves in a direction other than anticipated. It is difficult to create situations with risk-free combinations such as the one in the previous example.

Example

Netting the Butterfly: You sold two calls last month with a striking price of 40. The underlying stock's market value has declined to a point that the 35 calls are cheap, so you buy one to partially cover your short position. At the same time, you also buy a 45 call, which is deep out of the money. This series of trades creates a butterfly spread.

Trading costs makes butterfly spreads impractical when using a small number of options. The potential gain should be evaluated against the potential loss, trading costs, and ongoing exposure to risk.

Butterfly spreads involve either calls or puts. A bull butterfly spread will be most profitable if the underlying stock's market value rises, and the opposite is true for a bear butterfly spread.

A detailed butterfly spread, with defined profit and loss zones, is shown in Figure 9.14. In this example, the following transactions are involved:

Sell two June 40 calls at 6 (+$1,200).
Buy one June 30 call at 12 (−$1,200).
Buy one June 50 call at 3 (−$300).

The net cost is $300. This butterfly spread will either yield a limited profit or result in a limited loss. The potential yield often does not justify the strategy, since trading costs will not offset the limited potential profit. That is why the butterfly spread is often created in increments rather than all at once. Instead of executing the trades in the example, it might be more practical to simply buy one June 50 call and pay $300. In that alternative, you still have a limited potential loss ($300) but you also gain unlimited profit potential.

Table 9.4 summarizes profit and loss status at various prices of the underlying stock, using the previous example. It is based on values at expiration and assumes no remaining time value. If the stock's market value rises to $50 or more, the short position losses will be offset by an equal number of long position profits. And if the stock's market value declines, the maximum loss is $300, the net cost of opening these positions.

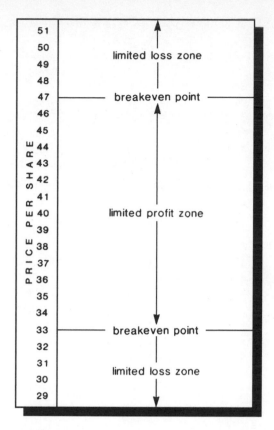

FIGURE 9.14 Butterfly spread profit and loss zones.

A variation on the butterfly is the *condor spread*. This is similar to the butterfly because it contains a bull and bear spread in combination; but with the condor, the striking prices of the short call and short put are not identical.

A similar variation on the use of multiple options is the *strap*. Also called a *triple option*, the strap consists of one long put and two calls (or vice versa).

condor spread
a variation of the butterfly spread using different striking prices in the short positions on either side of the middle range.

When the calls outnumber the puts, the position benefits if and when the underlying stock's market value rises. When the reverse is true, the position will benefit when the stock value declines. Because the in-the-money value of the heavier position will grow by two points, a favorable movement will quickly outpace the position cost. If the stock's price moves in the opposite direction,

TABLE 9.4 Profits/Losses for Butterfly Spread Example

Price	June 30	June 40	June 50	Total
$51	+ $900	−$1,000	−$200	−$300
50	+ 800	− 800	− 300	− 300
49	+ 700	− 600	− 300	− 200
48	+ 600	− 400	− 300	− 100
47	+ 500	− 200	− 300	0
46	+ 400	0	− 300	+ 100
45	+ 300	+ 200	− 300	+ 200
44	+ 200	+ 400	− 300	+ 300
43	+ 100	+ 600	− 300	+ 400
42	0	+ 800	− 300	+ 500
41	− 100	+ 1,000	− 300	+ 600
40	− 200	+ 1,200	− 300	+ 700
39	− 300	+ 1,200	− 300	+ 600
38	− 400	+ 1,200	− 300	+ 500
37	− 500	+ 1,200	− 300	+ 400
36	− 600	+ 1,200	− 300	+ 300
35	− 700	+ 1,200	− 300	+ 200
34	− 800	+ 1,200	− 300	+ 100
33	− 900	+ 1,200	− 300	0
32	−1,000	+ 1,200	− 300	− 100
31	−1,100	+ 1,200	− 300	− 200
30	−1,200	+ 1,200	− 300	− 300
29	−1,200	+ 1,200	− 300	− 300
Lower	−1,200	+ 1,200	− 300	− 300

the single offsetting option will partially offset the cost (and if price movement is severe enough, it could recapture the entire cost).

strap
an option strategy, also called a triple option, involving purchase of one put and two calls (hoping the stock's price will rise) or the purchase of one call and two puts (anticipating a stock's price decline).

triple option
alternative name for the strap.

In some brokerage account arrangements, you can reduce your trading cost by arranging for a *multileg options order*. This applies when several option positions are going to be opened at the same time, and the orders will be placed for a single commission rather than being charged a fee on each option position.

Any combination involving separate or offsetting options can be designed so that profits will be taken at specific points, either using stop orders or through careful tracking of the combination's status. However, in taking partial profits, you should be careful to not expose yourself to unintended risks. For example, if a short position is protected by an offsetting long position, the risk is minimal. But if the long position is closed without also closing the short position, additional risk is created.

multileg options order
a type of order allowed by some brokerage firms in which a strategy involving several options is opened for a single transaction fee, rather than for separate minimum fees on each option.

long hedge
the purchase of options as a form of insurance to protect a portfolio position in the event of a price increase; a strategy employed by investors selling stock short and needing insurance against a rise in the market value of the stock.

Hedge Strategies

Whenever options are bought or sold as part of a strategy to protect another open position, the combination of positions represents a hedge.

The Two Types of Hedges

A *long hedge* protects against price increases. A *short hedge* protects against price decreases.

Example

Trimming the Hedge: You are short on 100 shares of stock. This puts you at risk in the event the market value of that stock were to rise. You buy one call on that stock, which hedges your short stock position.

Example

Allowing the Hedge to Grow: You own 100 shares of stock and, due to recent negative news, you are concerned that the market value could drop. You do not want to sell the shares, however. To hedge against the risk of lost market value, you have two choices: Buy one put or sell one call. Both positions hedge the 100 shares. The put provides unlimited protection because it would increase in value for each in-the-money point lost in the stock's value. The call provides limited downside protection, only to the extent of the points received in premium.

short hedge

the purchase of options as a form of insurance to protect a portfolio position in the event of a price decrease; a strategy employed by investors in long positions who need insurance against a decline in the market value of the stock.

An example of a hedge, with defined profit and loss zones, is shown in Figure 9.15. In this case, you sold short 100 shares of stock at $43, and hedged that position with a May 40 call bought at 2. The cost of hedging your short position reduces potential profits by $200, but protects you against potentially greater losses without requiring that you close the position. The risk is eliminated until the call expires. At that point, there are three choices:

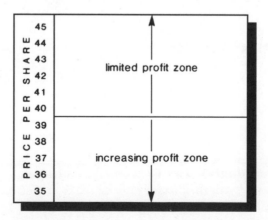

FIGURE 9.15 Long hedge profit and loss zones.

TABLE 9.5 Profits/Losses from the Long Hedge Example			
Price	Stock	Call	Total
$45	−$200	+$300	+$100
44	− 100	+ 200	+ 100
43	0	+ 100	+ 100
42	+ 100	0	+ 100
41	+ 200	− 100	+ 100
40	+ 300	− 200	+ 100
39	+ 400	− 200	+ 200
38	+ 500	− 200	+ 300
37	+ 600	− 200	+ 400
36	+ 700	− 200	+ 500
35	+ 800	− 200	+ 600

1. Close the short position to eliminate risk.

2. Replace the call with another, later-expiring one.

3. Do nothing since perception of the risk attributes might have changed.

In this example, if the underlying stock's market value increases, then profit potential is limited to the offsetting price gap between the stock's market value and the call's premium value. If the stock's market value falls, the short stock position will be profitable, with profits reduced by two points for the call premium you paid.

Table 9.5 summarizes this hedged position's overall value at various stock price levels.

Hedging beyond Coverage

One of the disadvantages to the hedge is that potential profits may be limited. A solution is to modify the hedge to increase profit potential, while still minimizing the risk of loss.

A *reverse hedge* involves providing more protection than needed to cover another position. For example, if you are short on 100 shares of stock, you need to purchase only one call to hedge the position. In a reverse hedge strategy, you buy more than one call, providing protection

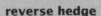

reverse hedge
an extension of a long or short hedge in which more options are opened than the number needed to cover the stock position; this increases profit potential in the event of unfavorable movement in the market value of the underlying stock.

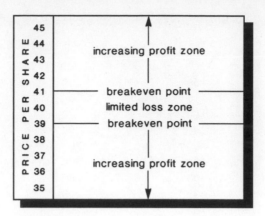

FIGURE 9.16 Reverse hedge profit and loss zones.

for the short position *and* potential for additional profits that would outpace stock losses 2 to 1, for example; with three calls, the ratio would be 3 to 1. Three calls applied against 200 shares of stock would produce a ratio of 3 to 2. The ratio can also be negative. For example, using two calls against 300 shares of stock provides a 2 to 3 negative reverse; you mitigate the potential loss, but you don't offset the entire potential loss.

An expanded example of a reverse hedge with defined profit and loss zones is shown in Figure 9.16. In this example, you sold short 100 shares of stock at $43 per share, and the value now has declined to $39. To protect the profit in the short position and to insure against losses in the event the price rises, you bought two May 40 calls at 2.

This reverse hedge solves the problem of risk in the short stock position, while also providing the potential for additional gain in the calls. In order for this profit to materialize, the stock's value would have to increase enough points to offset your cost in buying the calls. This hedge creates two advantages. First, it protects the short position in the event of unwanted price increase in the stock. Second, the 2-to-1 ratio of calls to stock means that if the price were to increase in the stock, the calls would become profitable.

Smart Investor Tip

The reverse hedge protects an exposed position while adding the potential for additional profits (or losses). This makes the hedge more than a form of insurance.

TABLE 9.6 Profits/Losses from Reverse Hedge Example			
Price	Stock	Call	Total
$45	−$200	+$600	+$400
44	− 100	+ 400	+ 300
43	0	+ 200	+ 200
42	+ 100	0	+ 100
41	+ 200	− 200	0
40	+ 300	− 400	− 100
39	+ 400	− 400	0
38	+ 500	− 400	+ 100
37	+ 600	− 400	+ 200
36	+ 700	− 400	+ 300
35	+ 800	− 400	+ 400

Table 9.6 summarizes this position's value as of expiration at various stock prices.

The reverse hedge works to protect paper profits in long positions as well. For example, you may own 100 shares of stock which has risen in value. To protect against a possible decline in market price, you may buy two puts, a reverse hedge that would produce 2-to-1 profits in the puts over decline in the stock's value. You may also sell two calls for the same reason. One would be covered while the other would be uncovered. Or, looking at this another way, the hedged position would be one-half covered overall. If the stock's market value were to fall, the calls would lose value, providing downside protection to the extent of the total premium received. However, if the stock were to rise, profits in the stock would be reduced by losses in the calls. As with short positions, you can use options for partial hedging. For example, if you own 500 shares of appreciated stock, selling four calls (or buying four puts) provides you with a 4 to 5 ratio protecting against lost market value. You can also view this as having 400 shares hedged and another 100 shares without a hedge.

Hedging Option Positions

Hedging can protect a long or short position in an underlying stock, or it can reduce or eliminate risks in other option positions. Hedging is achieved with various forms of spreads and combinations. By varying the number of options on one side or the other, you create a *variable hedge*, which is a hedge involving both long and short positions. However, one side will contain a greater number of options than the other.

Example

Three to One—Nice Odds: You buy three May 40 calls and sell one May 55 call. This variable hedge creates the potential for profits while completely eliminating the risk of selling an uncovered call. If the underlying stock's market value were to increase above the level of $55 per share, your three long positions would increase in value by three points for every point in the short position. If the stock's market value were to decrease, the short position would lose value and could be closed at a profit.

variable hedge
a hedge involving a long position and a short position in related options, when one side contains a greater number of options than the other. The desired result is reduction of risks or potentially greater profits.

This particular situation would be difficult to create all at once with a net credit, because the lower striking price calls would probably cost more than the higher-priced short position call. However, the variable hedge may be created in stages as a response to changing conditions. You can limit the risk exposure when short positions exceed long, by combining LEAPS and shorter-term options. A long LEAPS offset by soon-to-expire short position calls, for example, provides a return of premium and limited time at risk.

Long and short variable hedge strategies, with defined profit and loss zones, are shown in Figure 9.17. In the long variable hedge example, you buy three June 65 calls for 1, paying $300; and you sell one June 60 call for 5. Net proceeds are $200. This long variable hedge strategy achieves maximum profits if the underlying stock's market value rises. Above the striking price of 65, long call values would increase three points for every point increase in the underlying stock. If the stock's market value decreases, all of the calls lose value and the net $200 proceeds will be all profit. The short June 60 call could also be closed at a net gain.

Table 9.7 summarizes this position's value as of expiration at various stock price levels. The problem in this strategy is that the short positions expire later than the long positions; in most circumstances, this is the most likely way to create a credit in a variable hedge. So you need to experience price movement that creates an acceptable profit before expiration of the long position options, or be prepared to close out the short positions once the long positions expire, to avoid exposure to the risk of exercise.

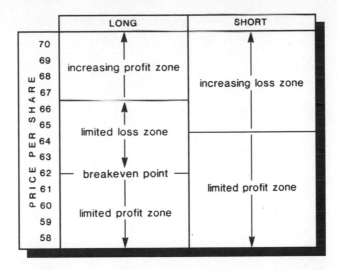

FIGURE 9.17 Variable hedge profit and loss zones.

The previously discussed Figure 9.17 also shows an increasing loss zone and limited profit zone in the example of a *short* hedge. In that case, you sold five June 60 calls for 5, receiving $2,500; and you bought three June 65 calls for 1, paying $300; net proceeds were $2,200. This short variable hedge strategy is a more aggressive variation than the long example, with more proceeds up front and a corresponding higher risk level overall. When the offsetting long and short call positions are eliminated, two short calls remain uncovered. A decline in the

	TABLE 9.7 Profits/Losses from the Long Variable Hedge Example		
Price	Stock	Call	Total
$70	+$1,200	−$500	+$700
69	+ 900	− 400	+ 500
68	+ 600	− 300	+ 300
67	+ 300	− 200	+ 100
66	0	− 100	− 100
65	− 300	0	− 300
64	− 300	+ 100	− 200
63	− 300	+ 200	− 100
62	− 300	+ 300	0
61	− 300	+ 400	+ 100
60	− 300	+ 500	+ 200
59	− 300	+ 500	+ 200
58	− 300	+ 500	+ 200

TABLE 9.8 Profits/Losses from the Short Variable Hedge Example

Price	Stock	Call	Total
$70	−$2,500	+$500	−$2,000
69	− 2,000	+ 400	− 1,600
68	− 1,500	+ 300	− 1,200
67	− 1,000	+ 200	− 800
66	− 500	0	− 500
65	0	− 300	− 300
64	+ 500	− 300	+ 200
63	+ 1,000	− 300	+ 700
62	+ 1,500	− 300	+ 1,200
61	+ 2,000	− 300	+ 1,700
60	+ 2,500	− 300	+ 2,200
59	+ 2,500	− 300	+ 2,200
58	+ 2,500	− 300	+ 2,200

value in the underlying stock would create a profit. However, an increase in the stock's market value creates an increasing level of loss. Beyond striking price, the loss is two points for every point of movement in the stock's price. Outcomes for this short hedge at various price levels of the stock are summarized in Table 9.8.

Partial Coverage Strategies

One variation of variable hedging involves cutting partial losses through partial coverage. This strategy is known as a *ratio write*. When you sell one call for every 100 shares owned, you have provided one-to-one coverage. A ratio write exists when the relationship between long and short positions is not identical. The ratio can be greater on either the long side or the short side. See Table 9.9.

TABLE 9.9 Ratio Writes

Calls Sold	Shares Owned	Percent Coverage	Ratio
1	75	75%	1 to $3/4$
2	150	75	2 to $1^1/2$
3	200	67	3 to 2
4	300	75	4 to 3
5	300	60	5 to 3
5	400	80	5 to 4

Example

Ratio Write or Wrong: You own 75 shares of stock and you sell one call. Because some of your shares are not covered, this overall position actually consists of two separate positions: 75 shares of stock are long, and one call is short. In practice, however, in the event of exercise, your 75 shares would satisfy three-quarters of the assignment. You would need to buy 25 shares at the striking price. Your short position is 75 percent covered. The ratio write is 1 to $^3/_4$.

Example

Covered plus Uncovered: You own 300 shares of stock and you recently sold four calls. You have two positions here: 300 shares that are associated with covered calls; and one uncovered short call. In practice, however, you have created a 4 to 3 ratio write.

Smart Investor Tip

The ratio write is appropriate when you are willing to accept some of the risk. When you think the chances of loss are minimal, the ratio write can be utilized to reduce overall costs.

An expanded example of the ratio write, with defined profit and loss zones, is shown in Figure 9.18.

In this example, you buy 50 shares of stock at $38 per share and you sell one September 40 call for 3. This creates a partially covered call. Half the short call risk is offset by the 50 shares. The other half of the risk is uncovered. If the value of the underlying stock rises, the risk is cut in half in the event of exercise. If the stock's market value falls, a loss in the stock will be offset by premium received from selling the call; there are three points of downside protection. A summary of this strategy is shown at various prices of the stock at expiration in Table 9.10.

ratio write
a strategy for covering one position with another for partial rather than full coverage. A portion of risk is eliminated, so that ratio writes can be used to reduce overall risk levels.

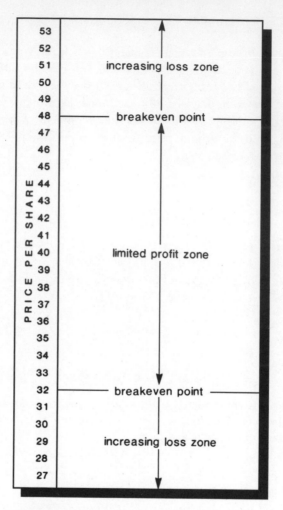

53	
52	
51	increasing loss zone
50	
49	
48	breakeven point
47	
46	
45	
44	
43	
42	
41	
40	limited profit zone
39	
38	
37	
36	
35	
34	
33	
32	breakeven point
31	
30	
29	increasing loss zone
28	
27	

PRICE PER SHARE

FIGURE 9.18 Ratio write profit and loss zones.

Straddle Strategies

While spreads involve buying and selling options with different terms, straddles are the simultaneous purchase and sale of options with the same striking price and expiration date.

Middle Loss Zones

A *long straddle* involves the purchase of calls and puts at the same striking price and expiration date. Because you pay to create the long positions, the result is

TABLE 9.10 Profits/Losses from the Ratio Write Example

Price	50 Shares of Stock	Sept. 40 Call	Total
$50	+$600	−$700	−$100
49	+ 550	− 600	− 50
48	+ 500	− 500	0
47	+ 450	− 400	+ 50
46	+ 400	− 300	+ 100
45	+ 350	− 200	+ 150
44	+ 300	− 100	+ 200
43	+ 250	0	+ 250
42	+ 200	+ 100	+ 300
41	+ 150	+ 200	+ 350
40	+ 100	+ 300	+ 400
39	+ 50	+ 300	+ 350
38	0	+ 300	+ 300
37	− 50	+ 300	+ 250
36	− 100	+ 300	+ 200
35	− 150	+ 300	+ 150
34	− 200	+ 300	+ 100
33	− 250	+ 300	+ 50
32	− 300	+ 300	0
31	− 350	+ 300	− 50
30	− 400	+ 300	− 100

a middle-zone loss range above and below the striking price, and profit zones above and below that zone.

Example

Back in the Straddle Again: You open a long straddle. You buy one February 40 call for 2; and you buy one February 40 put for 1. Your total cost is $300. If the underlying stock's value remains within three points above or below the striking price, the straddle will lose money. If the stock's market value moves higher or lower by more than three points from striking price, then the long straddle will be profitable.

Another example of a long straddle is summarized with defined profit and loss zones in Figure 9.19. In this example, you buy one July 40 call for 3 and one July 40 put for 1; total cost is $400. The long straddle strategy will be profitable if the underlying stock's market price exceeds the four-point range on either side of the striking price.

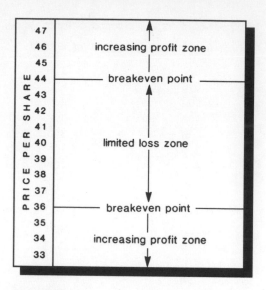

FIGURE 9.19 Long straddle profit and loss zones.

long straddle
the purchase of an identical number of calls and puts with the same striking prices and expiration dates, designed to produce profits in the event of price movement of the underlying stock in either direction, adequate to surpass the cost of opening the position.

The four points required on either side of the striking price emphasize the most important fact about long straddles: The more you pay in overall premium, the greater the required stock point movement away from striking price. It does not matter which direction the price moves, as long as its total point value exceeds the amount paid to open the position. Table 9.11 summarizes the outcome of this example at various stock price levels.

You have some flexibility in the long straddle. Since both sides are long, you are free to sell off one portion at a profit while holding on to the other, without increasing risk. In the ideal situation, the stock will move in one direction and produce a profit on one side; and then it will move in the opposite direction, enabling you to profit on the other side as well. A long straddle may be most profitable in highly volatile stocks, but of course, premium value of the options will tend to be greater as well in that situation. To show how the price swing can help to double profit potential, let's say that the stock's price moves up two points above striking price. The call can then be sold at a profit. If the stock's

	TABLE 9.11 Profits/Losses from the Long Straddle Example		
Price	50 Shares of Stock	Sept. 40 Call	Total
$47	+$400	−$100	+$300
46	+ 300	− 100	+ 200
45	+ 200	− 100	+ 100
44	+ 100	− 100	0
43	0	− 100	− 100
42	− 100	− 100	− 200
41	− 200	− 100	− 300
40	− 300	− 100	− 400
39	− 300	0	− 300
38	− 300	+ 100	− 200
37	− 300	+ 200	− 100
36	− 300	+ 300	0
35	− 300	+ 400	+ 100
34	− 300	+ 500	+ 200
33	− 300	+ 600	+ 300

market value later falls three points below striking price, the put can also be sold at a profit. The strategy loses if the stock's price remains within the narrow loss range, and time value premium offsets any minor price movements. In other words, time works against you as a buyer; and when you buy both calls and puts, you have to contend with time value on both sides of the transaction.

Middle Profit Zones

In the previous example, two related long positions were opened, creating a middle loss zone on either side of the striking price. The opposite situation—a middle profit zone—is created through opening a *short straddle*. This involves selling an identical number of calls and puts on the same underlying stock, with the same striking price and expiration date. If the stock's market price moves beyond the middle profit zone in either direction, this position would result in a loss. Short straddles offer the potential for profits when stocks do not move in an overly broad trading range, and when time value premium is higher than average.

short straddle
the sale of an identical number of calls and puts with identical striking prices and expiration dates, designed to produce profits in the event of price movement of the underlying stock within a limited range.

Less volatile stocks also tend to contain lower time value, whereas more volatile stocks have higher time value and higher risks with short straddles. Because time value decreases as expiration approaches, the advantage in this position is the same as for sellers of calls and puts individually—time works for the short seller.

Example

Straddling with Anticipation: You open a short straddle. You sell one March 50 call for 2 and one March 50 put for 1; total proceeds are $300. As long as the underlying stock's market value remains within three points of the striking price—on either side—the position will remain profitable. But if a change in current market value of the stock exceeds the three-point range, the short straddle will produce a loss.

The problem with the short straddle is that one side or the other is always at or in the money, so the risk of exercise is constant. The previous example does not allow for the transaction costs. In a practical application, the profit zone would be smaller for single options. The best outcome for this strategy, assuming that exercise does not take place, is that both sides will lose enough time value so that they can both be closed at a profit. Considering that the profit margin will be slim and risks are considerable, you need to evaluate whether this two-sided short position would be worth the risk. As with other examples of advanced strategies, the short straddle is likely to result from opening one position and later adding the other.

Smart Investor Tip

For each and every strategy with limited profit potential, always ask the critical question: Is it worth the risk?

An example of a short straddle with defined profit and loss zones is shown in Figure 9.20. In this example, you sell one July 40 call at 3, and one July 40 put at 1; total proceeds are $400. This creates a four-point profit zone on either side of the striking price.

The short straddle in this example creates a middle profit zone extending four points in both directions from striking price. Unless the stock's market value is at the money at the point of expiration, the likelihood of exercise on one side or the other is high. Table 9.12 summarizes the outcome of this short straddle at various stock price levels.

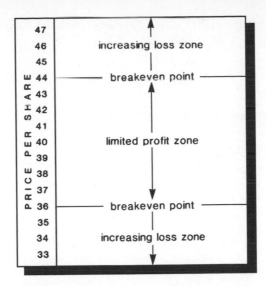

FIGURE 9.20 Short straddle profit and loss zones.

Actual profits and losses have to be adjusted to allow for trading costs on both sides of any position. A thin margin of profit can be entirely wiped out by those fees, making more elaborate option strategies less than practical, notably when using only single options. To compare outcomes of long and short straddles, refer to Figure 9.21, which shows profit and loss zones in a side-by-side format for each strategy.

Theory and Practice of Combined Techniques

Advanced option strategies expose you to the risk of loss, which could be significant especially when short positions are involved. If you do decide to employ any of these strategies, remember the following seven critical points:

1. *Brokerage fees are part of the equation.* Transaction fees reduce profit margins significantly, especially when you are dealing in single-option increments. A marginal potential profit could be wiped out by fees, so approach advanced strategies from a practical point of view.

2. *Early exercise can change everything.* Buyers have the right of exercise at any time, so whenever your short positions are in the money, you could face early exercise. What seems a straightforward, easy strategy can be thrown into complete disarray by early exercise.

TABLE 9.12 Profits/Losses from the Short Straddle Example

Price	July 40 Call	July 40 Put	Total
$47	−$400	+$100	−$300
46	− 300	+ 100	− 200
45	− 200	+ 100	− 100
44	− 100	+ 100	0
43	0	+ 100	+ 100
42	+ 100	+ 100	+ 200
41	+ 200	+ 100	+ 300
40	+ 300	+ 100	+ 400
39	+ 300	0	+ 300
38	+ 300	− 100	+ 200
37	+ 300	− 200	+ 100
36	+ 300	− 300	·0
35	+ 300	− 400	− 100
34	+ 300	− 500	− 200
33	+ 300	− 600	− 300

3. *Potential profit and risk are always related directly to one another.* Many options traders tend to pay attention only to potential profits, while overlooking potential risks. Remember that the greater the possibility of profit, the higher the potential for losses.

4. *Your degree of risk will be limited by your brokerage firm.* As long as your strategy includes short positions, your brokerage firm will restrict your exposure to risk—because if you cannot meet assignment obligations, the firm will be stuck with a loss.

5. *You need to thoroughly understand a strategy before opening positions.* Never employ any strategy before you understand how it will work out, given all possible outcomes. You need to evaluate risks carefully, not only for the most likely results but for the worst-case possibilities.

6. *Using LEAPS options vastly increases the flexibility of combinations.* Combination strategies can also be designed to avoid exercise risk or naked option writing risk, by employing longer-term LEAPS options. A net debit position could be transformed into a net credit position with repeated short-position offsetting sales over as long a period as three years.

7. *It doesn't always work out the way it was planned on paper.* When working out an option strategy on paper, it is easy to convince yourself that a particular strategy cannot fail, or that failure is only a remote possibility. Remember that option premium changes are not completely predictable, and neither are stock prices.

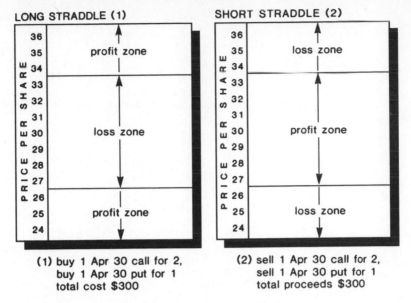

FIGURE 9.21 Comparison of long and short straddle strategies.

Options add a new dimension to your portfolio. You can protect existing positions, insure profits, and take advantage of momentary opportunities. However, every potential profit is associated with an offsetting risk. The market is efficient at least in that regard: Pricing of options reflects the risk level, so while a price is an opportunity, it also reflects exposure to the inherent risk in opening a position. Only through evaluation and analysis can you identify strategies that make sense for you, that protect your stock positions, and that you believe have a reasonable chance of producing profits at risk levels you are willing to undertake.

The next chapter helps you test out strategies without putting money at risk. Even the most complex options strategies may contain risks you cannot always anticipate. By first going through the exercise of setting up a model portfolio and then paper trading (moving through transactions without any money at risk), and can try out any strategy and gain trading experience.

Paper Trading: A Test Run of the Theory

Risk is present in all forms of investing. One of the troubling aspects to any new investing idea is this basic risk, and with options the lack of knowledge or experience adds to the overall risk. Anything new you try invariably will involve placing money on the line, even when you lack the experience to know for sure that the concepts will actually be profitable. So anyone new to options trading faces a dilemma: How do you gain experience without placing capital at unacceptable risks? And how do you *know* if a risk is acceptable until you try a trade for the first time?

This problem keeps many people away from options altogether. Few traders are willing to gain actual experience if that means losing money along the way. Few people will simply acknowledge that loss is the price they pay to gain experience; in fact, the experience you are able to gain profitably is far more satisfying. But even if you are dubious about options trading due to misunderstood or unknown risk, there is an easy solution. You can educate yourself about a variety of trading strategies, even the most exotic ones, by using a free service offered on many financial web sites. This feature, called *paper trading*, lets you place trades with a fictitious starting portfolio of cash, and see how it comes out.

paper trading
online "mock trading" of stocks and options using a hypothetical sum of cash to test strategies in a realistic environment but without placing real money at risk.

> ### Smart Investor Tip
>
> Paper trading works best when it simulates a real-world environment. This should include limitations on portfolio size, timing, risk, and level of transaction you are allowed to execute.

Different web sites offer you a variety of features for paper trading. Selection criteria should include the following:

- *Ease of use.* The most important feature for any web site is how easy it is to use. No one enjoys having to struggle with a complex or slow web site. Later in this chapter, several sites are reviewed that offer a variety of easy-to-use features.

- *Realism.* Your paper trading experience should approximate the real trading environment as much as possible. So rules should apply just as they do in your trading account with a broker.

- *Trading level distinctions.* In the real world, brokers are going to assign you a trading level based on your knowledge and experience and also on the cash level in your account and volume of trading activity. A paper-trading web site should provide you with one of two trading capabilities. First, if you use a site that restricts your trading activity, you will learn to function within your level of experience. Second, if you are allowed to execute any risk level of trade, you will quickly learn firsthand about risk and how some options theories end up being very costly. So pick a site that provides you with the level of experience you seek—realistic based on your knowledge level, or unlimited based on your desire to try even advanced and exotic strategies.

- *Ability to trade both stocks and options.* You want a paper-trading site to provide you with a realistic trading environment, even though you will only be making mock trades. In order for paper trading to provide you with valuable experience, it should be as close as possible to the real world of stock and options trading. You should be allowed to trade both, so that you can experience the cash limitations, risk dynamics, and interaction between stocks and option values.

- *Provision of valuable support services.* A site offering paper trading is most valuable when it offers additional services. These include educational service including publications, articles, and useful links. Many sites have options glossaries or bookstores, links to options market experts, and stock and options quotation services. The more extensive the level of additional services, the greater the value to a paper-trading site.

The Case for Paper Trading

Why should you paper trade? Of course, using a site with many valuable support features will invariably help everyone, but why not go directly to real-time trading? Even if you agree that paper trading makes sense, why not paper trade on a brokerage site? Because some online services offer modeling features to one degree or another, some might think it makes sense to simply paper trade where they will eventually trade with real money.

Smart Investor Tip
Using a nonbrokerage paper-trading site is a good form of discipline. It keeps you from the temptation to enter real-money trades before you are ready.

The reasons to paper trade as a first step, apart from a brokerage account, include:

- *Paper trading with a brokerage could be too tempting.* It might seem convenient to open a brokerage account and paper trade for a while, until you are comfortable with a range of options trades. But because real-time trades are also available, it is all too easy to abandon paper trading and go for the money. Without experience in a range of possible outcomes, this could be a costly mistake. It is human nature to fall into a habit of watching the market and seeing opportunities come and go while you paper trade. "If I had only put money into that last week . . ." is a dangerous and self-defeating way of thinking about options. Remember, on the long side you have to fight the odds because three-quarters of all options expire worthless. On the short side, you need to know what you're doing before entering a two-part trade (covered call) or, even more so, a naked position. This is why you should use a paper-trading service that restricts your trades to the same trading level you will experience when you begin trading for real. When you open your brokerage account, you are asked to fill out and submit an options-trading application, and based on your information and account dollar level, the brokerage firm will limit your trading. First-time traders will be allowed to open long positions only, or to write covered calls; more advanced strategies won't be allowed. To get experience in these advanced ideas, paper trading will be your only initial outlet.

Smart Investor Tip

An options-trading application is a brokerage firm's way to ensure that anyone trading options has been screened in advance.

- *Using real money before you have experienced the outcome of a trade is risky.* Many people begin studying options by reading books or observing the market. But a theory about how a trade will work out is not the same as putting real money at risk. A lot of first-time options traders focus on exotic, complicated, and high-risk trades, so that experience comes at a price, usually meaning losing money. With paper trading, you can try the most exotic, high-risk strategies you want without actually risking any loss. While you should approach paper trading seriously, it does provide you with a risk-free method for finding out the true risk level of a particular strategy.

Smart Investor Tip

Many options strategies look good on paper. But when you execute a trade, the experience might be far different than you expected. This is why paper trading is a sensible starting point.

- *Once you start trading for real, especially using a discount brokerage service, you have little or no support.* The advantage of discount services is that trades are executed for very little cost. In fact, the combined cost of opening and closing an option position is usually under a quarter point ($25), sometimes less. This also assumes you trade a single contract. Trading multiple contracts lowers the per-option cost even more. But this savings also comes without any advice or guidance, so you have to find your own way. Options traders, of course, should be able to execute their own trades and also to make their own decisions without help. But everyone needs to start somewhere, and paper trading is an excellent way to begin. Think of paper trading as learning to ride a bike. The training wheels are useful and they help avoid serious injury. At some point, the training wheels have to come off, but not until you are ready.

Smart Investor Tip

Some investors depend on the safety net of a commission-based broker. But options investors should be prepared to proceed on their own. Paper trading helps you gain experience in trading without the risk *and* without the advice many investors are accustomed to having available.

- *The mechanics of options trading take some getting used to.* The very fact that options expire makes them much different from the buy-and-hold strategy of stocks. Many aspects associated with options trading, including margin requirements and limitations, matching of risk with financial resources, and even the details of placing trades properly, all require a degree of practice. For example, many first-time options traders make the expensive mistake of entering a buy instead of a sell, or vice versa. Paper trading helps you to master the oddities of the market by trying out even advanced trades in a simulated environment.

Smart Investor Tip

The devil is in the details. Options trading in concept might seem quite easy, but in practice any type of mistake can be expensive. Paper trading is a good forum for making these mistakes.

There are three types of web sites offering paper trading:

1. *Free paper trading on sites selling other products.* A site that offers more than mere paper trading is valuable because it lends support to your trading activity, especially if good learning tools are included. Some sites offering paper trading also promote products they are selling. There is nothing wrong with selling products online and, in fact, many marketing sites view free services like paper trading, quotations, and articles as good inducements for traders to visit.

2. *Subscription sites for options traders.* Other sites specialize in paper trading but also offer valuable services as a specific options-related educational service. Many options traders will be willing to pay for paper-trading services because the value in these added services is worth the money.

3. *Options sites providing paper trading and many other services.* A third type of site offers paper trading as well as many other support services, tutorials and articles, and links to education. Because such a site (see the CBOE in the next section) is aimed specifically at options trading, it is informative and full of valuable resources.

Four Sites Worth Checking

Following are four sites worth checking out. They offer an array of different services, levels of use, and conveniences. Each site should be visited in order to see exactly what is offered and whether it will work for you.

www.e-opts.com

This site is subscription based, but it offers its members much more than just paper trading. A number of additional resources for novice traders makes this site worth checking into. As a site dedicated to paper trading (rather than one offering paper trading as one of many benefits), e-opts is easy to use and includes real-time quotes.

When you trade with real money, you buy and sell based on current prices and, of course, within the limitations of cash and margin accounts. This site imitates the reality of how trading occurs by setting up a portfolio with a specific dollar value, and then inviting you to trade stocks and options. If and when your proposed trade exceeds monetary limitations, you are not allowed to proceed. Some other paper-trading sites allow you to add dollar values to your fictitious portfolio, but that contradicts the purpose to paper trading, which is to see what it is like to enter transactions in a real environment.

An especially valuable feature is the glossary. Throughout the site, if you position your cursor over a highlighted option term you do not understand, its definition pops up. This is not only convenient; it also adds value to the learning experience you need while paper trading.

www.investopedia.com

This is a multiresource site that offers an easy-to-use dictionary, articles and tutorials, professional exam preparation, reports, quotes, and financial calculators—as well as free paper trading.

From the home page, go to the link for "stock simulator" and enter the "Investopedia games" area. Choose the game that includes both stock and options trading. By participating in a game, you are ranked according to the profitability of stock and options trades you enter. This makes paper trading interesting, because it enables you to compete against other investors.

The stock simulator starts you out with a mock portfolio valued at $100,000. This is a nice, tidy sum to begin your portfolio. However, for most individuals, starting out with such a large amount of capital is not realistic. One frustrating aspect of getting into options trading is that for most people, the limitations of capital prevent extensive trading activity. So in that respect, paper trading with a $100,000 portfolio does not approximate a real-world environment for the majority of people.

The system also requires a form of diversification. No one position can exceed 50 percent of your total portfolio value, so that you have to put the cash to work in two or more different stocks and/or option positions.

www.eztradeclub.com

This site sells software aimed at investors and offers free paper trading as a feature of the site. From the home page, link to "trading console" to open an account.

Your initial mock trading portfolio can range between $3,000 and $20,000. It makes sense to create a portfolio that is approximately the same size as the real-money portfolio you will eventually create for yourself. This site also allows you to specify whether you want to work out of a cash account or a margin account. If you pick margin trading, you can exceed cash limitations when you trade, but only according to actual margin rules and restrictions.

This site has a lot on it, and the paper-trading area is not as user friendly as some other sites. However, it does enable you to model your portfolio to a similar level to that of the "real cash" portfolio you expect to have later. Options traders will have some frustration, however. Unless you set your account up as a margin account, you will not be allowed to write covered calls. So if you open up with a cash account (as most people wanting to explore option strategies are likely to do initially), this paper-trading site will not provide you with the flexibility you will need and want.

www.cboe.com

The Chicago Board Options Exchange (CBOE) is the site where options are traded and cleared. Located in Chicago, the exchange is an interesting one, and its web site offers an array of tools and features specifically aimed at options traders.

From the home page, link to "trading tools" and then to "virtual trading tool." One of the most interesting features of the free CBOE paper-trading page is that it asks you to set up your own trading level. It sets this based on your experience, interests, and skill levels. So as long as you set up the account to honestly reflect your personal experience and knowledge, the site will impose the same restrictions on you as those of a real brokerage firm.

You can also set up the dollar amount of your portfolio from $5,000 and up. You should establish your account to start out at the level you are likely to start in a real trading account, so that your paper-trading experience will take place in an environment similar to the one you'll experience later on, using actual cash.

The CBOE also offers extensive and easy-to-use options quotes. If you do not yet have a brokerage account, this feature is very valuable. Many financial web sites offering free quotes are limited to stocks and are not set up for ease of use in options trading. The CBOE is an exception. Its options listings are accessible by linking to "quotes" and then to "delayed option chains." The delayed chain link is practical for most people. It lists all calls and puts on a specified stock on a single page. This feature is valuable because you don't need to know the symbol for an option in advance, a problem many options traders have to struggle with. Quote symbols used to be simple, but after the introduction of long-term equity anticipation security (LEAPS) options, they became quite complex. So the CBOE system is just as convenient as most brokerage listing systems.

Proceeding with a Paper-Trading Plan

To get started in paper trading for options, you may want to take three steps at the same time:

1. *Open a brokerage account or continue with the account you already have.* If you have an existing brokerage account where you trade stocks, continue that activity while you follow the next two steps. If you have not yet begun to trade on any level, open a free brokerage account after researching the terms and trading costs of several brokerage firms.

2. *Complete an options-trading application with your brokerage firm.* Download or request an options-trading application. This form asks you to specify the number of trades you execute per year and your level of experience in options trading. If you are a novice, you will be assigned a low level and probably be allowed only to open long call or put positions, at least as a start. But once you have gained some experience, you can apply to be upgraded to the next level.

3. *Find a paper-trading site that fits your needs and begin actively trading options.* Check out several paper-trading sites and find one that is flexible enough for the kind of trading you want to try. Also, make sure it works. You can open a free account on several sites and navigate your way through the paper-trading feature before deciding whether to remain with a site or not. Try to think of your paper trades as real; avoid the problem of not taking the paper-trading activity seriously. Begin with a specific portfolio amount and see what kind of net returns you realize through paper trading. That is the only way to ensure that once you begin putting actual money into trades, you will know what to expect.

The next chapter expands the whole question of strategies, risk levels, and the use of options. By applying options as a tool in specialized trading strategies, you achieve many benefits: You can expand your trading with options because they cost a fraction of stocks, limit your overall risks, and use puts for short-side positions without having to go short.

Chapter

Options for Specialized Trading: Leveraging the Technical Approach

Most people think about options trading as an isolated and separate strategy. Options are used to speculate or to hedge existing stock positions, and, for many traders, that is the full extent and value of options. But options are so flexible and convenient that they can be used in numerous specialized situations as well.

A popular system in use today is *swing trading*. This is an excellent technical trading method for anyone who wants to become involved in short-term market plays, normally lasting between two and five days. Swing traders use charting to identify a buy or sell *setup* and then time their decisions for small but consistent profits.

swing trading
a system based on a two- to five-day cycle, involving buying and selling positions based on predictable price movements and in response to buy and sell setup signals.

setup
in swing trading, a signal indicating that a stock has reached a short-term high level (a sell setup) or a short-term low level (a buy setup). By taking action upon recognizing a setup, swing traders make small but consistent profits.

Options are perfect devices for swing traders, and for one simple reason. If you swing trade using stocks, your potential range of trades is severely limited and involves significant risks, at least on the short side. For example, if you want to swing trade using lots of 100 shares, a $25 stock demands a $2,500 commitment, but an option on the same stock will be available for a small fraction of that cost. An $85 dollar stock requires $8,500 in available cash to place at risk but, again, an option on the same shares will cost far less.

Smart Investor Tip

The leveraging feature of options makes swing trading practical, affordable, and less risky than using stock. This is an example of how options favor short-term traders.

With these important distinctions in mind, the swing-trading strategy is perfectly set up for options in place of stock. Remember these key points:

- *Swing traders are not interested in long-term investing.* A swing trader wants to create extremely short-term profits by moving in and out of positions in two- to five-day trading ranges. Because they are not interested in the long term, swing trading and options are a good match.

- *Because options cost less than stock, the range of possible swing trades is expanded with the use of options.* Imagine starting a swing-trading strategy with $10,000 available. Using stocks, you could trade four stocks in the range of $20 to $25. If you have to go short, you would be required to keep cash on hand to cover margin requirement. However, with the same $10,000, you could trade many more stocks, avoid the margin requirement involved with going short, and still make the same profits on each trade.

- *Swing traders want to open both buy and sell positions, meaning they may have to short stock. But with options, swing traders can buy puts instead of selling stock.* Many swing traders simply avoid opening short positions in stock because the risk is so significant. So they cut out half of their potential trades, and limit activity only to the buy side. With options, you can go long on calls and puts, meaning both sides can be involved without extra risk.

- *Swing trading is set up for very short-term positions, meaning this is a perfect strategy for in-the-money options that will expire within one month.* You are not likely to hear of very many options strategies where in-the-money options about to expire are favored above all others. But swing traders intend to be in positions for only two to five days, so soon-to-expire options are perfect for this purpose. Because time value will be at or near zero in these options, the cost of long positions will be limited to intrinsic value. Swing traders will want to use in-the-money options because they need the point-for-point price reaction, and options scheduled to expire in a month or less (but with current market value of the stock only a few points from striking price) are ideal.

- *Options present much lower risk than stock positions.* Swing traders are not going to time their decisions perfectly. No one is right 100 percent of the time. So in the use of long or short stock, the potential risks are significant. In fact, because swing traders want to move in and out of positions in only a few trading days, having capital tied up in positions beyond that time prevents swing traders from realizing their full potential and translates to many lost opportunities. In those cases where the timing is wrong, using soon-to-expire options is lower risk because less cash is involved. A missed timing situation does not destroy the strategy.

Swing-Trading Basics

A swing trader depends on the three emotions that dominate the stock market: greed, fear, and uncertainty. These emotions cause virtually all of the short-term price aberrations that make swing trading a profitable technical strategy. Swing traders try to ignore the tendency to react emotionally to price movement, using logic to take advantage of market overreactions. When prices of stocks rise quickly, "the market" (the overall investing market, that is) tends to act out of greed, buying up shares to get in on the anticipated profits. The majority is often wrong, meaning that many people buy shares at the very top of a short-term price swing.

Smart Investor Tip
Swing traders bet against majority thinking, which often leads to exceptional profits, because the majority is usually wrong.

When prices of stocks fall, investors fear further declines and want to cut losses. So the tendency is to sell shares at the very bottom of the short-term price swing. And after a period of price movement, stock prices may move into a very brief period of uncertainty. At these times, trading range narrows as traders wait out the next price movement. During uncertain times, some inexperienced investors become impatient and buy or sell impulsively.

All of these conditions present profitable opportunities, and this is where swing trading works best. Rather than timing decisions emotionally, swing traders tend to do the opposite of the majority. They attempt to time their sales for the price peaks, and time their purchases for the price bottoms. When prices settle down and the market is uncertain, swing traders wait out the period, moving focus to other stocks and practicing patience rather than making buy or sell decisions impulsively.

Swing traders buying and selling stock have to limit their activity based on cash available (on the long side) and margin credit (on the short side). So they typically can swing trade using odd lots only and limiting their participation to only a handful of stocks. In some cases, swing traders can afford to play only one or two stocks at a time, based on their capital restrictions. This is unfortunate because it means having to miss many opportunities. Options solve this problem while reducing risks *and* setting the stage to play both sides of the price swing without having to ever go short.

Smart Investor Tip

Swing trading with options presents a double advantage: You can be involved in many stocks at the same time, while costs and risks are lower than when shares of stock are used.

One argument against using options for swing trading is that they expire. But this should not be an issue because swing trading ideally works in a very short time frame. There is no need to tie up capital in buying (or selling) 100 shares of stock, when a single option contract provides the same dollar profit when price movement takes place.

Example

A Swinging Idea: In January 2007, Wal-Mart (WMT) was trading in the mid-40s and its trading range for 52 weeks had been $42 to $54 per share. Using the traditional method for measuring volatility, the stock was at 24 percent (range divided by low price). You wanted to swing trade this stock. To buy 100 shares, you would have needed more than $4,700 (on January 10, the stock was trading between $47 and $48 per share). To go short, you would have had to assume the risk of selling short, and had at least $2,400 in your account to cover the margin requirement.

Now consider using extremely short-term options. On January 10, slightly more than one week remained until expiration of the January options. There were only seven trading days remaining. This is a perfect scenario for extremely short-term in-the-money options for swing trading. Assuming a current setup signal occurred, you might anticipate a price rise (meaning you want to buy a call) or decline (meaning you want to buy a put). The January 45 call was about 2.5 points in the money, and was selling on January 10 for $2.37. This is virtually all intrinsic value. The January 47.50 put was selling that day for 0.60. So whether you believed in this situation that the price would rise or fall in the next six trading days, options are clearly much cheaper than 100 shares of stock.

The example makes a strong case for swing trading. But remembering that those options are going to expire in only six trading days, buying either the call or the put must be done only if and when a strong setup signal was present.

Smart Investor Tip

You can use options very close to expiration—even a matter of days—based on the swing-trading ideal of five or fewer trading days in any open position. But you also have to be willing to get in and out quickly or to accept small losses.

In most options strategies, you have to be concerned about the timing of a buy or sell decision primarily due to expiration, so the majority of strategies present a dilemma. On the long side, you want cheap options close to the money with a long time until expiration. On the short side, you seek high-time-value options with as short a time as possible until expiration. Swing trading contradicts these requirements, primarily because it is designed to work only within a few trading days.

In swing trading, you do not have strong feelings about companies one way or the other. You are trading emotions, not stocks. So when you find a setup to buy, you buy; and when you find a setup to sell, you sell. It's that simple. As a swing trader, you are exploiting the overreactions of the market at large and seeking very short-term profits based on identifiable setup signals. In the next section, the Wal-Mart example is revisited and the question of setup signals is explored in detail to show how this works.

The Setup Signal

Swing trading depends on the setup, a buy or sell signal based on at least three days' worth of indications. Setups occur as well in combinations. In other words, a short-term trend requires at least a three-day price and pattern movement in one direction, ending with a clear reversal signal. It also requires a combination of setup indicators.

candlestick charts
technical charts for stocks summarizing a stock's daily trading range, opening and closing prices, and price direction. The candlestick is used in many trading systems, including swing trading.

Swing traders do well using *candlestick charts* to spot these setups. The candlestick chart is based on an ancient Japanese system originally used centuries ago to track rice prices. Today, Internet-based services offer candlesticks on most listed stocks and save time by computing the indicators for you. The candlestick employs a relatively simple pattern that reveals the opening and closing prices, trading range, and direction of price movement for the trading day (or other period).

While the candlestick tracks the stock's market price, the setup signals you can derive from the candlestick can be employed to time buy and sell decisions using options. As long as you use minimally in-the-money options with a short time to go until expiration (meaning there will be little or no time value remaining), the use of options will track option price movement very closely.

Smart Investor Tip

The reason to use close-to-expiration options is to maximize the point-for-point price movement. If there is any time value remaining in the option, swing-trading models will not work.

upper shadow
on a candlestick formation, the line defining the extent of a day's trading range. The line extends above the opening or closing prices for the day.

Candlestick charts consist of a series of boxes (squares and rectangles) with single lines rising above and below. A white or blank box indicates the price rose on that day, and a black box occurs when the price direction is downward. The box borders the day's opening and closing prices. The lines extending above and below represent the trading range for the day and are named the *upper shadow* and the *lower shadow*. For example, if a stock opened at

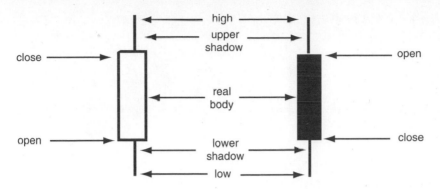

FIGURE 11.1 The candlestick.

$23 per share and closed at $26, but had prices as high as $28 and as low as $21, the candlestick for that day would consist of a white box (because the price rose from opening to closing). The rectangle would be bordered between $23 and $26, the opening and closing prices. And the lines would extend below the box down to $21 and above the box up to $28. The attributes of candlesticks are summarized in Figure 11.1.

The buy or sell setup is found when a clearly established trend comes to an end. The setup anticipates price movement in the opposite direction and may be seen in the emergence of one or more patterns. Important patterns to know include:

lower shadow
on a candlestick formation, the line defining the extent of a day's trading range. The line extends below the opening or closing prices for the day.

- *Three or more days of clearly identified uptrend or downtrend movements.* This is the clearest of all setup signals. A minimum of three days is required. An *uptrend* occurs when you see three or more trading days consisting of a series of higher highs, offset with higher lows in price. For example, a price range over three days of $23 to $26, $24 to $28, and $26 to $29 meets these criteria. A *downtrend* also occurs over three or more days, and consists of a series of lower highs and lower lows. For example, the price pattern of $29 to $26, $28 to $24, and $25 to $23 establishes a three-day downtrend.

uptrend
in swing trading, a series of three or more days consisting of higher highs offset by higher lowers.

uptrend   downtrend

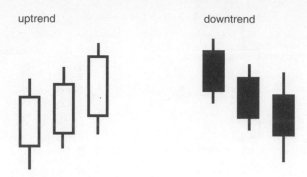

FIGURE 11.2   Uptrend and downtrend candlestick patterns.

downtrend

in swing trading, a series of three or more days consisting of lower highs and lower lows.

The terminology is somewhat confusing, but once you see the series on a candlestick chart, the pattern becomes completely clear. The fact that uptrends consist of a series of white or clear boxes makes an uptrend jump right out and, of course, the black boxes in a downtrend are equally visible. As long as the size and shape of those boxes exceed the boxes of the previous day (so that both top and bottom are higher in an uptrend or lower in a downtrend), the pattern is clearly set. The three-day uptrend and downtrend are demonstrated in Figure 11.2.

Smart Investor Tip

Short-term trends are easily identified. They open, close, and move in the same direction for three or more days.

narrow range day (NRD)

in a candlestick chart, a trading day with an exceptionally small trading range.

- *Look for the setup following the three-day pattern.* The setup will usually consist of either a *narrow-range day* (*NRD*) or a day with exceptionally high volume. The NRD is easily recognized; the rectangle and shadows are quite small.

An NRD is considered a strong signal that the established trend may be ending. This is especially true when accompanied by a high-volume day. So when you see (1) a trend lasting three days or more, (2) an NRD, and (3) exceptionally high volume on the same day as the NRD, that combination gives you the strongest setup possible. On the upside, it is a sell signal; on the downside, it is a buy signal.

Smart Investor Tip

A narrow-range day signifies price consolidation at the end of a trend. When this occurs *with* unusually high volume, it is the clearest possible setup, indicating time to take action.

Testing the Theory

The two- to five-day price trends and setups can be tested by reviewing a typical candlestick chart. Figure 11.3 is a good example.

This is a 30-day candlestick chart for Wal-Mart, which was the stock used in an example earlier in this chapter. The latest few days of this chart did not present a clear signal in either direction; but look at the activity from December 26 (the trading day after December 22) through January 4. In these six trading days, there was a clear uptrend and sell signal. Five uptrend days ended with a peak in prices and exceptionally high volume. The following day was an NRD

FIGURE 11.3 Wal-Mart (WMT).
Source: Candlestickchart.com, © 2007 the RediNews Network. Used with permission.

day, which is recognized by the virtual flat line in place of a more obvious trading *range*. This means that opening and closing prices were quite close together. A stronger signal would have involved the NRD and high volume in a single day. But if you had bought a call in late December, the development of this uptrend pattern ending on January 4 would have provided a clear sell signal.

Smart Investor Tip

It is not any one signal that indicates time to take action, but a combination of an established short-term trend with a reversal signal. That is what swing traders depend on before making a move.

A clearer pattern emerged for Apple, the well-known computer company, during the period of December 2006 through early January 2007. Figure 11.4 shows a one-month candlestick chart for the company.

The range of trades marked off includes four days of declining price, followed by two uptrend days. There are five aspects to this pattern, all signaling an end to the downtrend:

1. *Consecutive downtrend days.* The stock had fallen in value for four days in a row. This is the preliminary signal that, in fact, the short-term

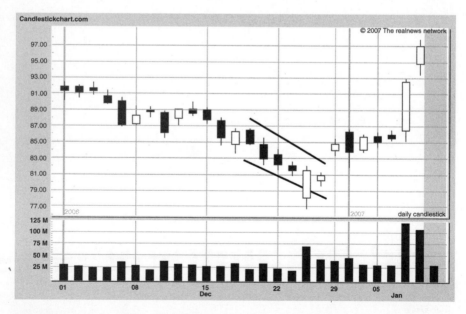

FIGURE 11.4 Apple Inc. (AAPL).
Source: Candlestickchart.com, © 2007 the RediNews Network. Used with permission.

downtrend is probably coming to an end, and the most common pattern swing traders seek.

2. *A narrowing trading day.* On December 26, a down day also showed a narrowing range, but it was not necessarily an NRD. You would expect an NRD to be quite thin (like the last day shown on the chart, for example).

3. *A reversal in direction with higher volume.* December 27 was a day when price rose for the first time in five trading days, and volume picked up as well.

4. *A second narrowing trading day.* December 28 was yet another up day and also with relatively narrow trading.

5. *A price gap.* Chart watchers invariably point to a *gap* as significant. In the case of Apple, after the signals indicating that the downtrend had ended, the stock's price gapped between December 28 and 29. This is a strong indication that the stock will be rising in price, and it foreshadowed trading over the next seven to eight trading days.

gap
a trading pattern in which the range between days includes a gap in price, with the second day's trading range opening above the highest price of the previous day or below the lowest price of the previous day.

In using options for swing trading, the signal that the downtrend had ended was clear by December 27 or 28. If you had bought a call on one of those days, especially one in the money and due to expire in the near future, you would have made a profit within eight trading days. For example, on December 27, when the stock opened under $79 per share, the January 80 call was selling for approximately 4 ($400). On January 11 (the last day on the chart and an NRD following a strong uptrend), the same call was worth 15.80, nearly 400 percent higher.

Of course, hindsight is always perfect in swing-trading situations being reviewed. At the time, the price decline followed news that Apple CEO Steve Jobs may have been awarded stock options without proper approval. The stock's price was reacting to the news, so the price decline caused a lot of fear among Apple investors. However, swing traders are supposed to ignore the news and just trade the price patterns and investor emotions. In this situation, the signals that the downtrend had ended were quite strong, and five separate indicators provided strong *confirmation* of

confirmation
a signal providing support for another signal, reinforcing the belief that a trend is ending and about to reverse.

that fact. Even so, using options the maximum risk in this situation would have been less than $500 for a single January call, far less than the purchase price of $7,900 for 100 shares. A comparison of the percentage return also bolsters the argument favoring the use of options over stock. A profit of $1,180 on 100 shares bought at $79 per share would be 15 percent, but the profit on a 4.50 option would be 262 percent. The option would have required less capital, involved less risk, and created a far higher return.

Smart Investor Tip
The more confirmation you have that an established short-term trend is on the verge of reversing, the better. But if you wait too long—even one day—you could also miss the opportunity.

This leverage feature is compelling. A swing trader faces the constant problem of capital limitation. With a finite amount of money, you can swing trade only a limited number of stocks if you are going to be buying shares. But slightly in-the-money, soon-to-expire options are quite cheap. In the example earlier in this chapter, when Wal-Mart stock was selling at about $48 per share, the closest in-the-money call was available for 2.37, or about 5 percent of the stock's price. The next-expiring in-the-money put was at 0.60, or about 1 percent of the stock price. So your capital is easily leveraged with options in place of stock. Rather than having to buy 100 shares for $4,800, you could put $237 into a call and have the same potential upside profit; or invest only $60 in a put for the same downside potential (not to mention avoiding the risk of selling shares short).

A Strategic View of Options for Swing Trading

The success of a swing-trading program relies on following the rules: identifying the setup after an uptrend or downtrend and acting quickly to take advantage of the short-term price swing. But many stock-related considerations should be kept in mind as well, including:

- *Selection of stocks based on value.* No matter what potential profits you might earn using options for swing trading and other strategies, it remains a sensible approach to limit your trading activity to high-value stocks. Using the relatively logical and simple theory of *value investing*, you may limit your options trading to stocks that also offer long-term growth and profits for well-managed companies.

- *A stock's price volatility.* Options traders face a dilemma when considering strategies like swing trading. The strategy will not work on the exceptionally safe stocks because, by definition, they tend to trade only in a narrow price range. So the opportunities for even moderate price volatility are simply not there. At the same time, exceptionally volatile stocks are difficult to predict. Even trying to apply the principles of swing trading to erratic stock trends is difficult and risky, so swing traders also want to avoid risky stocks. The ideal stock is one with moderate volatility, that is likely to experience price swings of a few points within a few days, but not likely to go through wide swings in *either* direction due to high market interest and high market overreaction to news and rumor.

Smart Investor Tip

No matter what options strategies you employ, limiting your activity to high-quality companies is simply smart investing. Those stocks will be more predictable, less volatile, and better for all types of option trading.

- *Price history (recent) and potential.* The definition of various volatility levels is invariably based on past price performance. But the potential price history can be further clarified by checking the size of the stock's recent trading range. Stocks with relatively narrow trading ranges of 10 points or less are excellent candidates for swing trading in the $40 to $80 price range. These stocks display historical volatility of 12.5 percent to 25 percent. If this range has been consistent, it is reasonable to extrapolate the same volatility levels into the future. This may oversimplify the task, however. In an ever changing market, yesterday's sedate stock may be tomorrow's most volatile, and vice versa. But investors and traders have to rely on trends and trust them. Without the trend, you would have no basis for selecting one stock over another for swing-trading purposes.

- *The price-to-earnings (P/E) ratio of the stock.* The P/E ratio tells you how much the market anticipates future price appreciation. So a P/E multiple of 20 represents a price per share 20 times higher than last year's earnings per share. The P/E can be used to limit the range of stocks you consider for swing trading. An exceptionally high P/E often indicates that the market has driven the stock's price too high, that enthusiasm is higher than justified. An exceptionally low P/E ratio is a symptom of a lack of interest in the stock. The P/E ratio may foreshadow future volatility as well. High-P/E stocks will tend to overreact to marketwide price movements and be highly volatile. Low-P/E stocks will tend to underreact, making them poor candidates for swing trading. With this in mind, limiting a stock portfolio to those with P/E ratio between 10 and 20, for example, will help avoid companies with overpriced stocks as well as those lacking the moderate price volatility swing traders desire. The range of 10 to 20 for P/E ratio is subjective, but if you check typical P/E ranges, you will find that this range represents the midrange of stocks. Historically, a P/E of 15 has been considered the "norm" for the market's P/E ratio, and the stocks in the S&P 500 have often ranged between 15 and 20, but in more volatile markets, such as the year 2002, the P/E range for the S&P 500 rose as high as 45.

Smart Investor Tip

Picking a range of P/E in which to consider stocks is a matter of personal preference. The multiples between 10 and 20 are reasonable, but some investors will prefer P/E ranges far higher.

The history of the S&P 500 collective P/E over several years is summarized in Figure 11.5

Smart Investor Tip

For a good overview of financial and economic indicators as part of your portfolio analysis, check www.bullandbearwise.com. Indicators such as P/E as well as broader indications classified as "bullish" or "bearish" help you to gauge the current market mood.

- *Fundamental and technical tests of the company and stock.* Any stock you pick for options trading as part of a swing-trading strategy should also pass a few basic fundamental and technical tests. You may develop

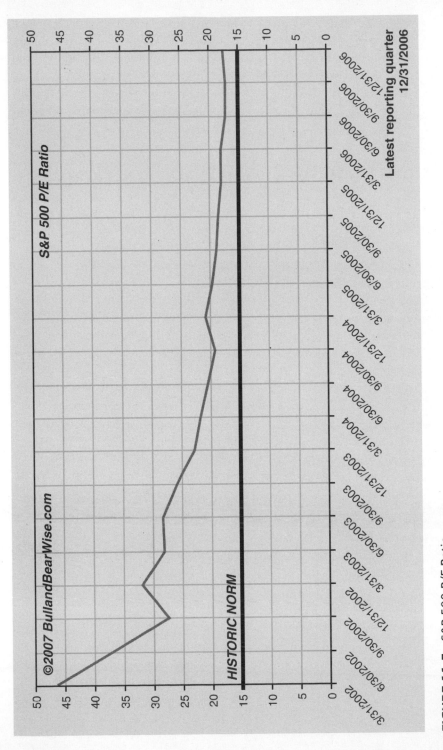

FIGURE 11.5   S&P 500 P/E Ratio.

Source: © 2007 BullandBearWise.com. Used with permission.

your own short list of essential tests. On the fundamental side, these should include tests of working capital, the trend in debt versus equity capitalization, revenue, and net return. On the technical side, you will want to test price history and volatility, expressed in terms of the volatility percentage and breadth of the trading range for stocks at various price levels.

Options Used for Other Trading Strategies

day trader
an individual who trades within a single day, usually closing positions before the end of the trading day, and often making such trades on high volume.

pattern day trader
any individual executing four or more transactions on the same security within five consecutive trading days; these traders are required to maintain no less than $25,000 in their brokerage accounts.

Swing trading is only one of many possible trading strategies in which options can play a valuable role. In fact, swing trading is an extension of a better-known strategy called *day trading*. The day trader typically moves in and out of positions within a single trading day, so that the open positions do not extend from one day to the next. Day traders also tend to be high-volume traders, moving in and out of positions frequently and on the same stock, often tracking prices minute to minute. Day trading is perfectly suited to options in the same way and for the same reasons as swing trading: greater leverage and lower risk. Because day trading is extremely short term in nature, cheap options near expiration and slightly in the money are real bargains. With little or no time value, options enable day traders to control 100 shares of stock per contract, for only a fraction of the cost of trading stock. The risks are limited as well, due to lower investment requirements and the ability to use calls and puts equally in long positions.

Day traders are able to avoid a margin requirement, and this has caused problems for regulators. Under the rules, margin requirements are based on positions open at the end of each trading day. So a day trader could avoid having to meet margin requirements while still placing a large amount of capital into positions, as long as those positions were closed before the end of the day. Because this practice can lead to large losses for the trader as well as for the brokerage firm, a qualification was enacted and applied to day traders. Anyone who trades on high volume (meaning moving in and out of the same positions four or more times within five consecutive trading days) is classified as a *pattern day trader*. Anyone meeting this standard is required to leave at least $25,000 in their account. If they do not maintain the required level, they will not be allowed to execute further trades once the pattern day trader status is triggered.

Smart Investor Tip

Swing trading is the perfect solution for avoiding being classified as a pattern day trader. The typical entry and exit takes at least three days, so executing four trades within five days under these guidelines would be unlikely.

Swing- and Day-Trading Advanced Strategies

Most examples used in this book involve single option contracts, for the sake of clarity. However, swing and day trading do not necessarily have to be limited to single contracts to control 100 shares of stock. Especially when option premium levels are quite low, using multiple contracts saves on brokerage fees while increasing profit potential. In addition, using multiple contracts vastly expands your strategic potential for swing trading, including taking partial profits while keeping the remainder of a position open, and expanding swing trading into more advanced options strategies such as straddles and spreads.

For example, one popular online brokerage firm (Charles Schwab) charges $9.95 for a single option trade, plus $0.75 per contract. However, when multiple contracts are involved, the savings are substantial:

Number of Options	Transaction Fee
1	$10.70
2	11.45
3	12.20
4	12.95
5	13.70

At five contracts, the cost per option is only $2.74. So substantial transaction cost savings are going to be realized when trading in multiple option contracts. But there are other and more important reasons to use multiple contracts. It adds flexibility to swing- and day-trading strategies. Example of how you can vary your strategies with multiple contracts include:

- *Take partial profits.* In many cases when swing trades are executed, you face a dilemma. Do you take your profits even when setup signals are not present or do you wait? Because no system is perfect, you will at times miss profit opportunities by waiting one day too long. But with the use of multiple contracts, you can sell part of your holdings and keep the balance in the position. When profits are exceptional, this enables you to make a profit on the entire position, while keeping a portion in play and awaiting the setup signal.

- *Partial exercise.* As a holder of a long call, you have the right to exercise or to sell. For example, if you are swing trading on a stock you might want to also own, multiple contracts open the possibility of combining strategies. You can sell part of the overall position to gain a profit on the swing trade and exercise the remainder. This strategy is valuable when you realize that the stock was selling at a great price a few days earlier. With a long call in hand, you can buy at the striking price and then hold the stock for the long term (or revert to a covered call strategy, for example).

- *Add more option contracts in times of price momentum.* From time to time, a stock's price not only moves in one direction, but gains momentum. For example, you might open a single-contract position only to later get a *second* setup signal going in the same direction. You can simply wait out the trend or buy additional option contracts based on the strong momentum of the stock's price.

Multiple contracts give you greater flexibility in a swing- or day-trading program, while also enabling you to execute trades for very little additional cost. Yet another interesting twist involves combining a swing-trading strategy with covered calls.

One of the great advantages in using options rather than stock is that you can use puts instead of the high-risk shorting of stock. But there is a mirror strategy of this, and it involves using covered calls instead of buying puts. If you do not own shares of stock and you reach a sell setup point, the obvious move is to buy puts. Then, when the stock declines, the put becomes profitable. However, if you also own stock, you can write covered calls rather than buying puts. This provides you with a double advantage.

First, the covered call is safer than the long put because time value is involved. As time value declines, your short call becomes less valuable and can be closed out (bought to close) at a profit. Second, you have to pay money for the long put, but when you write a covered call, it produces cash that goes into your account.

Smart Investor Tip

Covered calls are conservative strategies in their own right. But as part of a swing-trade strategy, covered calls make even more sense because they are tied to a sell setup. You can take profits within a few days without having to sell stock. This approach also produces cash rather than spending it.

You might consider many options-trading strategies to work as swing trades. But the strategy itself is invariably based on short-term price swings identified with specific setup signals. Swing-trading signals improve your profitability even when using options near expiration. In all strategies, however, the simple analysis of profits is never complete until you also calculate the tax consequences involved. The next chapter explains the oddities of option-based tax rules.

12

Risk and Taxes: Rules of the Game

All this worldly wisdom was once the unamiable heresy of some wise man.
—Henry David Thoreau, *Journal*, 1853

A tremendous opportunity awaits anyone who considers including options in their portfolio. When you review the broad range of possible uses for options, it becomes clear that they can serve the interests of a wide spectrum of investors. At the same time, you need to recognize the broad range of risks in option investing, and also to remember the complexity of income tax rules. As an options trader, your status as a stock investor could be affected by the option-related decisions that you make.

You will ultimately decide to employ options only if you conclude that they are appropriate, given your own financial and personal circumstances. If your risk tolerance and goals contradict the use of options in your portfolio, then you should avoid them altogether. Options might provide you with a convenient form of diversification, protection, or income—or all of these in various combinations. Identification of risk has to include not only knowing about *high* risk and how to avoid it, but also knowing how to contend with the risks of taking too little action. Risk comes in many forms and has to be managed constantly.

Identifying the Range of Risk

In any discussion of risk, a starting point should be a discussion of *information* risk. Are you getting valid information? If you have listened to analysts in the past, or followed the crowd in deciding when to buy or sell, then you have been operating with the wrong information. But if you have picked stocks carefully and based your choices on analytical criteria (fundamental, technical, or a combination of both) then your decisions can be made based on facts rather than on the more common standards: rumors, opinions, and unsupported claims. Even the analysts' "target price" announcement is arbitrary and baseless. The popular practice of identifying earnings ranges and target price ranges has deceived many investors into making decisions for all the wrong reasons.

Beyond the problems of information risk, you will also want to remain vigilant and watch for the whole range of risks you face whenever you are in the market. Options address the entire spectrum of risk tolerance profiles and can be used in combinations of ways to supplement income, insure other positions, leverage future long positions, or modify exposure to loss. To determine how to use options in your portfolio, first go through these three steps:

1. *Study the full range of possible option strategies.* Before opening any positions in options, prepare hypothetical variations and track the market to see how you would have done. Become familiar with valuation and changes in valuation by watching a particular series of options over time.

2. *Identify your personal risk tolerance levels.* Before picking an option strategy, determine what levels of risk you can afford to take. Set standards and then follow them. Be prepared to abandon outdated ideas and perceptions of risk, and continually refresh your outlook based on current information.

3. *Identify and understand all of the risks associated with options trading.* Consider every possible risk, including the risk that a stock's market price will not move as you expect, or that a short position could be exercised early. In option investing, risk levels depend on the position you assume. For example, as a buyer, time is the enemy; and as a seller, time defines your profit potential.

The risk in each and every option position is that the underlying stock will do one of two things. It may move in a direction you didn't expect or want; or it may fail to move enough for a position to be profitable. A study of profit and loss zones before opening positions is a smart tactic, because it helps you to define whether a particular decision makes sense.

Margin and Collateral Risks

You may think of margin investing as buying stock on credit. That is the most familiar and common form. In the options market, margin requirements are different and margin is used in a different way. Your brokerage firm will require that short positions be protected, at least partially, through collateral. The preferred form of collateral is ownership of 100 shares of stock for each call sold; if you are short on puts, your broker will require cash or securities to be left on deposit to provide for the cost of stock in the case the short put is exercised.

Whenever you open uncovered short positions in options, cash or securities will have to be placed on deposit to protect the brokerage firm's position. The level required is established by minimum legal requirements, subject to increases by individual brokerage firms' policies. Any balance above the deposit represents risk, both for the brokerage firm and for you. If the stock moves in a direction you do not desire, the margin requirement goes up as well. In that respect, margin risk could be defined as leverage risk.

Personal Goal Risks

If you establish a goal that you will invest no more than 15 percent of your total portfolio in option speculation, it is important to stay with that goal. This requires constant review. Sudden market changes can mean sudden and unexpected losses, especially when you buy options and when you sell short. Getting away from the goals you set is all too easy.

Your goal should also include identification of the point at which you will close positions, either to take profits or to limit losses. Avoid breaking your own rules by delaying, hoping for favorable changes in the near-term future. This is tempting, but it often leads to unacceptable losses or missing a profit opportunity. Establish two price points in every option position: *minimum gain* and *maximum loss*. When either point is reached, close the position.

Smart Investor Tip
Options traders, like gamblers, can succeed if they know when to fold.

Risk of Unavailable Market

One of the least talked about risks in any investment is the potential that you will not be able to buy or sell when you want to. The discussion of options strategies is based on the basic idea that you will be able to place orders whenever you want to, without problems or delays.

The reality is quite different in some situations. When market volume is especially heavy, it is difficult and sometimes impossible to place orders when you want to. In an exceptionally large market correction, volume will be heavy as investors scramble to place orders to cut losses. So if you trade by telephone, your broker's lines will be overloaded and those who do get through will experience longer than usual delays—because so much business is taking place at the same time. If you trade online, the same problem will occur. You will not be able to get through to the online brokerage web site if it is already overloaded with traders placing orders. In these extreme situations, your need to place orders will be greater than normal, as it is with all other investors. So the market may be temporarily unavailable.

Risk of Disruption in Trading

Trading could be halted in the underlying stock. For example, if rumors about a company are affecting the stock's market price, the exchange may halt trading for a day or more. When trading in stock is halted, all related option trading is halted as well. For example, a company might be rumored to be a takeover candidate. If the rumors affecting price are true, when the trading halt is lifted, the stock may open at a much higher or lower price than before. As an options investor, this exposes you to potentially significant risks, perhaps even preventing you from being able to limit your exposure to loss by offsetting the exposed side of the transaction. You will be required to wait until trading reopens, and by then it might be too late. The cost of protecting your position might be too high, or you might be subjected to automatic exercise.

Brokerage Risks

A serious potential risk is the individual action of your broker. If you use a discount brokerage or online trading service, you are not exposed to this risk, because the role of the broker is limited to placement of orders as you direct. However, if you are using a broker for advice on options trading, you are exposed to the risk that a broker will use his or her discretion, even if you have not granted permission. Never grant unlimited discretion to someone else, no matter how much trust you have. In a fast-moving market, it is difficult for a broker with many clients to pay attention to your options trades to the degree required. In fact, with online free quotations widely available, you really do not need a full-commission broker at all. In the Internet environment, commission-based brokerage is becoming increasingly obsolete. As an options trader, you may want to consider using an order placement service and moving away from the practice of paying for brokerage services.

Yet another risk, even with online brokerage accounts, is that mistakes will be made in placing orders. Fortunately, online trading is easily traced and documented. However, it is still possible that a "buy" order goes in as a "sale," or vice versa. Such mistakes can be disastrous for you as an options trader. If you trade by telephone or in person, the risk is increased just due to human error. If you trade online, check and double-check your order before submitting it.

Trading Cost Risks

A calculated profit zone has to be reduced, or a loss zone increased, to allow for the cost of placing trades. Brokerage trading fees apply to both sides of every transaction. If you trade in single-option contracts, the cost is high on a per-option basis. Trading in higher increments is economical because the cost of trading is lower on a per-option basis.

This book has used examples for single contracts in most cases to make outcomes clear; in practice, such trading is not always practical because the trading fees require more profit just to break even. A thin margin of profit will evaporate quickly when trading costs are added into the mix.

When you buy and then exercise an option, or when you sell and the option is exercised by the buyer or the exchange, you not only pay the option trading fee; you also have to pay for the cost of transacting the shares of stock, a point to remember in calculating overall return. It is possible that if you're operating on a thin profit margin, it could be taken up entirely by trading fees on both sides of the transaction, so that cost has to be calculated beforehand. In general, single-contract trades involve about one-half point for the combined cost of opening and then closing the option position; so you need to add a half-point cushion to allow for that. The calculation changes as you deal in multiple contracts, in which trading costs on a per-contract basis are going to be far lower.

Lost Opportunity Risks

One of the more troubling aspects of options trading involves *lost opportunity risk*. This arises in several ways, the most obvious being that experienced by covered call sellers. You risk the loss of stock profits in the event of price increase and exercise. Your profit is locked in at the striking price. Covered call writers accept the certainty of a consistent, better than average return and, in exchange, they lose the occasional larger capital gain on their stock.

lost opportunity risk (options)
the risk that covered call writers will lose profits from increased prices in stock because they are locked in at a fixed striking price.

Opportunity risks arise in other ways, too. For example, if you are involved in exotic combinations including long and short positions, your margin requirements may prevent you from being able to take advantage of other investment opportunities. You will often find yourself in an environment of moderate scarcity, so that you cannot seize every opportunity. Before committing yourself to an open position in options, recognize how your economic boundaries could limit your choices. You will probably lose more opportunities than you will ever be able to take.

Tax Consequence Risk

ordinary income
noninvestment income, subject to the full tax rate an individual pays and not qualified for exclusions or lower rates applicable to some forms of net investment income.

net investment income
an individual's taxable income from interest, dividends, and capital gains; distinguished from ordinary income by tax rate or potential tax exclusions.

In trading options, you need to take great care to ensure that you don't incur unintended consequences. This is as true when it comes to tax liabilities as anywhere else. The potential tax consequences include:

- *Poor timing of taxable outcomes.* You are going to need to perform careful tax planning to maintain control over the taxes due on your portfolio. This includes consideration of both federal and state taxes. Because so many options strategies are only marginally profitable, poor planning could result in new losses once taxes are considered in the overall outcome. For example, a small profit could result in extra tax liabilities, wiping out all of the gain. In this situation, you are exposed to risk while option positions are open, but you earn no profits.

- *Loss of favorable tax rates.* As you will see later in this chapter, some options positions automatically revert a long-term capital gain (with its lower maximum tax rate) to short-term capital gains (which are taxed at your full *ordinary income* tax rate). While *net investment income* is included on a person's tax return, it is often taxed at lower rates (long-term capital gains) or excluded from tax (qualified dividends).

- *Limitations on deductibility of losses.* Some types of advanced options trades are subject to limitations in deductibility. For example, in some cases involving two or more offsetting option positions, a loss portion cannot be deducted in the year incurred, but has to be deferred and offset against the rest of the position (more on this later in this chapter).

There are some obvious tax advantages to some trades, especially if they are timed properly. For example, if you sell a covered call not due to expire until next year, you receive funds at the time you open the position, but taxes are not applicable until the position is closed, expired, or exercised. But there is much more to tax planning and to tax risk. These tax risks in trading options can be quite complex, especially for anyone not completely familiar with how the tax rules work. Options taxation is exceptionally complicated, so before entering into advanced trading positions, consult with your tax adviser.

Evaluating Your Risk Tolerance

Everyone has a specific level of risk tolerance—the ability and willingness to accept risk. This trait is not fixed but changes over time. Your personal risk tolerance is influenced by several factors:

- *Investment capital*. How much money do you have available to invest? How much do you have committed to long-term growth, and how much can you spare for more adventurous alternatives?

- *Personal factors*. Your risk tolerance is significantly affected by your age, income, debt level, economic status, job, and job security. It changes drastically with major life events such as marriage, birth of a child, divorce, or death of a family member.

- *Your investing experience*. How experienced are you as an investor? No matter how much you study investing in theory, you do not really gain market experience until you place real money at risk.

- *Type of account*. Your risk tolerance depends on how and why you invest, and the type of account involved. If you invest in your personal account, you will have greater flexibility than in a retirement account, for example.

- *Your personal goals*. Every investor's goals ultimately determine how much risk is acceptable. Remember that definition of personal goals should dictate how you invest.

Smart Investor Tip
Risk tolerance is reflected in the way you invest. You will have a better chance of succeeding if you ensure that the risks you take are risks you can afford.

TABLE 12.1   Risk Evaluation Worksheet

Lowest Possible Risk

___	Covered call writing
___	Put purchase for insurance (long position)
___	Call purchase for insurance (short position)

Medium Risk

___	Ratio writing
___	Combined strategies
	___ Long ___ Short

High Risk

___	Uncovered call writing
___	Combined strategies
	___ Long ___ Short
___	Call purchases for income
___	Put purchases for income

The best investment decisions invariably are made as the result of thorough evaluation of the features of an investment or strategy, the most important being risk. The evaluation process helps you to avoid mistakes and focus attention on what will be beneficial, given your risk tolerance level. The risk evaluation worksheet for option investing in Table 12.1 will help you to classify options by degrees of risk.

Risk evaluation depends on your analysis of potential profits and losses under all possible outcomes. When considering an option strategy of any nature, first calculate potential profits in the event of expiration or exercise, and then set criteria for other features: maximum time value, time until expiration, the number of contracts involved in the transaction, target rate of return, and the price range at which you will close. Obviously, these criteria will be drastically different for buyers than for sellers, and for covered versus uncovered option writing. Use the option limits worksheet in Table 12.2 to set your personal limits.

Tax Ramifications in Trading Options

An especially complex area of risk involves taxes. If you are like most people, you understand how taxation works, generally speaking. When it comes to options, though, a few special rules apply that can decide whether a particular strategy makes sense.

TABLE 12.2 Option Limits		
Covered Call Sale Criteria		

Rate of Return If Unchanged		
Dividends	$___	
Call premium.	___	Total	$___
		Cost of stock	$___
		Gain	___%

Rate of Return If Exercised		
Dividends	$___	
Call premium	___	
Stock gain	___	Total	$___
		Cost of stock	$___+
		Gain	___%

Option Purchase Criteria

Maximum time value: ___%
Time until expiration: ___ months
Number of options: ___ contracts
Target rate of return: ___%
Sell level: increase to $___ or decrease to $___

Capital gains—taxable profit or loss from investments—are broken down into short-term or long-term. The normal treatment of capital gains is determined by your holding period. If you own stock for 12 months or more and then sell, your profit is treated as long-term gain or loss; a lower tax percentage is applied than to short-term capital gains (gains on assets owned less than 12 months). This rule applies to stocks and is fairly straightforward—until you begin using options as well. Then the capital gains rules change.

Here are 11 rules for option-related capital gains taxes:

1. *Short-term capital gains.* Generally speaking, any investment you hold for less than 12 months will be taxed at the same rate as your other income (your effective tax rate). After 2003, this rate may be as high as 35 percent. The rate is scheduled to rise in 2010 unless further legislation is passed to change that.

> **capital gains**
> profits from investments, taxed the same as other income if the holding period is less than one year, and at lower rates if investments were owned for one year or more.

short-term capital gains
profits on investments held for less than 12 months, which are taxed at the same rate as other income.

long-term capital gains
profits on investments held for 12 months or more, which are taxed at a rate lower than other income.

constructive sales
status when investors buy and sell in separate transactions, but involve substantially identical property; the holding of offsetting long and short positions may be taxed as a constructive sale even when no physical sale has occurred.

2. *Long-term capital gains.* For investments held for 12 months or more, a more favorable tax rate applies. The maximum rate of 15 percent on long-term gains applies to "net" capital gains (long-term capital gains less short-term capital losses). This rate lasts until the end of 2008 unless future revisions are made to make the favorable rates permanent.

3. *Constructive sales.* You could be taxed as though you sold an investment, even when you did not actually complete a sale. This constructive sale rule applies when offsetting long and short positions are entered in the same security. For example, if you buy 100 shares of stock and later sell short 100 shares of the same stock, it could be treated as a constructive sale. The same rules could be applied when options are used to hedge stock positions. The determining factors include the time between the two transactions, changes in price levels, and final outcomes of both sides in the transaction. This is a complex area of tax law; if you are involved with combinations and short sales, you should consult with your tax adviser to determine whether constructive sale rules apply to your transactions.

4. *Wash sales.* If you sell stock and, within 30 days, buy it again, it is considered a wash sale. Under the wash sale rule, you cannot deduct a loss when 30 days have not passed. The same rule applies in many cases where stock is sold and, within 30 days, the same person sells an in-the-money put.

5. *Capital gains for unexercised long options.* Taxes on long options are treated in the same way as other investments. The gain is short-term if the holding period is less than 12 months, and it is long-term if the holding period is one year or more. Taxes are assessed in the year the long position is closed in one of two ways: by sale or expiration.

6. *Treatment of exercised long options.* If you purchase a call or a put and it is exercised, the net payment is treated as part of the basis in stock. In the case of a call, the cost is added to the basis in the stock; and the holding period of the stock begins on the day following exercise. The holding period of the option does not affect the capital gains holding period of the stock. In the case of a long put that is exercised, the net cost of the put reduces the gain on stock when the put is exercised and stock is sold. The sale of stock under exercise of a put will be either long-term or short-term depending on the holding period of stock.

7. *Taxes on short calls.* Premium is not taxed at the time the short position is opened. Taxes are assessed in the year the position is closed through purchase or expiration; and all such transactions are treated as short-term regardless of how long the option position remained open. In the event a short call is exercised, the striking price plus premium received become the basis of the stock delivered through exercise.

8. *Taxes on short puts.* Premium received is not taxed at the time the short position is opened. Closing the position through purchase or expiration always creates a short-term gain or loss. If the short put is exercised by the buyer, the striking price plus trading costs becomes the basis of stock through exercise. The holding period of the stock begins on the day following exercise of the short put.

9. *Limitations of deductions in offsetting positions.* The federal tax rules consider straddles to be *offsetting positions.* This means that some loss deductions may be deferred or limited, or favorable tax rates are disallowed. If risks are reduced by opening the straddle, four possible tax consequences could result. First, the holding period for the purpose of long-term capital gains could be suspended as long as the straddle remains open. Second, the wash sale rule may be applied against current losses. Third, current-year deductions could be deferred until an offsetting "successor position" (the other side of the straddle) has been closed. Fourth, current charges (transaction fees and margin interest, for example) may be deferred and added to the basis of the long-position side of the straddle.

offsetting positions

in tax law, a straddle which creates a substantial diminution of risk; when positions are classified as offsetting, tax restrictions are applied on deductibility of losses or treatment of long-term gains.

10. *Tax treatment of married puts.* It is possible that a married put will be treated as an adjustment in the basis of stock, rather than taxed separately. This rule applies only when puts are acquired on the

qualified covered call
a covered call that meets specific definitions allowing an investor to claim long-term capital gains tax rates upon sale of stock, or to retain long-term holding period status. Qualification is determined by time to expiration, and by the price difference between current market value of the stock and striking price of the call.

same day as stock, and when the put either expires or becomes exercised. If you sell the puts prior to expiration, the result is treated as short-term capital gain or loss.

11. *Capital gains and qualification of covered calls.* The most complicated of the special option-related tax rules involves the treatment of capital gains on stock. This occurs when you use covered calls. The federal tax laws have defined *qualified covered calls* for the purpose of defining how stock profits are treated; it is possible that a long-term capital gain could be converted to short-term if an unqualified covered call is involved. The following section provides the details and examples of how qualification is determined.

Qualified Covered Calls—Special Rules

The tax rules applied when you write in-the-money covered calls are exceptionally complicated. There are several rules to keep in mind to determine whether your in-the-money covered call is qualified or unqualified. With a qualified covered call, your stock does not risk losing its long-term capital gains status; if the covered call is unqualified, then treatment of stock profits changes as a consequence.

If you write out-of-the money covered calls, there is no effect on the status of stock. The following explanation applies *only* when your covered calls are in the money at the time the transactions are opened.

The general rule governing in-the-money covered calls refers to time. The option must have more than 30 days until expiration. In addition, the striking price cannot be lower than the striking price immediately below the closing price of the stock on the day before you open the covered call.

Example

Mind-Boggling Limitation: You wrote two covered calls last week. The first one was written with a striking price of 30; the stock's previous day's closing price was 32. The call expires in two months. The second call was written with a striking price of 45 and the stock closed the day before at the price of 52. This call expires in three weeks.

The first call is qualified in both respects. The striking price is the first available striking price below the previous day's stock closing price; and the call is scheduled to expire longer than 30 days out.

The second call is unqualified in both respects. It is not the first available striking price below close (that would have been the striking price of 50). Also, the call is set to expire within the next 30 days.

The rules of qualification are more complex when the call has more than 90 days until expiration. Table 12.3 summarizes the qualification of covered calls given the stock's closing price in specific stock price ranges, and with various times until expiration.

TABLE 12.3　Qualification of Covered Calls

Previous Day's Stock Closing Price	Time until Expiration	Striking Price Limits
$25 or less	More than 30 days	One striking price below prior day's closing stock price (Exception: you cannot have a "qualified" covered call if striking price is lower than 85% of the stock price.)
$25.01 to $60	More than 30 days	One striking price below prior day's closing stock price
$60.01 to $150	31–90 days	One striking price below prior day's closing stock price
$60.01 to $150	More than 90 days	Two striking prices below prior day's closing stock price (but not more than 10 points in the money)
Over $150	31–90 days	One striking price below prior day's closing stock price
Over $150	More than 90 days	Two striking prices below prior day's closing stock price

---

Example

A Math Challenge: You own shares of stock in several corporations. You want to write covered calls in the money, but you want to ensure that all are qualified. One stock has current market value of $74 per share. To qualify a covered call, it must be one striking price below that level, or 70, if the call is set to expire within 31 to 90 days. If the call is set to expire beyond the 90-day limit, you can write a call two striking prices below the prior day's close, which is the 65 call. If you write any in-the-money calls other than these, they will be unqualified.

---

antistraddle rules

tax regulations that remove or suspend the long-term favorable tax treatment of stock when the owner writes unqualified in-the-money covered calls.

What happens when you write an unqualified call? The rules governing the consequences, which are also called the *antistraddle rules*, affect long-term capital gains qualification of stock. Following is a summary of five ways the rules work.

1. *No change for at-the-money or out-of-the-money covered calls*. No effect on the tax treatment of stock will be suffered if you write calls with striking prices at or above the closing price of stock.

2. *No change for qualified in-the-money covered calls*. As long as in-the-money calls fall within the rather limited qualification period (see the preceding Table 12.3), no effect will be experienced on the tax treatment of stock.

3. *Treatment of capital gains with unqualified covered call*. As a general rule, stock you own one year or more is taxed at lower long-term capital gains rates. But when you write an unqualified covered call against stock, the holding period is suspended. This means that counting up to the one-year holding period will not continue as long as the short option remains open.

Example

Coming Up Short: You have owned 100 shares of stock for 11 months. You write an unqualified covered call and your long-term holding period is suspended. Three months later, the call is exercised and you give up your stock at a profit. Even though you owned the stock for 14 months, your gain is treated as short-term. You sold an unqualified covered call, so the period required before long-term rates apply is suspended.

---

4. *Treatment of covered call losses when qualified.* Any losses on qualified covered calls are treated as long-term losses when the underlying stock profits are treated as long-term capital gains.

5. *Treatment of stock holding period when covered calls are closed.* If you sell a covered call at a loss within 30 days of the end of the tax year, you have to hold on to the stock for at least 30 days in order to have the call treated as a qualified covered call.

These rules are exceptionally complicated and the underlying reasoning for them is puzzling. It certainly requires you to use a qualified tax expert if you do engage in writing in-the-money covered calls. Additional problems may arise when you employ rolling techniques. For example, if you write a qualified covered call today, you satisfy the rules for treatment of the stock if and when the call is exercised. But what happens if the stock's price rises and you roll forward? The replacement option may end up being unqualified, based on several factors: the current price level of the stock, proximity of the stock's price to the call's striking price, and time until expiration. You could unintentionally replace a qualified covered call with an unqualified covered call.

If you are a typical investor, you view a roll as a single transaction: One option is replaced with another. But from the tax point of view, there are two separate transactions. When you close the original short position, you create a short-term capital gain or loss. When you open the second option, you may be either qualified or unqualified in the *new* option because it is a separate transaction.

You may question whether it is necessary to master the special and complex tax rules governing covered call qualification. However, the problem is very narrow in focus. It is only a potential problem if you write (or roll forward to) unqualified in-the-money positions. So as long as your calls are at the money or out of the money, you are not affected.

In some situations, you may view writing in-the-money calls as advantageous. For example, you can either sell stock at a profit augmented by option profits, or take advantage of stock price changes by profiting on intrinsic value price movement. If you have large unused *carryover capital losses*, you may also view the disqualification of stock status as an advantage. Because your annual losses are limited to $3,000, you can use a current-year stock

carryover capital losses
sums of capital losses from prior years that exceeded annual loss limitation levels; the annual maximum capital loss deduction is $3,000, and all losses above that level have to be carried over and applied in future tax years.

profit as an offset to carryover loss. In this case, you will not be concerned with the loss of long-term favorable treatment.

Example

The Absorption Factor: You had large losses in your portfolio in the years 2000 and 2001. In the current year, you still have over $50,000 in unused carryover capital losses. It will take many years to absorb these losses at the rate of $3,000 per year. However, by selling in-the-money covered calls you create numerous short-term profits, both in calls and in stock exercised against your in-the-money short calls. You view this as one way to shelter short-term profits. Current-year gains are applied against the large carryover loss, so you have no net tax consequences this year.

---

qualified retirement plans those plans qualified by the IRS to treat current income as deferred and free of tax in the year earned and, in many cases, also exempting annual contributions to the plan from current taxes.

There are two situations in which you will not be concerned about the loss of favorable long-term capital gains tax rates. First is when you have a substantial carryover loss. Because net investment income can be offset against past-year losses, current-year capital gains—even short-term gains—are fully protected from any taxes.

The second situation is when you are investing through an individual retirement account (IRA) or other retirement plan for which current income is not taxable. In these so-called *qualified retirement plans*, current income is free of tax, but in future years when withdrawals begin, all income is taxed at ordinary rates. Since you do not benefit from long-term gains rates within such plans, you are free to pursue even aggressive options strategies such as deep in-the-money covered calls.

Looking to the Future

Tax problems and strategies have been made very complex by the current tax rules and, hopefully, future reforms will simplify those rules or make them easier to follow. However, taxes are only one of the many challenges you face in deciding how to plan your investment portfolio, determine which risks are acceptable, and protect capital for your future.

Options, like all investments, should always be used in the context of your individual plans. This is one of the long-term problems with taking advice from individuals whose compensation depends on generating trades: They tend to think in terms of volume rather than starting from the point of view of what works for the client. You need to ensure that your options positions are a logical risk for your portfolio, based on your risk tolerance and personal investing goals.

Example

Defining Yourself and Your Goals: You have written down your personal investing goals, and have identified what you hope to achieve in the intermediate and long-term future. You are willing to assume risks in a low to moderate range. So all of your capital is invested in shares of blue-chip companies. In order to increase portfolio value, you consider one of the following two possible strategies:

Strategy 1: Hold shares of stock as long-term investments. Aim for appreciation and continuing dividend income.

Strategy 2: Increase the value of your portfolio by purchasing shares as described above, and waiting for a moderate increase in value; then begin writing covered calls. As long as your minimum rate of return if exercised or unchanged will always exceed 35 percent, you will write a call, and then avoid exercise through rolling techniques. If a call is exercised and stock is called away, you plan to reinvest the proceeds in additional purchases of other blue-chip company shares.

In this comparison, the rate of return from the second strategy will always be higher than the first, due to the yield from writing covered calls. A 35 percent rate of return is not unreasonable, because it includes the capital gain from selling shares in the event of exercise, and because calls can be closed and replaced repetitively. So an annualized double-digit rate is not only possible, it is likely under this strategy. In addition to providing impressive returns, writing covered calls also provides downside protection by discounting your basis in shares of stock.

An interesting point to remember about the covered call strategy, especially as described in strategy 2: The common argument *against* writing covered calls is that you may lose future profits in the event the stock's price rises dramatically, because your striking price locks you in. It is true that, were the stock's market value to climb dramatically, you would experience exercise and lose those profits. However, remember that well-selected stocks will also tend to be less volatile than average, so that the chances of such increases—while they can happen—are lower than average. In addition, covered call writers take their double-digit returns consistently in exchange for the occasional lost paper profit. The goal of long-term growth is not inconsistent with writing covered calls, as long as you have a plan and stick to it, and as long as exercised shares are replaced with other shares of equal growth potential.

Every form of investing contains its own set of opportunities and risks. If you lose money consistently in options, you will also tend to have the following characteristics: You do not set goals, so you do not have a preestablished plan for closing positions profitably. You do not select strategies in your own best interests, describing yourself as conservative while using options in a highly speculative manner. You believe in the fundamentals but you follow only technical indicators. You have not taken the time to define your risk tolerance level, so you do not know when the risks you are taking are too high. A popular maxim in the investing community is, "If you don't know where you're going, any road will get you there."

As a successful investor, you are focused. You take the time to define your goals carefully, and you define your risk tolerance level with great care. You also define yourself in terms of what works for you, and what doesn't work. This enables you to use strategies that make sense, and to resist temptation when you receive advice from others. You also tend to be patient, and you are willing to wait for the right opportunities rather than taking chances when conditions are not right.

Devising a personal, individualized strategy is a rewarding experience. Seeing clearly what you need to do and then executing your strategy successfully gives you a well-deserved sense of achievement and competence, not to mention control. You will profit from devising and applying options strategies based on calculation and observation. You will also benefit from the satisfaction that comes from mastering a complex investment field, and finding yourself completely in control.

The next chapter examines the potential use of options for specialized trading situations. Because calculations of marginal profits often do not include consideration of the tax consequences, you need to always keep the tax rules in mind when judging various strategic approaches to options trading.

13

Calculating the Return: A Complex Aspect to Options

The return on your options trades can be complicated. When you consider the various elements, including your basis and profit in stock, dividends you earn, and the time your stock and option positions remain open, this is no easy matter.

In Chapter 2, you found a useful summary for calculating return on various option positions. In this chapter, these same concepts are expanded upon and developed. There are several potential methods for return calculations, and the most important points to remember are: the method you pick has to be realistic, and annualization is a means for comparing similar risks, not to establish likely returns from options trades.

Finding a Realistic Method

Among the many methods available to you, some are exceptionally complex and involve theoretical valuation. The small increments of difference in these incremental returns versus the easier, faster, and more logical methods make them impractical. The options market is fast moving, and traders have to make decisions in the moment and based on return calculations and risk that are readily comprehended. Some of the methods used by academics do not have practical applications in the real world of options trading.

Smart Investor Tip

You can expand return and valuation calculations infinitely, but the more obscure the method, the less practical it becomes. It is useful to know about complex methods for valuation of options, but in the real world of trading, you will most likely prefer a simple method over a complex one.

Black-Scholes model
a formula used to estimate a fair price for an option contract, originated in 1973. The calculation takes into account the elements of time value, stock price variation, an assumed market interest rate, and the time left until expiration.

Two of the best-known modeling calculations are worth a brief explanation. The *Black-Scholes model* is named for Fischer Black and Myron Scholes, who together published a scholarly paper in 1973 explaining their theory. The calculation is beyond the scope of this book; however, it is designed to take into account the elements of time value, stock price variation, an assumed market rate of interest, and time remaining until expiration. The formula sets a fair price for options, and several variations of the original formula have evolved since 1973.[1]

Smart Investor Tip

Black-Scholes is a well-known model, but it is based on assumptions about interest rates and fixed expiration. Even with its variations, this model is too obscure for most applications.

One problem with the original Black-Scholes model is that it was based on European-style option expiration. Under the European rule, options can only be exercised immediately before expiration and not whenever the owner wants, as is the case with American-style options.

---

[1] Black, Fischer, and Myron Scholes. 1973. "The Pricing of Options and Corporate Liabilities," *Journal of Political Economy* 81(3):637–654.

An alternative calculation is known as the *binomial model*. This calculation was developed in 1979 and allows for possible exercise at different moments in an option's life. These times are selected between the current date and expiration to demonstrate how time valuation adjustment would be made. One major flaw in the binomial model, however, is that it assumes the stock's price is *always* reasonable; in other words, this model succeeds only if you also accept the premise of the efficient market theory. Clearly, in the volatile and emotional market environment, highly volatile stocks will not behave in an efficient manner, so that the binomial model is just that—a model. It is instructive, however, because it also assumes a risk-neutral posture in valuation of the underlying stock. If such efficiency worked in the real world, option valuation, risk analysis, and return calculations would be quite simple.[2]

binomial model
an option valuation formula developed In 1979 and based on selection of various times between valuation date and expiration. The formula is risk neutral but also assumes that the efficient market theory applies in all cases.

Smart Investor Tip

The binomial model would be excellent *if* the efficient market theory were realistic. But as anyone who has tracked the market knows, it is far from efficient.

Neither the Black-Scholes nor the binomial model will be able to provide a practical, realistic method for determining option values. However, in reviewing options for any trade you have in mind, the apparent value of an option at any time is best made in comparisons between other options on the same stock. You will consider time until expiration, the level of intrinsic versus time value, proximity between a stock's current value and the option's striking price, and then dollar value of the option itself. This process applies whether you are considering long or short positions; using calls, puts, or combinations of both; and willing to take high risks or only very conservative risks. The process is the same in any case.

In evaluating risk, you will also want to make a judgment call about the level of exposure versus the premium value of an option. For example, you might

[2]Cox, J. C., S. A. Ross, and M. Rubinstein. 1979. "Options Pricing: A Simplified Approach," *Journal of Financial Economics* 7:229–263.

not be willing to enter a covered call for only $200 over the next two months. However, if the stock's current market value is $20, that is a 10 percent return (60 percent annualized). If the stock is worth $60, the same option yields only 3.33 percent (20 percent annualized). All of the elements have to be brought into the decision, including the yield itself, dollar value of the option, time to expiration, and your risk profile.

Annualizing Models and Guidelines

Annualize returns, not to establish a realistic expectation for outcomes on similar transactions, or to set goals for yourself, but to ensure consistency in comparisons. A discussion of annualization beyond the obvious technique is worthwhile. The basic concept is easily comprehended: If you have two option profits, both at 10 percent, they are not necessarily equal. One held for six months will annualize at 20 percent; another held for 24 months annualizes at only 5 percent. So rather than attempting to compare two options with 10 percent returns, annualization enables you to make a valid time-based comparison. Clearly, developing a 10 percent profit in six months is far better because (in theory) you can create and duplicate the same outcome four times over a two-year period.

Smart Investor Tip
Annualizing stock-based returns is a smart way to ensure like-kind comparisons. The same principle does not apply to options returns, so annualizing does not provide you with a realistic expectation of future outcomes.

time value of money
the concept observing that earnings potential adds value to a sum of money. As long as money is put to use earning profit, the present discounted value of the future fund relies on (1) the interest rate, (2) compounding method, and (3) time involved until the final result can be achieved.

This preliminary view of annualization is completely valid when comparing compound interest in savings accounts, money market funds or certificates of deposit (or in calculating annual percentage rates on a home mortgage). The time value of money is fairly straightforward for most calculations of the *time value of money*, which is what annualization is all about. But when it comes to option return calculations, annualization can distort outcomes and even build unrealistic expectations.

For example, a sum of $100 invested in a savings account at 3 percent simple annual interest would grow to $103 in one year. A similar investment in stock may grow to $103 in months and, upon sale, earns the same amount but in half the time. Thus, looking back and comparing these two outcomes, the time value of money invested in that particular stock was twice that of the money left in the savings account.

Time value of money does not take into account varying degrees of risk, and this is where annualization is flawed regarding options. For example, you might take substantial risks in buying a long call for 3 ($300) and seeing in grow to a net of $400 in one month; and achieve exactly the same return writing a covered call and realizing a $100 profit in three months. While the first example annualizes at 400 percent, the second annualizes at only 133 percent. But the risk levels are substantially different, so annualizing does not make these outcomes truly comparative.

Smart Investor Tip

An annualized return can be comparative only when risks are also comparative. As a consequence, you cannot depend on annualized returns for dissimilar positions and expect to gain any reliable conclusions from the analysis.

You achieve a comparative annualized return only when you compare two transactions that are substantially the same, but for different options and stocks and over different time periods. For example, comparing any two long option positions (between calls, puts, or a mix with a call in one case and a put in another) is a substantially identical type of option transaction. The fact that the risk levels are essentially similar lends itself to the use of annualization as a useful device for ensuring that your comparisons are accurate.

You might vary long risks by selecting different timing until expiration, in-the-money versus out-of-the-money positions, or even proximity between striking price and market value of the underlying stock. But the point remains valid: Annualization with options is useful in comparing similar risks. It is not a reliable means for comparing dissimilar risk positions.

Because many option positions are exceptionally short term, it is also not realistic to point to a 400 percent annualized return (or even a 133 percent return) and call it typical. Many options promoters have pointed to such examples to sell seminar "get rich" programs, but that level of outcome is not going to repeat consistently. So another caveat about annualizing is that it should not be viewed as an approximation of returns you can reasonably expect to realize on typical transactions. It is useful as a means of return comparisons only when risk attributes are the same between the transactions annualized.

An Overview of Basic Calculation for Calls

net return
the percentage return on an investment, based on dollar amounts going in and coming out, after transaction fees.

On a realistic level, your calculations of returns on option trades should be possible with a desk calculator; it should be quick and easy; and the results should tell you all that you need to know immediately.

For all long positions, the basic calculations are very straightforward. To review, there are various terms used to describe an outcome, including "return on investment," "yield," and numerous other wording. The expression *net return* is useful because it is simple, but it qualifies the return. By "net," this expression means actual dollar values realized and expressed as a percentage. So transaction costs are deducted from both the buy and sell sides of the transaction, and the return is calculated based on dollars-in and dollars-out results, or the "net."

Example

The Safety Net: You purchase a call for 0.75 ($75) and also pay a brokerage fee of $12.50. Your basis in the long position is $87.50. Two months later, you sell for 1.5 ($150). Your brokerage firm deducts another $12.50 from proceeds and credits your account with $137.50. To calculate net return, first calculate the net profit:

$$\$137.50 - \$87.50 = \$50.00$$

Next, divide the net profit by the original net basis:

$$\$50.00 \div \$137.50 = 36.4\%$$

If you also want to annualize this return (to compare it to other long positions), you divide the percentage by the holding period (2 months) and multiply by 12 months:

$$36.4\% \div 2 \times 12 = 218.4\%$$

As with all other instances of annualizing returns, this should *not* be used to set a standard for outcomes in future long positions. It is useful only for comparisons between similar risk levels of trades.

The long position calculation is simple compared to calculations for short positions. In the short position, you sell first and realize a profit when one of three events occurs: (1) the position is closed when you enter a buy; (2) the option is exercised; or (3) the option expires worthless.

Smart Investor Tip

Calculating net return for long positions is simple because the levels of risk, capital requirements, and outcomes are well understood. The same argument is not true for short position net returns.

Short-position calculations for calls are complicated by three factors:

1. Different levels of capital have to be kept in your brokerage account for uncovered calls or puts.
2. When you write covered calls, you have to consider your basis in the stock as part of your capital at risk.
3. If a covered call is exercised, you have to consider gain on the option *and* gain or loss on the stock, as well as deciding whether to include dividends in your net return.

If you own stock and sell covered calls, you can perform one type of net return calculation separate and apart from the value or profit on stock. Assuming your purpose in selling the calls is to increase current income and not to force exercise, you may consider *only* call premium and calculate the return in one of four ways:

1. *You close the position and calculate option-based net return.* When you close a covered call, either to take a profit or to avoid or defer exercise, you can calculate net return in the same way you do for trading long options. The difference between sell and buy is divided by the net buy price, and the resulting percentage is your preannualized net profit or loss.

Example

Upside-Down Return: You sold a covered call four months ago and received a premium of 5 ($500). Net proceeds came to $487.50. Last week, you entered a buy to close order at 2 ($200). Net cost was $212.50. Your net return considering only the option transaction was $275 ($487.50 − $212.50). That was 129.4 percent based on the closing buy price. This is a somewhat unrealistic form of return, because the transaction occurs in reverse. You cannot, however, calculate the return based on the initial sales price of the option. This format may be useful for comparative purposes, but it does not give you a full view of how net return worked in this example.

2. *You close the position and calculate net return based on the entire position.* A different point of view for covered call returns is going to be based on outcome for the whole position, including option premium, capital gain or loss on the stock, and dividend income during the holding period. The calculation includes everything, and there is a justification for performing the calculation in this manner: Your selection of one striking price over another affects the outcome in case of exercise. Consider the difference between making a two-point capital *gain* or accepting a three-point capital *loss.* This comparison is valid if you choose between two striking prices when current value of the stock resides in between.

Example

A Striking Proposal: You may base potential profit or loss on the striking price of the option, regardless of your actual basis in the stock. You own 100 shares of stock you originally purchased at $32 per share. Today, the stock's value is at $42.50. You want to write a covered call and you have reviewed both 40 and 45 striking prices. The 40 call provides higher premium, but the 45 is also attractive and out of the money. So you calculate the total net return including dividends you will earn between now and expiration date; capital gain or loss (based on current value rather than original price), and the option premium.

Example

Your Basic Basis: Given the same facts as in the previous example, you may consider striking prices of 40 and 45, given the current value of stock at $42.50. However, in making the comparison, you use your original cost per share of $32. This enables you to judge the relative value of one option over the other in deciding whether to write the covered call.

***

Both situations are somewhat distorted because option profit or loss is combined with the stock capital gain. However, net returns aside, it is clear that the comparison has to be made in order to judge the viability of one striking price over the other.

3. *The covered call is exercised and you calculate option and stock profits separately.* The solution to the dilemma of mixing option, stock, and dividend

sources of net return is to perform analysis separately. So you use the stock basis to consider whether or not you actually want to create one level of profit or another. But when it comes to judging the results, you separate the stock and option profits.

Example

Separate but Equal: You are considering writing a covered call on stock you originally bought at $28 per share. Today, you can write calls with striking prices of 25 or 30, and both are attractively priced. However, in a separate analysis of each, you abandon the 25 striking price because, if exercised, that would create a capital loss in the stock of three points. The 25 call is available for 4.50 today. The combined income from stock and option would only be $150, whereas exercise of the 30 call would include three points of capital gain in the stock plus two points in the option. You calculate the potential profit or loss separately, but you use the comparison to eliminate the in-the-money call.

---

4. *Any covered call outcome is computed strictly on the basis of capital on deposit.* Yet another method for calculating option profits is based on the use of margin rather than actual basis in either stock or option. This *return on capital employed (ROCE)* is a cash-for-cash calculation when applied to options trading. Those investing solely in stocks often use this leveraged approach to analysis. For example, if you buy stock at $50 per share, you are required to have only $2,500 in your account, and the rest is loaned to you by your brokerage firm. The calculation of net return has to include the interest charged during your holding period; but the return is potentially higher because you have less cash committed to the position. If you net a five-point gain, that is 10 percent based on the stock's growth in value (from $50 to $55 per share). But if you have only $2,500 at risk, a five-point gain is 20 percent net return (assuming the return is net of interest expense).

return on capital employed (ROCE) in stock and options trading, net return based on cash left on deposit in a margin account, to include all forms of net return minus transaction costs and interest charged on the balance financed; leveraged return combining minimum margin requirements with borrowed funds.

The same approach can be used when you buy or sell options or when you write covered calls. You might have only half the stock's value on deposit with the balance on margin; you may also be required to leave only a portion of an option's value in your account in order to open an option position. The calculation of net return in this case is not going to be based on the movement of a number of points, but rather on the change in your actual cash position. It requires that you add together the stock capital gains, option profits, and dividend income, and deduct any losses as well as transaction and interest charged by your brokerage firm. The net income is not based on the prices of stock and option but on the amount of cash you had on deposit.

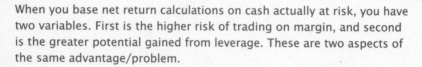

Smart Investor Tip

When you base net return calculations on cash actually at risk, you have two variables. First is the higher risk of trading on margin, and second is the greater potential gained from leverage. These are two aspects of the same advantage/problem.

The leveraged approach is going to produce much higher percentage gains, but they also involve greater risk. When you suffer net losses, you will be required to make up the difference in cash. For example, if you have $2,500 at risk on a $50 stock and it falls five points (10 percent), you will lose $500, or 20 percent of your cash on deposit. The same doubling effect applies to options as well. For example, if you deposit $200 to buy an option priced at 4 ($400) and it expires worthless, you not only lose your $200 on deposit; you also have to pay your brokerage firm another $200 plus transaction fees and interest. In that example, your net loss will exceed 100 percent.

Anticipating the Likely Return

Calculating potential profit or loss on a variety of trades demonstrates that you often operate on thin margins. The judgment call as to whether a particular strategy will or will not be profitable is often based on consideration of a single option contract. In practice, you can cut your transaction costs considerably by using multiple contracts. This also expands your potential secondary strategies.

You should not decide to use multiple contracts solely to reduce your costs, but that is one way to amend your calculation of profitability for a particular strategy. The use of multiple contracts also opens up the potential for advanced strategies and altering them, spreading or reducing risks, and creating a range of profitable outcome while better managing the chances of risk.

Return calculations are rather inflexible when based on single contracts. While examples using only one option clarify possible outcomes, in practice you have much greater flexibility and lower trading costs by trading in multiple contract increments.

In evaluating strategies, you will also benefit by calculating the *expected return*. This is the probability of several different outcomes, averaged to create a "most likely" outcome, and this is useful in determining whether a particular strategy is worth the risk.

expected return

the likely return from an option strategy, based on analysis of a range of possible outcomes, used to identify the most reasonable return a trader should expect to realize.

Example

Great Expectations: You are considering writing a covered call on stock you own. The stock recently rallied so you see a covered call as a way of taking profits in the event the stock falls. If the covered call is exercised, you are also willing to sell your stock at the striking price. You can receive 5 ($500) for a call expiring in three months that is today at the money. Because you expect the stock's price to retreat, this seems like a good plan. Expected return is based on a series of several possible outcomes:

1. The stock will continue to rise and the call will be exercised. You think there is a 25 percent chance that this will happen. In this case, your overall profit (including only call premium) would be 100 percent.

2. The stock will remain close to the striking price of the option but will not go in the money. You would wait for the option to lose half its value and then buy to close and take the net profit. For this, you believe there is only a 10 percent chance. Your profit in this case would be 50 percent (based only on the call's premium).

3. The stock will retreat back to previous trading levels and remain there, in which case you expect the option's premium to retreat to 2.5 or less. In that case, you would probably close the position and take your profits. This would also create a 50 percent profit. You believe there is a 40 percent chance this will occur.

4. The stock will retreat below previous trading levels and the option premium will fall drastically. In this outcome, you would be inclined to let the call expire worthless. This would create a 100 percent profit. You believe there is a 25 percent chance that this will happen.

Given these possible outcomes, expected return would consist of calculating the likely range of outcomes:

Likely Outcome	Return	Expectation	Result
A	100 %	25 %	25 %
B	50	10	5
C	40	40	16
D	100	25	25
Total		100 %	71 %

The expected return in this case is 71 percent. This is also based on the recognition of covered call writing as having good profit potential, but this example is limited to analysis of the option premium. It does not take into account the risks involving the stock. You may also want to think about the possibilities of the stock's rising far above the striking price (meaning the covered call strategy involves a lost opportunity) *or* falls below. That means that, if the stock's price were to retreat and remain lower, you would have lost the chance to sell at a profit when the price per share had been higher. So expected return might be further extended to include an evaluation of outcomes based on stock profit or loss as well. Exercise of a covered call at a striking price above original basis is invariably profitable. But a paper loss is a risk to consider, just as lost opportunity in the event of exercise.

Smart Investor Tip

Expected return is useful for identifying a range of likely outcomes. In situations where expected return is minimal given the range of risk, this calculation can be used to decide to not proceed.

You can take analysis of this type to any extent you desire. But at some point, options traders are going to need to make decisions and not spend excessive time on highly detailed theories about likely outcomes. Hopefully, before investing in any options positions, you will appreciate the range of risks as well as the potential profit or loss. But most options traders soon discover that they can take analysis only so far; eventually, they need to act, and often decisions have to be made quickly to take advantage of ever-changing price conditions.

Every options trader needs to calculate a practical and accurate outcome to the potential trades involved. Everything works out well on paper, of course; but when you consider the cost of transactions, interest on margin balances, and income taxes, you quickly realize that these are elements of risk. No one can predict every possible outcome; but you can improve your percentages in all forms of options trading by identifying and performing reliable forms of likely returns. The calculations do not need to be complicated, but they do need to be consistent and accurate.

Glossary

How often misused words generate misleading thoughts.
—Herbert Spencer, *Principles of Ethics*, 1892–1893

after-tax breakeven point   the point level at which you will break even on an option trade, considering the taxes due on capital gains you will be required to pay for trading options.

American-style option   an option that can be exercised at any time before expiration. All equity options and some index options are American-style.

annualized basis   a method for comparing rates of return for holdings of varying periods, in which all returns are expressed as though investments had been held over a full year. It involves dividing the holding period by the number of months the positions were open, and multiplying the result by 12.

antistraddle rules   tax regulations that remove or suspend the long-term favorable tax treatment of stock when the owner writes unqualified in-the-money covered calls.

approval level   a brokerage house's limitation on types of options strategies customers are allowed to enter, based on experience, knowledge, and account value.

assignment   the act of exercise against a seller, done on a random basis or in accordance with orderly procedures developed by the Options Clearing Corporation and brokerage firms.

at the money   the status of an option when the underlying stock's value is identical to the option's striking price.

auction market   the public exchanges in which stocks, bonds, options, and other products are traded publicly, and in which values are established by ever-changing supply and demand on the part of buyers and sellers.

automatic exercise   action taken by the Options Clearing Corporation at the time of expiration, when an in-the-money option has not been otherwise exercised or canceled.

average down   a strategy involving the purchase of stock when its market value is decreasing. The average cost of shares bought in this manner is consistently higher than current market value, so a portion of the paper loss on declining stock value is absorbed, enabling covered call writers to sell calls and profit even when the stock's market value has declined. (See Figure G.1.)

buy 100 shares per month

MONTH	PRICE	AVERAGE
Jan	$40	$40
Feb	38	39
Mar	36	38
Apr	34	37
May	27	35
Jun	29	34

buy 100 shares per month

MONTH	PRICE	AVERAGE
Jan	$40	$40
Feb	44	42
Mar	45	43
Apr	47	44
May	54	46
Jun	52	47

FIGURE G.1 Average down.   **FIGURE G.2** Average up.

average up   a strategy involving the purchase of stock when its market value is increasing. The average cost of shares bought in this manner is consistently lower than current market value, enabling covered call writers to sell calls in the money when the basis is below the striking price. (See Figure G.2.)

bear spread   a strategy involving the purchase and sale of calls or puts that will produce maximum profits when the value of the underlying stock falls.

beta   a measurement of relative volatility of a stock, made by comparing the degree of price movement to that of a larger index of stock prices.

binomial model   an option valuation formula developed in 1979 and based on selection of various times between valuation date and expiration. The formula is risk neutral but also assumes that the efficient market theory applies in all cases.

Black-Scholes model   a formula used to estimate a fair price for an option contract, originated in 1973. The calculation takes into account the elements of time value, stock price variation, an assumed market interest rate, and the time left until expiration.

book value   the actual value of a company, more accurately called *book value per share*; the value of a company's capital (assets less liabilities), divided by the number of outstanding shares of stock.

box spread   the combination of a bull spread and a bear spread, opened at the same time on the same underlying stock.

breakeven price   (also called the *breakeven point*) the price of the underlying stock at which the option investor breaks even. For call buyers, this price is the number of points above striking price equal to the call premium cost; for put buyers, this price is the number of points below striking price equal to the put premium cost.

breakout   the movement of a stock's price below support level or above resistance level.

bull spread   a strategy involving the purchase and sale of calls or puts that will produce maximum profits when the value of the underlying stock rises.

butterfly spread   a strategy involving open options in one striking price range, offset by open positions at higher and lower ranges at the same time.

buyer   an investor who purchases a call or a put option; the buyer realizes a profit if the value of stock moves above the specified price (call) or below the specified price (put).

calendar spread   (also called *time spread*) a spread involving the simultaneous purchase or sale of options on the same underlying stock, with different expirations.

call   an option acquired by a buyer or granted by a seller to buy 100 shares of stock at a fixed price within a specified time period.

called away   the result of having stock assigned. Upon exercise, 100 shares of the seller's stock are called away at the striking price.

candlestick charts   technical charts for stocks summarizing a stock's daily trading range, opening and closing prices, and price direction. The candlestick is used in many trading systems, including swing trading.

capital gains   profits from investments, taxed the same as other income if the holding period is less than one year, and at lower rates if investments were owned for one year or more.

capped-style option   an option that can be exercised only during a specified period of time; if the option's value reaches the cap level prior to expiration, it is exercised automatically.

carryover capital losses   sums of capital losses from prior years that exceeded annual loss limitation levels; the annual maximum capital loss deduction is $3,000, and all losses above that level have to be carried over and applied in future tax years.

chartist   an analyst who studies charts of a stock's price movement in the belief that recent patterns can be used to predict upcoming price changes and directions.

class   all options traded on a single underlying stock, including different striking prices and expiration dates.

closing purchase transaction   a transaction to close a short position, executed by buying an option previously sold, canceling it out.

closing sale transaction   a transaction to close a long position, executed by selling an option previously bought, closing it out.

collar   a spread strategy combining long stock, a covered call, and a long put, with both options out of the money. The collar limits potential gains and potential losses.

combination   any purchase or sale of options on one underlying stock, with terms that are not identical.

condor spread   a variation of the butterfly spread using different striking prices in the short positions on either side of the middle range.

confirmation   a signal providing support for another signal, reinforcing the belief that a trend is ending and about to reverse.

constructive sales   status when investors buy and sell in separate transactions, but involve substantially identical property; the holding of offsetting long and short positions may be taxed as a constructive sale even when no physical sale has occurred.

contingent purchase a strategy involving the sale of a put and willingness to accept exercise, which will result in purchasing 100 shares of stock. The strategy makes sense when the individual believes the striking price is a reasonable price for the stock.

contract a single option, the agreement providing the buyer with the terms that option grants. Those terms include identification of the stock, the cost of the option, the date the option will expire, and the fixed price per share of the stock to be bought or sold under the rights of the option.

contrarian an investor who recognizes the tendency for the majority to be wrong more often than right, who invests opposite popular opinion.

conversion the process of moving assigned stock from the seller of a call option or to the seller of a put option.

cookie jar accounting the practice of banking revenue or earnings in exceptionally high-volume years and booking them in later periods, to even out results consistently and to reduce fundamental volatility.

core earnings as defined by Standard & Poor's, the after-tax earnings generated from a corporation's principal business.

cover the ownership of 100 shares of the underlying stock for each call sold, providing sellers the ability to deliver shares already held, in the event of exercise.

covered call a call sold to create an open short position, when the seller also owns 100 shares of stock for each call sold.

credit spread any spread in which receipts from short positions are higher than premiums paid for long positions, net of transaction fees.

current market value the market value of a stock at any given time.

cycle the pattern of expiration dates of options for a particular underlying stock. The three cycles occur in four-month intervals and are described by month abbreviations. They are (1) January, April, July, and October, or JAJO; (2) February, May, August, and November, or FMAN; and (3) March, June, September, and December, or MJSD.

day trader an individual who trades within a single day, usually closing positions before the end of the trading day, and often making such trades on high volume.

debit spread any spread in which receipts from short positions are lower than premiums paid for long positions, net of transaction fees.

debt investment an investment in the form of a loan made to earn interest, such as the purchase of a bond.

debt ratio a ratio used to follow trends in debt capitalization. To compute, divide long-term debt by total capitalization; the result is expressed as a percentage.

deep in condition when the underlying stock's current market value is five points or more above the striking price of the call or below the striking price of the put. (See Figure G.3.)

deep out condition when the underlying stock's current market value is five points or more below the striking price of the call or above the striking price of the put. (See Figure G.3.)

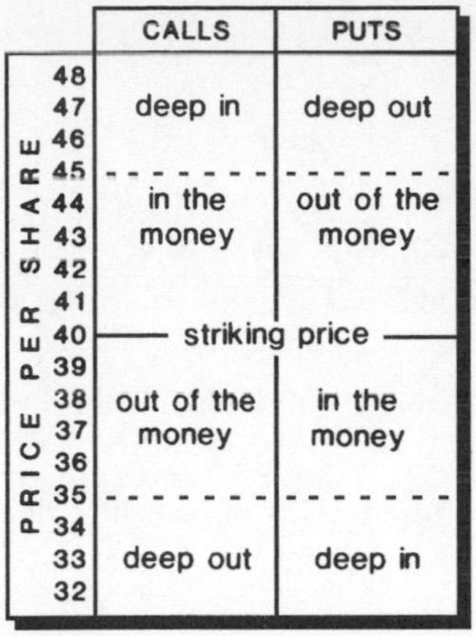

	CALLS	PUTS
48		
47	deep in	deep out
46		
45	- - - - - - -	- - - - - - -
44	in the	out of the
43	money	money
42		
41		
40	——— striking price ———	
39		
38	out of the	in the
37	money	money
36		
35	- - - - - -	- - - - - -
34		
33	deep out	deep in
32		

(left axis: PRICE PER SHARE)

FIGURE G.3 Deep in/deep out.

stock price change	OPTION PREMIUM CHANGE			
	1 point	2 points	3 points	4 points
1	1.00	2.00	3.00	4.00
2	0.50	1.00	1.50	2.00
3	0.33	0.67	1.00	1.33
4	0.25	0.50	0.75	1.00
5	0.20	0.40	0.60	0.80

FIGURE G.4 Delta.

deferred credit   an account listed under the liabilities section of a balance sheet, representing income to be recognized in future years.

delivery   the movement of stock ownership from one owner to another. In the case of exercised options, shares are registered to the new owner upon receipt of payment.

delta   the degree of change in option premium in relation to changes in the underlying stock. If the call option's degree of change exceeds the change in the underlying stock, it is called an *up delta*; when the change is less than in the underlying stock, it is called a *down delta*. The reverse terminology is applied to puts. (See Figure G.4.)

diagonal spread   a calendar spread in which offsetting long and short positions have both different striking prices and different expiration dates.

discount   the reduction in the basis of stock, equal to the amount of option premium received. A benefit in selling covered calls, the discount provides downside protection and protects long positions.

dividend yield   dividends paid per share of common stock, expressed as a percentage computed by dividing dividend paid per share by the current market value of the stock.

dollar cost averaging   a strategy for investing over time, either buying a fixed number of shares or investing a fixed dollar amount, in regular intervals. The result is an averaging of overall price. If market value increases, average cost is always lower than current market value; if market value decreases, average cost is always higher than current market value.

downside protection   a strategy involving the purchase of one put for every 100 shares of the underlying stock that you own. This insures you against losses to some degree. For every in-the-money point the stock falls, the put will increase in value by one point. Before exercise, you may sell the put and take a profit, offsetting stock losses, or exercise the put and sell the shares at the striking price.

downtrend   in swing trading, a series of three or more days consisting of lower highs and lower lows.

Dow Theory a theory that market trends are predictable based on changes in market averages.

early exercise the act of exercising an option prior to expiration date.

earnings per share a commonly used method for reporting profits. Net profits for a year or for the latest quarter are divided by the number of shares of common stock outstanding as of the ending date of the financial report. The result is expressed as a dollar value.

EBITDA a popular measurement of cash flow, an acronym for earnings before interest, taxes, depreciation, and amortization.

efficient market hypothesis a theory stating that current stock prices reflect all information publicly known about a company.

equity investment an investment in the form of part ownership, such as the purchase of shares of stock in a corporation.

European-style option an option that can be exercised only during a specified period of time immediately preceding expiration. Some index options are European-style.

exercise the act of buying stock under the terms of the call option or selling stock under the terms of the put option, at the price per share specified in the option contract.

expiration date the date on which an option becomes worthless, which is specified in the option contract.

expiration time the latest possible time to place an order for cancellation or exercise of an option, which may vary depending on the brokerage firm executing the order and on the option itself.

expected return the likely return from an option strategy, based on analysis of a range of possible outcomes, used to identify the most reasonable return a trader should expect to realize.

extrinsic value the portion of an option's premium generated from volatility in the underlying stock and from market perception of potential price changes until expiration date; a nonintrinsic portion of the premium value not specifically caused by the element of time.

fundamental analysis a study of financial information and attributes of a company's management and competitive position, as a means for selecting stocks.

fundamental volatility the tendency for a company's sales and profits to change from one period to the next, with more erratic change representing higher volatility.

GAAP acronym for Generally Accepted Accounting Principles, the rules by which auditing firms analyze operations, and by which corporations report their financial results.

gamma a measurement of the speed of change in delta, relative to price movement in the underlying stock.

gap a trading pattern in which the range between days includes a gap in price, with the second day's trading range opening above the highest price of the previous day, or below the lowest price of the previous day.

Greeks a series of analytical tests of option risk and volatility, so called because they are named for letters of the Greek alphabet.

hedge a strategy involving the use of one position to protect another. For example, stock is purchased in the belief it will rise in value, and a put is purchased on the same stock to protect against the risk that market value will decline.

hedge ratio alternate name for the delta, the measurement of changes in option value relative to changes in stock value.

horizontal spread a calendar spread in which offsetting long and short positions have identical striking prices but different expiration dates.

incremental return a technique for avoiding exercise while increasing profits with written calls. When the value of the underlying stock rises, a single call is closed at a loss and replaced with two or more call writes with later expiration dates, producing cash and a net profit in the exchange.

in the money the status of a call option when the underlying stock's market value is higher than the option's striking price, or of a put option when the underlying stock's market value is lower than the option's striking price. (See Figure G.5.)

insider information any information about a company not known to the general public, but known only to people working in the company, or with nonpublic knowledge about matters that will affect a stock's price.

intrinsic value that portion of an option's current value equal to the number of points that it is in the money. One point equals one dollar of value per share; so 35 points equals $35 per share. (See Figure G.6.)

iron condor the combination of a long strangle and a short strangle on the same underlying stock. The cost is reduced due to offsetting premium payments and receipts; and it is practical as long as short position exercise costs do not exceed long position profits.

know your customer a rule requiring brokers to be aware of the risk, knowledge level, and capital profile of each client, designed to ensure that recommendations are suitable for each individual.

last trading day the Friday preceding the third Saturday of the expiration month of an option.

PRICE PER SHARE	CALLS	PUTS
59		
58	in the	
57	money	
56		
55	— striking price —	
54		
53		in the
52		money
51		

FIGURE G.5 In the money.

STOCK VALUE	STRIKING PRICE	INTRINSIC VALUE
$38	$35	$3
43	45	0
41	40	1
65	65	0
21	20	1

FIGURE G.6 Intrinsic value.

LEAPS   Long-term Equity AnticiPation Security, a long-term option contract that works just like standardized options, but with expiration up to three years.

leverage   the use of investment capital in a way that a relatively small amount of money enables the investor to control a relatively large value. This is achieved through borrowing—for example, using borrowed money to purchase stocks or bonds—or through the purchase of options, which exist for only a short period of time but enable the option buyer to control 100 shares of stock. As a general rule, the use of leverage increases potential for profit as well as for loss.

liquid market   a market in which buyers and sellers are matched to one another, and the exchange absorbs any imbalances between the two sides.

listed option   an option traded on a public exchange and listed in the published reports in the financial press.

lock in   to freeze the price of the underlying stock by selling a covered call. As long as the call position is open, the writer is locked into the striking price, regardless of current market value of the stock. In the event of exercise, the stock is delivered at the locked-in price.

long hedge   the purchase of options as a form of insurance to protect a portfolio position in the event of a price increase; a strategy employed by investors selling stock short and needing insurance against a rise in the market value of the stock.

long position   the status assumed by investors when they enter a buy order in advance of entering a sell order. The long position is closed by later entering a sell order, or through expiration.

long straddle   the purchase of an identical number of calls and puts with the same striking prices and expiration dates, designed to produce profits in the event of price movement of the underlying stock in either direction, adequate to surpass the cost of opening the position.

long-term capital gains   profits on investments held for 12 months or more, which are taxed at a rate lower than other income.

loss zone   the price range of the underlying stock in which the option investor loses. A limited loss exists for option buyers, since the premium cost is the maximum loss that can be realized.

lost opportunity risk (options)   the risk that covered call writers will lose profits from increased prices in stock, because they are locked in at a fixed striking price.

lost opportunity risk (stock)   the risk stockholders experience in tying up capital over the long term, causing lost opportunities that could be taken if capital were available.

lower shadow   on a candlestick formation, the line defining the extent of a day's trading range. The line extends below the opening or closing prices for the day.

margin   an account with a brokerage firm containing a minimum level of cash and securities to provide collateral for short positions or for purchases for which payment has not yet been made.

margin requirement the maximum amount of outstanding risk investors are allowed to hold in their portfolio, or the maximum unfunded dollar level allowed when trading on margin.

market value the value of an investment at any given time or date; the amount a buyer is willing to pay to acquire an investment and what a seller is also willing to receive to transfer the same investment.

married put the status of a put used to hedge a long position. Each put owned protects 100 shares of the underlying stock held in the portfolio. If the stock declines in value, the put's value will increase and offset the loss.

money spread alternate name for the *vertical spread*.

multileg options order a type of ordered allowed by some brokerage firms in which a strategy involving several options is opened for a single transaction fee, rather than for separate minimum fees on each option.

multiple the P/E's outcome, the number of times current price per share is above annual earnings per share; for example, if the P/E is 10, then current price per share is 10 times higher than the latest reported earnings per share.

mutual funds investment programs in which money from a large pool of investors is placed under professional management. For a fee, management invests in stocks and bonds. Mutual funds may be set up to pay a sales loan to salespeople, often called financial advisers; or they may be no-load, meaning investors can buy shares directly and not pay commissions.

naked option an option sold in an opening sale transaction when the seller (writer) does not own 100 shares of the underlying stock. (See Figure G.7.)

naked position status for investors when they assume short positions in calls without also owning 100 shares of the underlying stock for each call written.

narrow-range day (NRD) in a candlestick chart, a trading day with an exceptionally small trading range.

net basis the cost of stock when reduced by premium received for selling covered calls; the true net cost of stock after discounting original cost.

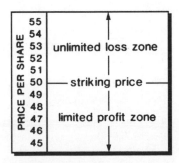

FIGURE G.7 Naked option.

net investment income   an individual's taxable income from interest, dividends, and capital gains, distinguished from ordinary income by tax rate or potential tax exclusions.

net return   the percentage return on an investment, based on dollar amounts going in and coming out, after transaction fees.

odd lot   a lot of shares that contains fewer than the more typical *round lot* trading unit of 100 shares.

offsetting positions   in tax law, a straddle which creates a substantial diminution of risk; when positions are classified as offsetting, tax restrictions are applied on deductibility of losses or treatment of long-term gains.

opening purchase transaction   an initial transaction to buy, also known as the action of "going long."

opening sale transaction   an initial transaction to sell, also known as the action of "going short."

open interest   the number of open contracts of a particular option at any given time, which can be used to measure market interest.

open position   the status of a trade when a purchase (a long position) or a sale (a short position) has been made, and before cancellation, exercise, or expiration.

option   the right to buy or to sell 100 shares of stock at a specified, fixed price and by a specified date in the future.

orderly settlement   the smooth process of buying and selling, in full confidence that the terms and conditions of options contracts will be honored in a timely manner.

ordinary income   noninvestment income, subject to the full tax rate an individual pays and not qualified for exclusions or lower rates applicable to some forms of net investment income.

out of the money   the status of a call option when the underlying stock's market value is lower than the option's striking price, or of a put option when the underlying stock's market value is higher than the option's striking price. (See Figure G.8.)

paper profits   (also called *unrealized profits*) values existing only on paper but not taken at the time; paper profits (or paper losses) become realized only if a closing transaction is executed.

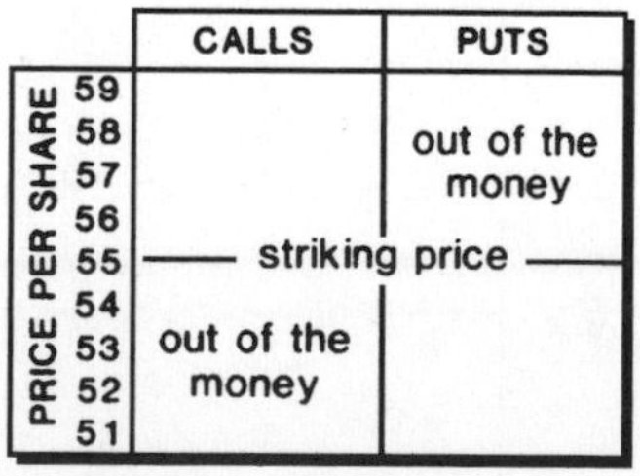

	CALLS	PUTS
59		out of the
58		money
57		
56		
55	— striking price —	
54		
53	out of the	
52	money	
51		

PRICE PER SHARE

FIGURE G.8 Out of the money.

paper trading online "mock trading" of stocks and options using a hypothetical sum of cash, to test strategies in a realistic environment but without placing real money at risk.

parity the condition of an option at expiration, when the total premium consists of intrinsic value and no time value.

pattern day trader any individual executing four or more transactions on the same security within five consecutive trading days; these traders are required to maintain no less than $25,000 in their brokerage accounts.

premium value the current price of an option, which a buyer pays and a seller receives at the time of the transaction. The amount of premium is expressed as the dollar value of the option, but without dollar signs; for example, stating that an option is "at 3" means its current market value is $300.

price/earnings ratio a popular indicator used by stock market investors to rate and compare stocks. The current market value of the stock is divided by the most recent earnings per share to arrive at the P/E ratio.

profit margin the most commonly used measurement of corporate operations, computed by dividing net profits by gross sales.

profit zone the price range of the underlying stock in which the option investor realizes a profit. For the call buyer, the profit zone extends upward from the breakeven price. For the put buyer, the profit zone extends downward from the breakeven price.

pro forma earnings "as a matter of form" (Latin), a company's earnings based on estimates or forecasts with hypothetical numbers in place of known or actual revenues, costs, or earnings.

prospectus a document designed to disclose all of the risk characteristics associated with a particular investment.

pump and dump action by an individual holding shares of a company. It involves spreading false rumors in order to get people to buy shares and increase the price of stock, and then selling shares at a profit.

put an option acquired by a buyer or granted by a seller to sell 100 shares of stock at a fixed price within a specified time period.

put to seller action of exercising a put and requiring the seller to purchase 100 shares of stock at the fixed striking price.

qualified covered call a covered call that meets specific definitions allowing an investor to claim long-term capital gains tax rates upon sale of stock, or to retain long-term holding period status. Qualification is determined by time to expiration, and by the price difference between current market value of the stock and striking price of the call.

qualified retirement plans those plans qualified by the IRS to treat current income as deferred and free of tax in the year earned and, in many cases, also exempting annual contributions to the plan from current taxes.

quality of earnings a measurement of the reliability of financial reports. A high quality of earnings means the report reflects the real and accurate operations of a corporation and may be used reliably to forecast likely future growth trends.

random walk   a theory about market pricing, stating that prices of stocks cannot be predicted because price movement is entirely random.

rate of return   the yield from investing, calculated by dividing net cash profit upon sale by the amount spent at purchase.

ratio calendar combination spread   a strategy involving both a ratio between purchases and sales and a box spread. Long and short positions are opened on options with the same underlying stock, in varying numbers of contracts and with expiration dates extending over two or more periods. This strategy is designed to produce profits in the event of either price increases or decreases in the market value of the underlying stock.

ratio calendar spread   a strategy involving a different number of options on the long side of a transaction from the number on the short side, when the expiration dates for each side are also different. This strategy creates two separate profit and loss zone ranges, one of which disappears upon the earlier expiration.

ratio write   a strategy for covering one position with another for partial rather than full coverage. A portion of risk is eliminated, so that ratio writes can be used to reduce overall risk levels.

ready market   a liquid market, one in which buyers can easily sell their holdings, or in which sellers can easily find buyers, at current market prices.

realized profits   profits taken at the time a position is closed.

Regulation T   a Federal Reserve Board (FRB) rule defining customer cash account minimum levels based on strategies employed.

relative volatility   the degree of volatility in comparative form, such as between portfolios or between a specific stock and other stocks or markets.

resistance level   the highest trading price, under present conditions, above which the price of the stock is not likely to rise.

return if exercised   the estimated rate of return option sellers will earn in the event the buyer exercises the option. The calculation includes profit or loss in the underlying stock, dividends earned, and premium received for selling the option. (See Figure G.9.)

exercise price 40
purchase price 38
May 40 call sold for 3
dividends earned $80

call premium	$300
dividend income	80
capital gain	200
return	$580
	15.3%

FIGURE G.9   Return if exercised.

basis in stock $3,800

sold May 40 call	$300
dividends earned	80
total	$380
return	10.0%

FIGURE G.10 Return if unchanged.

return if unchanged the estimated rate of return option sellers will earn in the event the buyer does not exercise the option. The calculation includes dividends earned on the underlying stock, and the premium received for selling the option. (See Figure G.10.)

return on capital employed (ROCE) in stock and options trading, net return based on cash left on deposit in a margin account, to include all forms of net return minus transaction costs and interest charged on the balance financed; leveraged return combining minimum margin requirements with borrowed funds.

reverse hedge an extension of a long or short hedge in which more options are opened than the number needed to cover the stock position; this increases profit potential in the event of unfavorable movement in the market value of the underlying stock.

rho a calculation of the effect of interest rate trends on option valuation; a long-term analytical tool rather than one of immediate value.

risk tolerance the amount of risk that an investor is able and willing to take.

roll down the replacement of one written call with another that has a lower striking price.

roll forward the replacement of one written call with another with the same striking price, but a later expiration date.

roll up the replacement of one written call with another that has a higher striking price.

round lot a lot of 100 shares of stock or of higher numbers divisible by 100, the usual trading unit on the public exchanges.

sales load a commission charged when a financial adviser places a client's capital into a load mutual fund.

sector a specific segment of the market defined by product or service offered by a company. Factors affecting value (cyclical, economic, or market based) make each sector distinct and different from other sectors, also affecting option valuation.

seller an investor who grants a right in an option to someone else; the seller realizes a profit if the value of the stock moves below the specified price (call) or above the specified price (put).

sensitivity the degree of change in an option's value based solely on the time remaining until expiration.

series   a group of options sharing identical terms.

setup   in swing trading, a signal indicating that a stock has reached a short-term high level (a sell setup) or a short-term low level (a buy setup). By taking action upon recognizing a setup, swing traders make small but consistent profits.

settlement date   the date on which a buyer is required to pay for purchases, or on which a seller is entitled to receive payment. For stocks, settlement date is three business days after the transaction. For options, settlement date is one business day from the date of the transaction.

share   a unit of ownership in the capital of a corporation.

short hedge   the purchase of options as a form of insurance to protect a portfolio position in the event of a price decrease; a strategy employed by investors in long positions who need insurance against a decline in the market value of the stock.

short position   the status assumed by investors when they enter a sale order in advance of entering a buy order. The short position is closed by later entering a buy order, or through expiration.

short selling   a strategy in the stock market in which shares of stock are first sold, creating a short position for the investor, and later bought in a closing purchase transaction.

short straddle   the sale of an identical number of calls and puts with identical striking prices and expiration dates, designed to produce profits in the event of price movement of the underlying stock within a limited range.

short-term capital gains   profits on investments held for less than 12 months, which are taxed at the same rate as other income.

sideways strategies   option strategies designed to produce maximum gains when the underlying stock is expected to exhibit lower than average volatility.

speculation   the use of money to assume risks for short-term profit, in the knowledge that substantial or total losses are one possible outcome. Buying calls for leverage is one form of speculation. The buyer may earn a very large profit in a matter of days, or could lose the entire amount invested.

spread   the simultaneous purchase and sale of options on the same underlying stock, with different striking prices or expiration dates, or both.

straddle   the simultaneous purchase and sale of the same number of calls and puts with identical striking prices and expiration dates.

strangle   a strategy in which an equal number of long calls and puts are bought (long strangle) or sold (short strangle). These terms include different striking prices but the same expiration date, and it will be profitable only if there is a large price movement in the underlying stock.

strap   an option strategy, also called a triple option, involving purchase of one put and two calls (hoping the stock's price will rise) or the purchase of one call and two puts (anticipating a stock's price decline).

striking price   the fixed price to be paid for 100 shares of stock, specified in the option contract; the transaction price per share of stock upon exercise of that option, regardless of the current market value of the stock.

suitability   standard by which a particular investment or market strategy is judged. The investor's knowledge and experience with options represent important suitability standards. Strategies are appropriate only if the investor understands the market and can afford to take the risks involved.

supply and demand   the market forces that determine the current value for stocks. The number of buyers represents demand for shares, and the number of sellers represents supply. The price of stocks rises as demand increases, and falls as supply increases.

support level   the lowest trading price, under present conditions, below which the price of the stock is not likely to fall.

swing trading   a system based on a two- to five-day cycle, involving buying and selling positions based on predictable price movements and in response to buy and sell setup signals.

synthetic position   a strategy in which stock and option positions are matched up to protect against unfavorable price movement. When you own stock and also buy a put to protect against downward price movement, it creates a synthetic call. When you are short on stock and buy a call, it creates a synthetic put.

tangible book value per share   the net value of a company, computed by subtracting all liabilities from all assets, and further reducing the net by all intangible assets. The net of tangible assets is then divided by the number of outstanding shares of common stock.

tau   a measurement of an option's premium value in relation to the underlying stock's changes in volatility.

tax put   a strategy combining the sale of stock at a loss—taken for tax purposes—and the sale of a put at the same time. The premium received on the put offsets the stock loss; if the put is exercised, the stock is purchased at the striking price.

technical analysis   a study of trends and patterns of price movement in stocks, including price per share, the shape of price movements on charts, high and low ranges, and trends in pricing over time.

terms   (also called *standardized terms*) the attributes that describe an option, including the striking price, expiration month, type of option (call or put), and the underlying stock.

theta   a measurement of an option's value based on time until expiration.

time value of money   the concept observing that earnings potential adds value to a sum of money. As long as money is put to use earning profit, the present discounted value of the future fund relies on (1) the interest rate, (2) compounding method, and (3) time involved until the final result can be achieved.

triple option   alternative name for the strap.

time value   that portion of an option's current premium above intrinsic value. (See Figure G.11.)

TOTAL PREMIUM	INTRINSIC VALUE	TIME VALUE
$4	$3	$1
2	0	2
4	1	3
1	0	1
3	1	2

FIGURE G.11 Time value.

stock exercised at
$40 (basis $34),
held for 13 months

option premium	$ 800
dividends	110
capital gain	600
total	$1,510
13 months	44.4%
annualized	41.0%

FIGURE G.12 Total return.

total capitalization   the combination of long-term debt (debt capital) and stockholders' equity (equity capital), which in combination represents the financing of corporate operations and long-term growth.

total return   the combined return including income from selling a call, capital gain from profit on selling the stock, and dividends earned and received. Total return may be calculated in two ways: return if the option is exercised, and return if the option expires worthless. (See Figure G.12.)

trading range   the price range between support and resistance; the current price area where stock purchase and sale levels occur.

uncovered option   the same as a naked option—the sale of an option not covered, or protected, by the ownership of 100 shares of the underlying stock.

underlying stock   the stock on which the option grants the right to buy or sell, which is specified in every option contract.

upper shadow   on a candlestick formation, the line defining the extent of a day's trading range. The line extends above the opening or closing prices for the day.

uptrend   in swing trading, a series of three or more days consisting of higher highs offset by higher lowers.

value investing   an approach to picking stocks based on actual value of the company rather than on price or price targets.

vega   a name sometimes applied to the calculation of tau.

variable hedge   a hedge involving a long position and a short position in related options, when one side contains a greater number of options than the other. The desired result is reduction of risks or potentially greater profits.

vertical spread   a spread involving different striking prices but identical expiration dates.

volatility   an indicator of the degree of change in a stock's market value, measured over a 12-month period and stated as a percentage. To measure volatility, subtract the lowest 12-month price from the highest 12-month price, and divide the answer by the 12-month lowest price. (See Figure ??.)

volume   the level of trading activity in a stock, an option, or the market as a whole.

wash sale rule   a provision in the tax code prohibiting the deduction of a loss if the security position is reopened within 30 days from the date of the sale.

wasting asset   any asset that declines in value over time. An option is an example of a wasting asset because it exists only until expiration, after which it becomes worthless.

whipsaw   a price trend in stocks when the price moves in one direction and then reverses and moves in the opposite direction.

writer   the individual who sells (writes) a call or a put.

Recommended Reading

Ansbacher, Max. 2000. *The New Options Market*, 4th ed. New York: John Wiley & Sons.

Cohen, Guy. 2002. *Options Made Easy*. Upper Saddle River, N.J.: Financial Times/ Prentice Hall.

Fontanills, George A. 1999. *Trade Options Online*. New York: John Wiley & Sons.

Friedentag, Harvey C. 2000. *Stocks for Options Trading: Low-Risk, Low-Stress Strategies for Selling Stock Options—Profitably.* Boca Raton, Fla.: CRC Press.

Jabbour, George, and Philip Budwick. 2004. *The Option Trader Handbook: Strategies and Trade Adjustments*. Hoboken, N.J.: John Wiley & Sons.

Johnston, S. A. 2003. *Trading Options to Win: Profitable Strategies and Tactics for Any Trader.* Hoboken, N.J.: John Wiley & Sons.

Kaeppel, Jay. 2002. *The Option Trader's Guide to Probability, Volatility, and Timing.* Hoboken, N.J.: John Wiley & Sons.

Kolb, Robert W. 2001. *Understanding Options*. New York: John Wiley & Sons.

———. and James, A. Overdahl. 2003. *Financial Derivatives*, 3rd ed. Hoboken, N.J.: John Wiley & Sons.

McMillan, Lawrence G. 1993. *Options as a Strategic Investment*, 3rd ed. New York: New York Institute of Finance.

———. 2002. *Profit with Options: Essential Methods for Investing Success.* New York: John Wiley & Sons.

———. 2004. *McMillan on Options*, 2nd ed. Hoboken, N.J.: John Wiley & Sons.

Natenberg, Sheldon. *Option Volatility and Pricing: Advanced Trading Strategies and Techniques*. New York: McGraw-Hill.

Schaeffer, Bernie. 1997. *The Option Advisor*. New York: John Wiley & Sons.

Thomsett, Michael C. 2004. *The LEAPS Strategist*. Columbia, Md.: Marketplace Books.

———. 2005. *Options Trading for the Conservative Investor*. Upper Saddle River, N.J.: Financial Times/Prentice Hall.

Trester, Kenneth R. 2003. *101 Option Trading Secrets*. Stateline, Nev.: Institute for Options Research.

Index